Folk Culture
in a
World of
Technology

D1453980

Folklore Studies in Translation
GENERAL EDITOR, DAN BEN-AMOS

Advisory Board

German Volkskunde: *A Decade of Theoretical Confrontation, Debate, and Reorientation (1967–1977),* translated and edited by James R. Dow and Hannjost Lixfeld.

The European Folktale: Form and Nature by Max Lüthi, translated by John D. Niles.

The Fairytale as Art Form and Portrait of Man by Max Lüthi, translated by Jon Erickson.

Nordic Folklore: Recent Studies, edited by Reimund Kvideland and Henning K. Sehmsdorf (in collaboration with Elizabeth Simpson).

Kalevala Mythology by Juha Y. Pentikäinen, translated and edited by Ritva Poom.

Folk Culture
in a
World of
TECHNOLOGY

Hermann Bausinger

TRANSLATED BY

Elke Dettmer

INDIANA UNIVERSITY PRESS

Bloomington and Indianapolis

Library of Congress Cataloging-in-Publication Data

Bausinger, Hermann.
[Volkskultur in der technischen Welt. English]
Folk Culture in a world of technology / Herman Bausinger ;
translated by Elke Dettmer.
p.   cm.
Translation of: Volkskultur in der technischen Welt.
Includes bibliographical references and index.
ISBN 0-253-31127-6
1. Folklore. 2. Popular culture. 3. Civilization, Modern.
4. Folklore—Germany (West) 5. Germany (West)—Popular culture.
I. Title.
GR40.B3313   1990
398—dc20   89-15492
                                                CIP

1 2 3 4 5   94 93 92 91 90

CONTENTS

Foreword

The translation of *Volkskultur in der technischen Welt* is long overdue. When the book was first published, in 1961, it was not even reviewed in the major English and American folklore journals. Seven years later, when American scholars convened to discuss folklore in the urban experience, a closely related subject, they did not make a single reference to Bausinger's ground-breaking book (see *The Urban Experience and Folk Tradition*, edited by Américo Paredes and Ellen J. Stekert [Austin: University of Texas Press, 1971]). In spite of the increased research on urban folklore and ethnography during the seventies and eighties, references to *Volkskultur in der technischen Welt* in folklore journals in English continue to be sparse and far between. While in Germany, twenty-five years after its original publication, Campus Verlag reprinted the book in a popular format, demonstrating its vitality and relevance to current general intellectual trends and specific folklore studies, folklorists in England and the United States hardly acknowledged Bausinger's theoretical study and rarely benefited from it, even when they addressed similar issues. Once again the language hurdle has hindered scholarly communication in folklore.

The relevance of Bausinger's theoretical approach to modern studies is evident from the increased research in the past thirty years on such subjects as urban folklore, in residential, industrial, and corporate contexts; the modern legend; popular culture; folklore revival; and the display of, and trade in, tradition as exotica for tourists. While each of these areas has been the subject of numerous analytical and descriptive studies, so far only Bausinger has sought to treat them within a unified and systematic theory that conceives of them as responses to the emergence of technology. In contrast to the common lament about the passing of traditional societies in the face of advances in technology, Bausinger theorizes and demonstrates that while man's environment changes, the dynamics of tradition may be transformed but they do not disappear. He proposes a theory of expansion, rather than disintegration, of traditional culture in the age of technology.

From that perspective the book is nothing short of revolutionary. With it Bausinger ushered folklore studies into the modern world, forcing them to confront and cope with the changes that are occurring in modern society. He robbed folklore of its romantic naiveté and idealization of traditional life. The city, with its congested streets, polluted air, and multi-ethnic population, becomes in his theory as much a ''natural environment'' for folklore as the open fields, clear sky, and tradition-steeped peasantry of the countryside. The very tension between city and country that manifests itself in nostalgia and has been a motivating force in the emergence of folklore studies turned out to be in Bausinger's theory a function of the technical world. Similarly, tradition, that keystone concept of folklore, gains significance in Bausinger's theory not as the prime but as the final cause of folklore in society. Tradition is not passed on from generation to generation in language, art, and music as a time-honored body of knowledge and values. Rather, it is in a constant stage of disarray, about to disintegrate under the pressures of change; and members of the society strive to restore and maintain it in new rituals, displays, and diverse forms of entertainment—constructed and if necessary invented—or the revival of old ones. Bausinger anticipated Eric Hobsbawm and Terence Ranger (the editors of *The Invention of Tradition* [New York: Cambridge University Press, 1983]), by considering tradition not as a cultural given but as a cultural construct.

Bausinger's book is bursting with ideas that are as fresh today as they were thirty years ago, and three concepts stand out among them: denationalization, expansion, and commodification of folklore. While the idea of the expansion of folklore, in terms of its spatial, temporal, and social dimensions, serves Bausinger as his principal analytic concept, the notions of denationalization and commodification (which are not his terms) are of no lesser significance.

Denationalization does not refer to a process of folklore in traditional culture but to an attitude a modern society could, or should, establish toward folklore. It reflects an evaluation of folklore—or in this case a disvaluation—by the society, underscoring the significance a people attribute to, or detract from, folklore and tradition. While in the past folklore has been valued as essential to the nationhood of a people, Bausinger argues that as a prerequisite for its adequate analysis, folklore has to be devalued of its national significance. In contrast to romantic perception, Bausinger advocates the study of folklore not as a means for the discovery of nationhood but as a way of analyzing and understanding human behavior. The association between nationalism and folklore, which has its origins in humanistic romanticism, has been incorporated into modern political ideologies. Political parties in power have distorted the initial romantic evaluation of folklore as a source and a representation of the spirit of a nation and have used it to sanction atrocities against other peoples. Bausinger realized that in order to salvage folklore from the clutches of narrow nationalism, particularly as it was conceived and practiced in Nazi Germany, it was necessary to denationalize it, to divorce it from the idea of nationhood, and to consider it as a subject of inquiry and as a social science. He prefers to consider folklore as a subdiscipline of sociology.

By making this choice Bausinger brought into the fold of folklore, a field that thrives on interdisciplinary connections, an area with which folklore had had only limited contact. Sociologists saw only a negligible value in folklore, and folklorists, with a few exceptions, have not realized the analytical potential sociology holds in addressing their issues (Kenneth Thompson, "Folklore and Sociology," *Sociological Review* 28 [1980]:249–275). Even Bausinger does not apply to his cultural analysis any specific sociological theory or method. He conceives the alliance between the two disciplines in having a common subject matter: the urban scene, a domain that is new for folklore but which sociology has treated for many years. This newly proposed shared area for research weights the balance in favor of sociology rather than, say, anthropology. While at present the research territories of these two social sciences are shifting, and rural sociology and urban anthropology are both well-established areas, issues of urbanity, modernity, and technology that dominate sociological theory and method have made sociology a more appropriate field with which Bausinger could denationalize folklore.

The research shift from a rural to an urban environment has a denationalizing function as well. By making it Bausinger recognizes a dimension of folklore that romanticism obscured and focuses deliberately on a social situation that homogenizes ethnic and regional differences. In the urban experience both conservative and expansive forces operate on the traditional cultures that rural migrants infuse into the city. While for them the city does not serve as the melting pot it was once thought, the new contexts for social life have generated some new traditions of their own that are genuinely urban. These are traditions of the uprooted and the rerooted that have not been the subject of nationalist aspirations. Hence not only the method Bausinger employs but also the culture he analyzes has been denationalized.

Exploring folklore against the backdrop of romanticism, Bausinger formulates his theory of folklore in the technical world by employing a positive rather than a negative concept—expansion. He does not regard tradition in the urban environment and the technical experience as disintegrating but as expanding. This is not an entropic expansion into nothingness but a broadening of the communal scope of folklore into a diversified and complex set of relations; Bausinger explores them in terms of their spatial, temporal, and social dimensions. Folklore in the technological world loosens up and sheds some of its archaic, ritualistic, and mythical qualities that modernism sought in the "primitive" and traditional world. It is a post-modernistic folklore in which tradition is not only made self-conscious but often put up for sale. In its transformation from a communal to a societal base it became an object of multiple perspectives and different systems of evaluation. It has acquired new symbolic significances in which the spurious obtains a new genuineness in its new contexts, and the genuine loses its historical significance to become valued for its antiquity, which in turn can be faked.

This is an expansion of reference and relations. The pastoral tradition of the renaissance has reached new heights in a technological world whose inhabitants aspire for antiquity and ruralism. The diverse objects and performances that represent these qualities provide them with a symbolic stability and continuity that appears to be absent from the modern, rushed world. On the one hand the expansion of folklore is referential, reaching beyond a region, a period, and a class to include the exotic, the historic, and the socially distant; on the other hand it is also relational, as it is evaluated from an expanding perspective, acquiring different meanings by different members of the society at different periods of their lives. By expansion folklore has acquired divergent meanings that are subject to continuous transformations.

Befittingly, one of the final reincarnations of folklore in the modern world is as a marketable commodity. Bausinger first explored this stage of folklorism in Part III of *Volkskunde: Von der Altertumsforschung zur Kulturanalyse* (1971). This chapter has been translated and incorporated into the present volume even though it represents a later development of Bausinger's theory, for it is a logical extension of his earlier thought and is consistent with the analysis of folklore in the modern world as presented in *Volkskultur in der technischen Welt*. The commodification of folklore, known as folklorism (see Regina Bendix, "Folklorism: The Challenge of a Concept," *International Folklore Review* 6 [1988]:5–15), thus refers to the transformation of folklore into a tradable commodity, turning the tradition of a group into a source of income. While financial rewards for diverse kinds of productions and performances are an acceptable, even desirable, form of exchange in traditional societies, the commodification of tradition occurs in the sale of objects and the display of artistic forms, not for their own sake and function, but because they are imbued with the idea of tradition, either regional, ethnic, or national. The production of such goods is geared to achieve maximal marketability, and hence it appeals to the stereotypical notions of tradition in a particular region or among a specific ethnic group. Its producers aim at representing regionality or ethnicity rather than a specific art form, conforming to images their consumers and spectators have acquired. The commodified tradition is part of the export market in the form of souvenirs for tourists or of performing delegations to other countries.

Bausinger develops these three ideas of denationalization, expansion, and commodification into a thorough and insightful analysis of folklore in current urban society. He draws most of his examples from Germany, but his descriptions and theoretical formulations apply everywhere. One can provide examples of similar processes, albeit with modifications for local conditions, from Africa, Asia, Australia, and the Americas. His formulations are relevant to developing as well as developed countries. As urban centers emerge in reality, the value of home villages, home countries, and older traditions, either transmitted or invented, rise in people's imagination and aspirations. They become focuses of regional, ethnic, and national identity. As such, folklore in modern society can be a positive social force among peoples who strive to reconstruct their lives after they have been crushed by colonialism; but at the same time, in the hands of racist ideologues, it can turn into a monstrous negative force. We must all be on guard.

Dan Ben-Amos

Author's Preface

Critics may characterize this book as very German (and I shall not mistake that as a compliment). But its topics are of general interest and most of the chapters deal with developments and problems with which the whole Western world is well acquainted. There are, however, some unavoidable refractions for a North American reader, and I will try to comment on them. In the Old World, and especially in the middle of Europe, folk culture and research into folk culture have been different from American folk life, folklore, and their investigation. In a pointed way one could say that the United States of America was built up by "folk"; the American nation was the democratic result of strong popular movements. The country was won by physical labor; for the craftsmen and farmers their own culture was a means of self-assertion, and for ethnic groups folklore was a strong expression and support of their identities. Even after the penetration of wide parts of the country by technical progress, industrial work, and urbanization, sizable pockets of folk culture have survived all over the United States.

All this is lacking in Germany. The nation was built from above; it was, at best, a civic achievement. Folk culture was defined—which means evaluated and put within strict limits—by middle-class people. There were regional shadings and local peculiarities but no marked ethnic differences. German ethnogists and folklorists, as a rule, were not pioneers accompanying, observing, and listening to wandering settlers; they could be found less in the field than in archives and libraries and at their desks. The brothers Grimm, drawing their fairy tales in the main from educated people and compiling legends from old prints, marked a symbolic start. In Germany, folklore and folk life were not so much realities but anti-modernist constructions based on a regressive ideology and compensating for the alienation of modern life.

This is the point of departure for this book. There was an urgent need to disentangle and disenchant folk culture, to pierce the romantic façades and arrive at the deeper reasons for those constructions. In Germany, the performance of folk culture had long since drifted away from its original texture and context; the praise of the original and primary had become part of a secondary system closely connected with advertising and public-relations activities, with economic and political interests. In order to show these differentiations of "folklorism," a few chapters from my book *Volkskunde* have been added to this edition.

In North America things are different, to be sure. Intercultural comparisons emphasize the fact that Europeans seek salvation in the past, whereas Americans look forward to the future. But I guess that even in North America folk life and folklore have become nostalgic categories. Even here, folklorists are in danger of overrating the genuineness of their objects of study and of not being aware of the social and cultural transformations which have made the term *genuine* questionable. The discussion of the making of tradition, the production of fakelore, and the availability of folk culture has begun, and I think this book might well fit into this discussion and is therefore timely.

It is true that substantial parts of it were written almost thirty years ago and therefore there may be shortcomings. At that time, ethnographers looked at folk cultures as preindustrial pockets not even touched by technological changes— thus, I emphasized the interdependence of technological developments and the folk world, and the secondary naturalness of technological experiences. Now I would question that naturalness and the dangers of unchained technology. At that time folklorists joined in the naive enthusiasm for popular historical traditions. Thus, it seemed necessary to me to point out the artifical and regressive character of many reconstructions. Now I would concede that in spite of this necessary disillusionment part of those historicist ambitions is an acceptable means of reestablishing lost identities. At that time, folk culture was still predominantly understood as an agrarian foundation of the whole nation, and so I had to indicate that, on the contrary, it was a well-calculated part of modern mass culture. Now I would specify the (sub)cultural differentiations within our society which have assigned new functions and values to the (really or pretendedly) old traditions.

But such emphasis would not mean that the arguments of this book had to be withdrawn. It deals with a rather lengthy historical process: the rise and development of folk culture in, and as a counterpart of, modernization, and this overturning of preindustrial society and culture has established the framework and starting points for all further changes in this field. In Germany, a 1986 reprint of this book has given proof of its enduring efficacy. I hope that for American readers, too, it will not be merely an exotic trifle but will make a contribution to sharpening the concepts used in folkloristics and will encourge discussion.

I would like to thank the editors for including this book in their series and Elke Dettmer for her ascetic struggle with my style and the troublesome work of rendering the contents into readable English.

Hermann Bausinger

Translator's Preface

The provocative study *Volkskultur in der technischen Welt* was first published in 1961 and earned Hermann Bausinger the chair of the Folklore Department, since renamed *Empirische Kulturwissenschaft* (Empirical Cultural Science), at the Ludwig-Uhland-Institut, University of Tübingen. Now considered a classic of German folklore scholarship, the book provided an essential stimulus for the reorientation of *Volkskunde* (the discipline of folklore) in Germany in the late sixties and the seventies.[1] Until then *Volkskunde* was mainly concerned with preindustrial, pretechnological folk culture, i.e., with peasants, survivals, and relics. Bausinger's work showed that the technological world and folk culture are not mutually exclusive, and that folk culture, in fact, has been strongly influenced by modern developments.

Inevitably by now some of the references appear outdated; the enthusiasm for progress and technology, which forms part of this study, has meanwhile been replaced by more sceptical attitudes. Many of the examples from the author's southwest German environment are barely familiar to the translator from northern Germany and will be even less familiar to the American reader. However, the basic thesis remains relevant beyond the context of any specific examples—the expansion of formerly narrow and fixed horizons in our world of technology.

The last part of the present book, "Relics—and What Can Become of Them," was originally published in 1971 as Part III of Hermann Bausinger's unconventional textbook *Volkskunde*. It consists of an extended discussion of some aspects of folklorism *(Folklorismus)*, a concept of increasing interest to folklorists in North America.

In 1979, soon after the "Decade of Theoretical Confrontation, Debate, and Reorientation," to quote Dow and Lixfeld,[2] Hermann Bausinger was clearly the dominant figure at the biennial congress of the *Deutsche Gesellschaft für Volkskunde* in Kiel.[3] His *Volkskunde* has just been reissued in paperback and was prominently displayed. It was here that I encountered the idea of folklore as an applied cultural science and the concept of folklorism before I had even begun my folklore studies. A few months later, Alan Dundes at the University of California—Berkeley asked for a report on *Volkskultur in der technischen Welt*. The book profoundly influenced me. Eventually part of my thesis on Blue Jeans, a topic that was "not folklore" according to an unknown American reviewer, was included in a publication at Tübingen. Subsequently I met Hermann Bausinger and we corresponded. It was a most encouraging contact for a novice folklorist, for this outstanding and very active scholar was also humane and approachable. Beyond the scholarly challenge and service it represents, this translation is therefore also a work of gratitude and appreciation.

Early in my folklore studies I noticed the divergent paths recent folklore studies had taken in North America and in Germany. Moreover, I was frequently asked by Alan Dundes and by fellow students to translate or summarize from German folklore texts. Graduate students of folklore in North America are generally required to have a reading knowledge of German, but their skills are not usually sufficient to comprehend more elaborate texts. At the same time it is important for the discipline to be informed on an international basis, a task to which the series Folklore Studies in Translation is dedicated.

On the whole, the translation proved to be a rewarding, if difficult, undertaking. Inevitably some words and concepts do not translate well. Where they are retained in German (italicized), brief glosses are inserted within the text. In more-complicated cases a few translator's footnotes have been added. Bausinger's consistent use of (folk) cultural *Gut* and *Güter* presented a particularly difficult problem. After attempting to translate the term variously as "cultural expression," "property," "artifact," and the like, in the end stylistic concerns were overridden by the need to convey a precise technical meaning, namely that of "objectivations" of (folk) culture. Moreover, Dow and Lixfeld had set a precedent in their translation of Bausinger's essay "Critique of Folklorism Criticism."[4] Consequently the reader will encounter the somewhat unusual terms of cultural "good" and "goods" throughout the text.

Another difficult choice was to translate *einfaches Volk* as "simple folk," rather than the more idiomatic "common folk." However, Hermann Bausinger specifically refers to the "simple" *(einfache)* manner in which "the folk" accepts the most complicated matters of the world of technology. In fact, the meaning of *Volk* varies and depends greatly on the attitude and mood of the users, as well as on the social structure of their time. The oldest meaning of *Volk* is a distinct unit of warriors, an army; by the late middle ages *Volk* was used as a more general term for soldiers or troops; from the eighteenth century on this sense was becoming outdated, and *Volk* now referred to a group that was held together by some sort of bond, often under the leadership of one individual, or united by a certain profession or locality. At this time *Volk* acquired a social value, generally one of low esteem, particularly in colloquial speech. *Volk* further indicated the mass of the population, as contrasted with an upper class or ruling powers. However, in the Romantic era the pejorative meaning subsided when interest in the customs, songs, and tales of the *Volk* was growing, when the *Volk* was viewed as the unselfconscious, unadulterated, characteristic part of society, even as an organic collective. On another level *Volk* meant the population of a country which is united by common descent, language, and political system, and is thus differentiated from other similar communities; in the French Revolution this meaning of *Volk* acquired the ring of a political slogan, a meaning which received extreme emphasis in Nazi Germany and left postwar German *Volkskunde* with a difficult legacy.[5]

Several people have helped me with the translation. Thanks go first of all to my parents, who provided a few months of calm and financial security to begin the project. Graham Shorrocks of the Department of English Language and Literature, Memorial University, Newfoundland, made sure that I had not bitten off more than I could chew. His linguistic background, interest in folklore and meticulous work proved most valuable. I also appreciate the helpful comments and advice by Neil Rosenberg, David Buchan, and Peter Narváez of the Folklore Department, Memorial University. Roberta Buchanan helped to make the text more digestible for non-specialist English readers; and Paul Smith, visiting research fellow at Memorial University, provided additional insights. Friends and roommates supported me with their interest and patience. All are gratefully acknowledged.

Elke Dettmer

Acknowledgments

The English language edition of this book was made possible, in part, by a translation subsidy from INTER NATIONES.

The generous support of The L. J. Skaggs and Mary C. Skaggs Foundation has made the *Folklore Studies in Translation* series possible.

Folk Culture
in a
World of
Technology

INTRODUCTION

In the 1930s, Bertolt Brecht urged that the term *Volk* (folk) be replaced with *Bevölkerung* (population), since those who make this change "already refuse to endorse many lies." The request appeared in the pamphlet *Fünf Schwierigkeiten beim Schreiben der Wahrheit*[1] (Five Difficulties in Writing the Truth), printed in 1934 in an underground anti-fascist journal. Brecht's statement was a response to the one-sided politicization of the concept *Volk* within the Nationalist Socialist State. It remains relevant today even beyond that historical context. Although the concept "folk culture" has been retained as the familiar subject of the scholarly discipline of *Volkskunde*, and the historical development of the discipline makes it all but impossible to discard the word *Volk*, any study concerned with today's folk culture must acknowledge and consider this position.

In general, arguments within *Volkskunde* run counter to those of Brecht: "The population *(Bevölkerung)* of individuals merely organized in the State and therefore not fully developed in their vitality, their talents impoverished," is contrasted with "the healthy, organically related folk *(Volk)*, a lost ideal which is to be regained."[2] At first glance it seems as if concepts are merely being substituted. Brecht at least objects to *Volk* for reasons similar to those used here to argue against *Bevölkerung:* the word "indicates a certain uniformity," which is merely organized and ignores the interests of the individual. Nevertheless the difference in terminology is based on important reasons, and the fact that folklorists have made no attempt to avoid the ambiguity of the word *Volk* by replacing it with *Bevölkerung* is not accidental. Their reasons are found not only in the historical ties of *Volkskunde* to Herder and the Romantics, who elevated the concept *Volk* without, however, removing its ambiguity,[3] but above all in the influence of Wilhelm Heinrich Riehl on the development of *Volkskunde* as a scientific discipline.

A hundred years ago, Riehl questioned research limited to the specific subject areas of *Volkskunde:* "Such studies of frequently very childish and preposterous habits and customs, of house and farm, dress and shirt and kitchen and cellar by themselves are, in fact, complete rubbish. . . ."[4] The thought expressed here by Riehl is the one which even now frequently startles *Volkskunde* out of its complacent focus on the often rather harmless individual object. "By themselves" these studies do not mean anything; they must be related to each other and to a larger entity. Riehl defines this entity by indicating that these single studies "only receive their scholarly, as well as their poetic, sanction because of their relationship to the wonderful organism of an entire folk personality. The proposition, that of all things in the world mankind is man's most worthy object of study, applies in its fullest extent to this idea of nation." A tenet of enlightened humanitarianism, Pope's "proper study of mankind is man" is here fused with the "idea of the nation," and for *Volkskunde* this idea becomes the "focus of its scattered investigations."[5]

Although comparative, supranational considerations were increasingly emphasized in the following decades—particularly in contact and confrontation with
the field of ethnology—until "vulgus in populo"[6] generally becomes considered
the object of *Volkskunde*, the "idea of the nation" nevertheless remains alive in
the word *Volk*. It is a blend of national and social elements, the proportions of
which may differ. It always includes, however, both ingredients, and it is precisely this ambiguity which seems to have strengthened this position of the term
Volk within *Volkskunde*. The repeatedly revived aim of "changing *Volkskunde*
from the study of variants in the manner ridiculed by Riehl"[7] was generally satisfied by the concept *Volk*. The occasional blame *Volkskunde* receives for its lack
of categories is directly related to the dominant position the concept *Volk* has
achieved within it: this concept seemed to answer the demand for overarching
regularities and aspects the individual subjects of study have in common. For
decades the discussion of this concept dominated almost the entire theoretical
debate of *Volkskunde*.[8]

Currently the mere comparative study of variants is questioned even more because of the increasingly dynamic quality of cultural life. To restrict oneself to
positivist individual studies is less possible than ever. According to Friedrich
Georg Jünger, positivism is "always an occupation of quiet times."[9] No one will
criticize as vain musing today's search for categories which relate to the entire
folk culture. But the present state of affairs makes it impossible to refer to the
ambiguous concept *Volk* as a panacea. The following discussion does not avoid
the concept, but context and qualifications should leave no doubt that instead of
the sacrosanct ideal of an organic collective personality, *Volk* is here used to indicate the real world of the lower classes, the "simple folk."[10] This concept,
therefore, no longer confers "scholarly sanction" on the individual sectors of
folk life. On the contrary, it is more urgent than ever for *Volkskunde* to identify
common points of view for the manifestations of its various subfields, which are
so differentiated that they overlap with several other scholarly disciplines: narrative research, no doubt, impinges upon literary studies, folk drama research upon
conventional drama studies, the sector "house and farm" upon architectural history and settlement geography.

It seems very natural now to observe common characteristics in smaller and
more tangible social units than the folk: the village, the neighborhood, the family. None of these units can be considered absolute, however. Folk life and folk
culture take place within the social weave of larger and smaller groups, and not
every "folk good" is simultaneously a "village good," a "neighborhood good,"
or the like.[11] But above all, these are sociological approximations, not specifically folkloristic categories. Particularly in view of the strong and fruitful influence questions and methods of sociology have exerted on *Volkskunde*, it is useful
to investigate the basic differences between these branches of scholarship.[12] The
fundamental difference is not the opposition between *Gemeinschaft* (community)
and *Gesellschaft* (society), which in itself is purely sociological and which has
been rendered relative by recent research, but the fact that the objects of knowledge of sociology "are not objects tied to the substratum" but are interhuman
relations,[13] while *Volkskunde* from its beginning has focused on objects tied to

the substratum, on "goods" of folk culture. There exists a reciprocal influence, however, between social realities and cultural forms and expressions. This functional relationship is of great interest to the new *Volkskunde:* "Out of the study of the interplay between behavior and cultural good grows the knowledge of the actual sphere of life."[14] Folkloristic categories do not primarily attempt to comprehend the social bases or the motif-historical relationship of cultural expressions, but are concerned with the particular mentalities which produce specific cultural expressions based on specific social foundations.[15]

This study attempts to seek such categories for folk culture in the age of technology. One could well assume that the main difficulty in such an attempt is the fact that today's folk culture in particular is characterized by radically new elements that have never been known before and therefore are difficult to comprehend. However, when the object is investigated *sine ira* it becomes obvious that in part today's manifestations of folk culture are deeply rooted in the history of ideas and in part they have striking historical parallels. It is at times difficult even to detect truly new elements, as they often consist merely of small shifts of emphasis. Any research single-mindedly concerned with entirely new aspects could only result in a catalogue of particular features brought into being by technological developments, but it would not provide an even approximately reliable overall picture of folk culture in the age of technology. Manifestations and disguises of archetypal elements that are conditioned over time, called "cultural-typical" elements by Carl Gustav Jung,[16] must be considered as well. Any pebbles from the long and lively stream of the history of ideas washed to the shore of the present may not be ignored simply because they do not pertain *exclusively* to the present.

The question of historical relationships has had to be neglected, or at least is often only alluded to, because this investigation, being more systematic than historical, does not trace the development of specific specialized areas of *Volkskunde* but seeks aspects that are overlapping and common to all or many of those areas, e.g., categories that are applicable to both folk narratives and folk architecture, to mention two widely separated branches. Obviously even such an attempt has to begin with concrete artifacts of specific branches of *Volkskunde*. Here they derive mainly from German studies, the field most familiar to the author. The examples and references, often taken from newspapers, are frequently located in southwest Germany. Without doubt this results in certain biases. Therefore factual or possible regional differences are repeatedly pointed out within this study. At the very least, the insights gained must be tested against other regions to ascertain whether they are more generally valid. However, compared to the regionally confined folk culture of earlier times, regional differences have become less important today.

It must be stated explicitly that the attempt, though informed by a great number of scholarly investigations, is not based on specific prior studies to any large extent. The transition from preindustrial peasant culture to the folk culture of the technological age has barely been noted by *Volkskunde*. Generally the folk culture of the more or less recent past has not been studied in and for itself, but was mainly investigated for survivals of earlier historical stages. Therefore few preliminary historical studies exist on which to base a *Volkskunde* of the present. An unbiased interpretation of the folk culture of the nineteenth century is just as desirable as a new folkloristic appraisal of the Enlightenment, which "is anything but a closed era, to be ridiculed with arrogance."[17]

The fact that this attempt leads into new territory may serve as an excuse for the fact that, as the Notes indicate, the material consulted was rather variegated and mixed, that an unhewn stone has been used here and there, and that many an important sidetrack has been ignored. For example, the many-layered concept of magic is used without thoroughly analyzing its components, and the sections on regressions and on archaisms touch only incidentally on the insights and questions generated by psychoanalysis. In some cases such a restriction consciously lends a certain emphasis; i.e., the "natural quality" of the technical realm is stressed in dialectical opposition to the emphasis on its unfamiliar and dangerous aspects that is common particularly within present-day *Volkskunde*.

The work remains open in many directions. Within the discipline of folklore major concerns are to question the relevance of the categories here assigned to the individual expressions and search for preliminary historical stages and regional characteristics. Now and again studies will be referred to that represent attempts in that direction. Above all, at the frontier of folklore studies, there are questions about the application of the knowledge gained as well as questions of evaluation, which are not explicitly addressed here. However, any arrangement by categories constitutes an evaluation in itself: "Intellectual understanding can never be separated from existential decision."[18] At the same time any such arrangement asks for and makes possible further evaluations and decisions. Amid the heat of the present-day skirmishes focusing on social-cultural criticism and the frantic prophesies of decline, and the equally frantic attempts at salvation, this investigation should show that studies of present-day folk culture can be carried out in a cool and deliberate manner.[19]

CHAPTER

1

THE TECHNICAL WORLD AS "NATURAL" ENVIRONMENT

FOLK WORLD AND TECHNICAL WORLD

In a recent book published in Cologne, the photographer Chargesheimer attempted to capture the life of a single old street in that city with pictures of children at play and old women, prostitutes and disabled people, small groups participating in carnival and Corpus Christi processions, in pubs and at the amusement park.[1] The epilogue by Heinrich Böll, "Streets Like This One," emphasizes the unwritten, rigid laws and the proud dignity of such streets. It concludes: "These streets can only live as a whole, not in particles, they are like colonies of plants which are nourished from secret roots; within them 'folk' is still alive—ancient, proud, inaccessible, and faithful to its laws."

Read in isolation, one would probably relate the last half sentence to an old, remote village rather than to a street of a large city and suspect that the source was the antiquated vision of a romanticizing popular poet. Within that domain such attributes for the "folk" are quite common. Obviously Böll is aware of this, and his comments should not be understood as a naive assessment but as a conscious, alienating transfer from that other realm. And yet these words are not intended as irony, but represent a sincere embracing of such streets. The reasons for this can hardly be reduced to a common denominator. Like the photographs, Böll's words show that the artist's loving devotion can produce beautiful, very individual, human pictures even from grim reality. Moreover, the poetry of poverty already has accumulated a lengthy literary tradition. When linking the text with a series of pictures, however, the relationship to reality must be stressed more strongly than the literary origins. Thus the social motivation, which recurs again and again in Böll's writing, and his passionate affection for the poor and the oppressed have to be considered. When reviewing Chargesheimer's photographs it strikes us that hardly a car, even less the owner of a car, appears in the pictures: a strange state of affairs for an urban street.

At this point the social motive touches on another one which is of special interest to us. To be sure, the world of technology is not foreign to Heinrich Böll. Nevertheless the evaluation seems to be based on an assumption of the sort that considers "folk" with its ancient laws is still unchanged in regions where the strong levers of technology have not yet been able to unhinge those old laws. Such an urban area has certainly not remained untouched by technology. As part of a large city it is directly a product of the Industrial Revolution. But within these quarters a certain condition has developed after the Industrial Revolution which may evoke the impression of an unchanging and enduring quality, compared to the very rapid mechanization of recent years and decades in other areas, including agriculture. Thus relic areas of the "folk" are no longer necessarily peasant villages, but urban quarters which seem to have been bypassed by the economic growth of the recent past: streets like this one, to which the old categories and attributes would still apply.

Even if Böll had not used the word "folk" so provocatively, the folklorist should still be concerned with this shift in emphasis. He notes uneasily that within his discipline very few attempts are made to tackle this problem. In fact, he finds distinct parallels to Böll's transfer of concepts. The recent development of *Volkskunde* has largely failed to address the formation of adequate new concepts and categories and has instead sought to match new objects and population groups with the old concepts.

Today the limitation of *Volkskunde* to the peasantry or to the rural population is rarely advocated in a theoretical sense. The last important theoretical statement which declares the German peasantry the sole subject of *Volkskunde* was made by Julius Schwietering in 1927.[2] At the same time he opened new paths for *Volkskunde* by elaborating on the functional method, as he shifted the focus from the rural cultural object to its social functions. Perhaps the conscious restriction to the peasantry is related to this methodological shift, which, in fact, opened the doors to sociology and could have made *Volkskunde* a subdiscipline of sociology, if it had not been firmly assigned a distinct subject matter. However, about that time the demand for an urban *Volkskunde* became more frequent and more emphatic. This demand never ceased even during the Third Reich, when the peasant world experienced an additional ideological reevaluation. To date it is still part of the permanent stock of programmatic statements so frequent within *Volkskunde*.

By contrast, practical studies of urban folklore are quite rare. For a long time the "Outline of the Folklore of Vienna" by Leopold Schmidt[3] was probably the only complete statement of its kind. Recently added are *Folklore of the City of Linz on the Danube* by Hans Commenda[4] and a few omnibus volumes,[5] but they do not substantially mitigate the discrepancy between theoretical demand and practice in this area. The discrepancy essentially derives from the very sketchy nature of the theoretical basis of urban folklore studies. Even the stereotypical limitation of the focus to large cities is suspicious. It fails to recognize the very broad transitional zone between the rural and the urban world, a transitional zone which not only characterizes the historical development from an agricultural to an industrial state, but which even today influences large parts of the industrial area.[6]

The demand for an urban folklore is frequently based on the opposition village-city as a dichotomy of ideal types. Often the urban folklorist is equipped only with the proven categories of peasant lore when he—somewhat flirtatiously at times—jumps across the intermediate zones. To that extent he remains close to those who want to limit *Volkskunde* to the world of the peasant. This is very obvious in the essay "Volkskunde der Grossstadt" (Folklore of the City) by Joseph Klapper.[7] He explicitly gives urban folklore the following mandate: "The inhabitants of the city have to regain such a vivid awareness of the idea of the crucial significance of blood and soil for the continued existence of *Volkstum*[8] that the influx to the large city is changed into a drawing away from it." Characteristically Klapper then has to evoke the multiple meanings of the concept *Volk* in order to save the city: the awareness of "the unity of the German folk" redeems the city "from the ban of alienation from the folk." To be sure, all this has to be considered in the context of the time. However, it was really only a striking escalation of ideas which had long been familiar to *Volkskunde* and which even today have not been entirely overcome by the discipline. Above all, many laymen tend to foster such ideas: here we are not merely concerned with the internal problem of a single discipline, but with questions which quite generally call forth answers or opinions, judgments or prejudices.

The problem of urban folklore—which requires an extensive assessment of individual studies to allow for a fruitful discussion—leads to a more general question. What emerges in this instance is similarly repeated in historical investigations of individual subject areas of folklore. After an exhaustive presentation of earlier eras they often fail to follow their object into the present. Instead they frequently end at the beginning or the middle of the nineteenth century, or they narrow down the formerly unbiased, broad perspective to a few "folklike" forms, e.g., to certain plays of religious consecration (in folk drama research) or to the songs of the Youth Movement (in folk song research). When confronted with such historical interpretations and with the opposition of village and city, the decisive question they ask is that of the relationship between folk world and technical world. Even this relationship is often understood as one of opposition. But where a sharp division is made between village and city, where categories of peasant lore are applied unquestioningly to studies of cities, or where the last hundred years remain ignored in comprehensive historical investigations, an unbridgeable gap is presumed, either explicitly or implicitly, to exist between folk world and technical world. At this point we must attempt to unravel and to test the complex of theoretical notions at the source of this assumption if we are to approach a really systematic presentation of the relationship between folk world and technical world, which, however, cannot be achieved here completely.

To begin with, one opinion considers the folk world as ahistorical but the technical world as historical in the highest degree. The thesis of the ahistorical quality of the folk world is perhaps most clearly expressed in Josef Dünninger's book *Volkswelt und geschichtliche Welt* (Folk World and Historical World),[9] which states: "*Volkstum* follows a different basic law from that of history. *Volkstum* is of eternal duration, timeless, realizing itself in the natural course of the year, unchangeable in its innermost aspects, imprinted and preordained from primordial beginnings, without time, but situated in space." Subsequently, however Dünninger specifies that "folkloristic phenomena have their history" and that "the contact and the fruitful argument" between folk world and historical world are the essential elements. Therefore to Dünninger *Volkstum* and folk world in their ahistorical permanence are idealized concepts. The category of permanence is always mythical in nature. In his later works Dünninger increasingly moves the historical aspects of folk life and folk culture to the forefront.[10] During recent years, wherever folklorists have conducted historical research supported by archival data, they have found a conspicuously strong dependence of folk culture on the trends of the time.[11] If folk world is understood as the true spiritual and material world of "simple folk" rather than the never-realized idea of timeless substance, then it is moved into the historical realm. When folk culture is compared to high culture, we can merely claim a relatively greater longevity of its goods—and even this has to be verified in each individual case.

However, the assumption that the technical world is historical must be qualified as well. The natural sciences as carriers of technical progress are searching precisely for permanently valid, ahistorical laws. Technology advances by a process of discovery,[12] i.e., it renders accessible and real that which potentially has always existed. Until the most recent past physics was also always an expression of metaphysics. "An experiment was the recognition of timeless associations."[13] Even Einstein attempted to hold on to the objectivity of physical occurrences. Only the Bohr-Heisenberg quantum theory turned physics from recognition of nature to recognition of our relationship to nature by a process of measuring: it is now part of the historical category.

It may be objected that these reflections apply only to the inner sphere of technology. Where technology exerts an external influence, it would hardly matter if it were understood as an expression of timeless laws or as something unique created by history. On the outside the strikingly rapid change of its manifestations—compared to the relative permanence of the folk world and its norms and forms—would threaten in each case to drag the latter into an all-too-swift transience, into the fast-turning machinery of historical change. This thought cannot be dismissed. It gives us a new starting point from which to dissolve the bare opposition between folk world and technical world. For much that is generally attributed to the technical world is valid only for the inner sphere of technology itself, while in its realization—insofar as technology determines and shapes the human world—it is dissolved or softened or modified.

This also applies to the notion which perhaps most decisively substantiates the opposition between folk world and technical world, i.e., the mechanical character of the technical world, which contrasts with the animated folk world. Wilhelm Grimm wrote about the *Märchen*: "For only where avarice and the rattling wheels of machinery stupefy any other thought does one think that one can dispense with them; they endure where a secure, customary order and life-style still prevail, where the connection between human emotions and surrounding nature is still perceived and the past is not torn from the present."[14] Such declarations remind us of early pieces of wisdom from the Far East, as, for example, the saying handed down from Chuang-tse, "I have heard my teacher say: If someone uses machines, then he conducts all his affairs in a machinelike manner; whoever conducts his affairs in a machinelike manner, develops a machine heart. But he who has a machine heart in his breast, loses his pure simplicity."[15] However, while the ancient Chinese saying grows out of a culture characterized by withdrawal from the world—a culture which was, in fact, capable of denying the impact of technical discoveries when they threatened to lead away from the basic source of nature—Wilhelm Grimm's remark was made in an era and culture concerned with mastering nature and with the scientific-technological conquest of the world. *Volkskunde,* which began under the sign of such declarations, was pushed into ever narrower corners in the course of the spread of technology and—more seriously—into an increasingly questionable attitude toward reality. The moral appeal of the Romantic era in the face of danger turned more and more into insincere zeal against reality.

Throughout this investigation it will be possible and necessary to examine the question of the mechanization of life through technology. At this point it can already be established that the transfer of mechanical notions to nonmechanical phenomena seems to be neither more frequent nor necessarily more dangerous than the reverse process. In fact, a closer look proves that sometimes quite opposite forces are engaged in those cases in which mechanization is suspected. This is true, for example, of current ideas of the state. Friedrich Georg Jünger comments, "The state increasingly is imagined as a technological control center comparable to a switchboard where one only has to press buttons and levers to produce results."[16] Without doubt this is the case; but this thought intersects with a second idea (and only then does it become truly dangerous), i.e., the organic idea, which makes the state seem like animated machinery, the whole larger than the sum of its parts, its processes anonymous and finally indisputable. While a machine necessitates service and interference, the organism functions by itself. However, this interpretation would require detailed investigation. Verification could be established, for example, if the high degree of technology typical of North America were proven to be matched by a particularly active responsibility for the state and a particularly sober insight into its organization.

In this context two further concepts, closely related to the problem of mechanization, that contribute to the argument for the opposition between folk world and technical world have already been mentioned: organism and organization, i.e., the world of folk defined as an organic structure, and the world of technology defined as organized construction. These concepts are not at all precise. In biology the ordering of the functions of an organism is referred to as organization.[17] On the other hand, it must be recognized that the application of the concept organism to a group of people has always represented a metaphorical extension, or to put it differently, is a threshold value.

The opposition touches on the one between *Gemeinschaft* (community) and *Gesellschaft* (society), which had long been fundamental to *Volkskunde,* for folklorists relied on the oppositional pair systematized by Tönnies to contrast the essentially "folklike" processes of communal life *(Gemeinschaftsleben)* with the manifestations of society *(Gesellschaft).* Sociology as well long remained spellbound by this antinomy, but has meanwhile thoroughly reexamined the matter.[18] The two concepts are no longer viewed as validating agents and "as substances, but merely as freely mobile characteristics of relationships . . . which under certain circumstances can even appear simultaneously within the same social constructs."[19] This means that *Volkskunde* research, too, must include groups which were formerly neglected,[20] and social forms pertaining to the technical world will have to be considered. Just as alliances, which have long represented the prototypes of "*Gemeinschaft*" for *Volkskunde,* are subject to forms of organization, so too do newer organizations like *Vereine* (voluntary associations) have "organic" links. The "partial shut-off effect" of technology[21] does not necessarily destroy holistic life and social forms.

The fluid transition between organism and organization touches on the relativization of the opposition between ahistorical and historical elements. It is based on the fact "that for human beings no domain of pure nature can be spatially isolated from their historical existence."[22] Finally the conceptual oppositions from which we proceed lead to fundamental concerns of anthropology. Largely these oppositions can be reduced to the opposition between rational and irrational; i.e., rational construction would prevail in the world of technology while the strongest impulses of the world of the folk would, according to this view, come from nonrational depths. But here, too, we must make qualifications in both cases. Above all, technology itself, with its clearly rational structure, must be distinguished from the technical world, in which this rational quality recedes at times to a rather dangerous degree. A precise investigation of the concept of consciousness as had been made, for example, by Otto Friedrich Bollnow,[23] brings us closer to this contrast. When dealing with technology, awareness is most often focused exclusively on the purpose, while "technology itself is not subjected to any questions." Therefore in a deeper sense this does not represent conscious action, but naive activity. Friedrich Georg Jünger quotes examples of the same problem: "The consciousness of a race car driver, a pilot, an operator of a diesel locomotive, is wide awake, yet only within a small sector limited by the night and dreamlike notions. It possesses that functional alertness that is directed toward the functions of the apparatus."[24] It even seems that this alertness is not so much directed toward the functions of the apparatus in use as toward a small section of reality which is encountered via the apparatus. "In this manner a man can at any time grow so intimately close to a bicycle, a car, or an airplane that these machines temporarily constitute an extension of his bodily scheme and consequently can no longer be counted as part of his environment."[25] It seems obvious that the sequence mentioned can be extended back beyond the bicycle to include the plow, the hammer, and any other tool technology. Even though it is necessary to distinguish the mechanical technology of our time from the mere tool technology of the craftsman and of handcrafted manufacture, the forms of awareness when using technology seem quite comparable in its various stages.

This explains why manifestations of technology are neither immune from nor even merely resistant to prerational forms of behavior and thought—a point which will be discussed in detail below. But if we question the entirely rational character of the technical world, then the irrational character of the folk world must be questioned as well. When soberly approached and exactly investigated, the processes of origin and tradition have proven to be neither entirely nor even predominantly rooted in nonrational elements. Mainly in more recent developments of folk culture are decidedly logical forms gaining ground: the wide dissemination of the joke[26] within folk narratives is only one example. The image of a "prelogical-associative" folk person, borrowed from a passing trend in anthropology, is no longer valid.

However, while the oppositions mentioned above are most often merely inherent in the contrast between folk world and technical world, the opposition between the nonrational forms of behavior of the simple folk and the, as it were, entirely rational world of today is stressed with conspicuous frequency. In the one case the contrast serves to proclaim the end of the folk world, in the other to offer proof that the technical world, after all, has not yet conquered all the territory. "The notion common folk is dead and will not even appear among us again in the form of a revenant," writes Max Rumpf, who gives the following reasons:

> Where the milker works with new production methods and better, cleaner utensils as part of the expert, successful conduct of the dairy business, the witch has no more cause to interfere maliciously and ungraciously with making butter. Indeed, in earlier times, when the open hearth fitfully lightened the darkness of the smoke-blackened walls and the beamed ceiling only here and there, and in the evenings drew the ever so credulous and ever so uneducated, naive folk of the house around it, it was time to tell ghost stories until the youngsters sitting on stools, filled with shudders and dread, pulled their legs up under their bodies to protect themselves from all the uncanny beings scurrying and fluttering about the room. But now, when pressing a button at once sends light as bright as day into the farthest corners of hall, parlor, or stable, poor souls no longer prowl through the room, and the house ghost no longer dares to leave its hiding place.[27]

On the other hand, in contradiction, many folklorists triumphantly point to mascots in cars, which are frequently installed for protection as well as for decoration. In both cases manifestations of "magic" are made to represent the whole folk world. That this limits the problem unduly need hardly be emphasized. However, the frequency of such arguments indicates that the question of "magic and technology" must become a pivotal point of an investigation that attempts truly to understand the folk culture of the world of technology.

THE MAGIC OF TECHNOLOGY

On January 12, 1417, during the great Church Council, a nativity play performed in Constance, as was usual, included the adoration of the Magi and ended with the murder of the children of Bethlehem. The description of the play emphasizes that the star which showed the way for the Magi was moved by machinery.[28] This is a small example of the very ancient and universal delight in elaborate mechanical contrivances, which certainly extends beyond the theatre.[29] However, it is most easily traced there; one only need remember the often intricate machinery employed on and behind the Baroque stage. Though partly meant to create illusions, it was not confined to this service, for it simultaneously delighted the public *as* machinery. While the artificiality of the machinery thus reached a certain climax during the Baroque period, the mechanization of the stage declined thereafter and for some time had no value in itself.

This transformation coincides with a transformation in the general evaluation of technical devices. Where these are of an order of magnitude that causes one to forget their mere servitude and perhaps even endangers it, fear of the machine as well as of its inventors can replace the delight. Philipp Adam Ulrich (1692–1748), a theologically trained teacher of jurisprudence, who was highly dedicated to the improvement of agriculture, constructed, among other things, a new mechanical plow and a threshing machine. His biographer, Franz Oberthür, reports how a "common legend" was linked to these inventions:[30] the plowing machine allegedly flung stones from their beds with such force and in such quantities that they descended on farmhand and ox like a downpour; the ox shied, and the farmhand worried about his head. And when Ulrich wanted to start his new threshing machine, his farmhand supposedly warned him "of injury, well-meaning and in guileless manner," whereupon Ulrich fired him in anger. The truth content of these legends—Oberthür assumes they are nothing but rumors—does not really matter to us. What is decisive here is the solid distrust which confronts technological inventions and places the machine into supratechnical, magical, or diabolical contexts—which probably explains the warning of the farmhand.

Certainly activities of superior intellects have always tended to be placed in a supernatural context. Thus Albertus Magnus was suspected of sorcery because of his unusual knowledge of the natural sciences, which placed him ahead of his time. Numerous legends evolved around Paracelsus, and Trithemius himself writes: "The same as happened to Albertus Magnus, who was considered a sorcerer by the folk because of the wonderful things he achieved with the aid of secret natural forces, may happen to me as well."[31] However, these men were in the field of tension between white and black magic. They admitted to practicing the art of magic, to harnessing "secret natural forces," and with only a small shift in emphasis their activities could gain the appearance of harnessing secret *super*natural forces. Certainly these "magical" experiments and arts represented a preliminary stage of the newer natural sciences. But if we merely acknowledge these as preliminary stages, we fail to recognize that magic originally represented a "holistic knowledge," a pansophy which cannot be separated from religion. By comparison the thinking of the newer natural sciences is much more rational and pragmatic. Earlier legends developed by a mere shift in emphasis from white to black magic; now legends evolve from a structure of thought that is different not only in degree but also in principle. Above all such legends and imaginary beliefs no longer focus on a few great personalities, but are spread along with the numerous technical apparatuses and machines.

However, fantasy does not ignite at the mere advent of machines, which are then placed in supernatural contexts. Such machines are often anticipated in the so-called technical legend,[32] which is by no means limited to such miracles as "a rope made of sand" or "stony strips for sewing," but also conceives of objects which are just about to move from the realm of utopia into the realm of reality. In one sense such technical legends definitely are precursors of technical developments. However, in another sense they provide a basis for resistance to machines, as soon as these evolve from the realm of legend and enter reality. Here scientific planning and technical construction are barely separated. It is revealing that a mere scientific calculation on paper can often generate ideas similar to actual technical construction. Jeremias Höslin was a parson who engaged in meteorological studies on the Schwäbische Alb (Jura Mountains of Swabia). When he publicized the results in 1784—"non eruditis, sed erudiendis"[33]—the booklet had to be preceded by a laborious advance report in which he deals with the rumors disseminated about him:

> Now I had predicted the ruin of some country abodes; now hunger and plague; now terrible thunder and hail storms; now the inevitable death at a certain age not only predicted, but most exactly calculated and confirmed; also the announcement of my own alleged death, which was detailed to the minute, and even circulated in my own neighborhood; and perhaps not all of such foolishness and interspersed evils has reached my ears. Because my weather forecasts, which I derived from the following principles, proved to be correct enough, although they were unappreciated by some, misunderstood by others, it so happened without any guilt on my part that a great many gullible or else superstitious people experienced utmost fear and apprehension and still do not know today what to think of such information. Although I protested against this a few years ago in the public newspaper, I nevertheless could not prevent renewed fantasies from entering here or there. I do not enjoy being counted as one of the new prophets, for I am certain that in the last analysis they deserve merely to be called fanatical dreamers, whereas I want to convince everyone that nothing is closer to my heart than the well-being and the contentment of my sublunar fellow citizens and that it will remain my most pleasant task to promote these according to my ability.

The nearness of technical facts to—mostly evil—magic is expressed particularly clearly in the many reports and stories accompanying the introduction of the railroad. Philipp Matthias Hahn is a key figure in southwest Germany. At each of the locations in which he was active, the prediction of the railroad has been ascribed to him. Shortly after the opening of the line from Stuttgart to Ludwigsburg, a man from Feuerbach said that Hahn, then a parson in Kornwestheim, predicted that soon one would be able to drive without horses.[34] In Erdmannshausen too someone related a prophecy of the railroad. As written in the local chronicle by Willi Müller,[35] "A very simple-minded man who lived here during the last century once predicted that coaches would run without horses at the edge of the road in the Murrtal. Only after the railroad was actually built there, was the prediction remembered." In the region of the Fildern, Hahn's place of birth, a time was predicted as well "when the coaches run without horses."[36] At the inauguration of the Onstmettingen Talgangbahn (valley railroad line) in 1901, a festive greeting mounted above the workshop of mechanic Kern read: "What long has been predicted by forefather Hahn now stands completed before us—the steam railroad."[37]

All these narratives mention a "prophecy" and on one occasion the "visionary mind" of Hahn. Thus he was credited with miraculous powers beyond those of common people. By contrast the problem of the steam railroad found in Hahn's posthumous works sounds very sober:

> I read about Potter's engine in a paper lent to me by Professor Oetinger [*Schauplatz der Maschinen*, Exhibition of Engines], of the great force exerted by the pressure of the atmosphere and the steam and in my mind I immediately placed a smaller model of the engine onto a coach to move it simply by means of fire and water, without further help, at any speed you like across mountains and valleys. However, I lacked the financial means to attempt this on a small scale.[38]

Thus oral tradition expanded into the miraculous, and it cloaked in the twilight of secrecy what had had its origin in one of Hahn's sober technical reflections. Hahn was an uncommonly versatile and ingenious thinker, and it is not surprising that hardly anyone could follow all his ideas. It is precisely his realistic technical thoughts and experiments which account for the fact that so many of his conversations and actions entered the realm of legend. Many members of his pastoral communities and many people in the region regarded Hahn, who also practiced the art of palmistry, as a miracle worker and even asked him for medical help.

Max Englemann, so far Hahn's only biographer, who also researched his tremendous technical ability, comments:

> A primitive mind readily spins the thread of monstrosity around a person who intends to brew the philosopher's stone in his chemical kitchen, who at night searches for the aspect, and who can render lightning harmless by an iron rod on his roof. Such a man must also be able to cure all diseases. And Hahn must have been occupied extensively with medical remedies. A man who believed he was possessed by the devil was cured of "worms" by Hahn. Hundreds of sick people came to him for advice and remedies. . . . A foolish maidservant recovered after he gave her laxatives and "stirred the cauterization with his finger in the spoon." Frequently women who had a crush on him seem to have approached him by way of seeking advice about various indispositions. They generally had to undergo blood-letting or purging.[39]

That patients visited him for reasons other than "having a crush on him" or simply wanting to meet the educated man who was credited with enhanced knowledge because of his studies, is shown by the fact that many people came to ask him for lottery numbers. Sometimes they begged him on their knees, and at times he weakened enough to tell them random numbers just to get rid of them. It was not just the rational scientist that was sought here, but at least *also* the miracle worker, the magician, the sorcerer. The fact that Hahn, like many another inventor of that time, also acted as priest and chaplain did not interfere with this assessment, but may instead have enhanced it in many cases.[40] Most importantly, this encouraged a situation where not all such technical innovations were considered *evil* magic.

Nevertheless the "magical"[41] misunderstanding of technical phenomena mentioned above is always accompanied by an undercurrent of warning and admonition. At most the salutary greeting above the mechanic's workshop in Onstmettingen at the turn of the century celebrates the predicted coach without horses unconditionally. Other narratives express the fear that something "uncanny" is involved. Related legends interpret the railroad as well as other technical phenomena as signs of the impending end of the world.

One might imagine that this resistance to technical facts and ideas would diminish with increasing education. That only applies to a point. A glance at primitive cultures shows that technological factors were often accepted with the greatest of ease. However, such acceptance represents only a superficial assimilation, i.e., a "halfway situation."[42] That is obviously the case where technological equipment is simply imitated: for example, in New Guinea Papuas erected a "radio station" with antennas made from bamboo canes and vines while others sat in "offices" and imitated such activities as writing and reading.[43] In many cases technical facts merely confirmed already existing general beliefs. Technology simply places in the real external world that which earlier belonged to dreams and myths. The airplane confirms the ability of the medicine man to "fly." An operation seems to repeat the cultlike ritual of death and revival.[44] There is no doubt here that technical phenomena intrude shocklike into the mental framework. "All of tradition from now on is misunderstood as the reporting of events of actual external reality. The ability to have psychic experiences suffers because of the expectation of finding these experiences in external reality." But there is no resistance to technology as a consequence. This makes the connection between magic and technology visible. As formulated by Ortega, "magic is in fact a technology, even if a failed and illusory one."[45]

The peoples of eastern Asia have included technology in their "mythical-magical order of existence" as well.[46] In Japan small Shinto shrines were erected to the "God of Petroleum," sanctuaries were built for the "Sulphur-Kami," and an electrical power station was dedicated to the fox god, "so that the great God Inari of Takahashi, who demands reverence because he confers power, can be worshipped here in addition to his main temple." Gerhard Rosenkranz cites additional examples which demonstrate how it is precisely the distance from modern technology—part of that firm religious and spiritual order of such a different kind—which prepares the way for the acceptance of technical phenomena. Here, too, a smooth transition is evident in the functional relationship between magic—in the widest sense—and technology. Commenting on the order of existence of Asian peoples, Rosenkranz writes "that within it magic plays a role similar to that played by technology in the secular world, i.e., the role of grasping the external world and of overcoming its resistance."[47] Resistance to technology seems to occur much earlier when it intrudes into a world that is less firmly established and, more importantly, that on the whole is more "realistic," where the supernatural orders of magic and of religion no longer have to refer all new phenomena to their center to make them part of tradition. Resistance in such cases does not seem to originate mainly from the uneducated classes, but is offered by the conservative educated class.

A detailed examination of the remarks made by German writers about contemporary technological innovations during the nineteenth century might confirm this. However, such material must be tested carefully. Words connoting magic could conceal very definite ideas or else be nothing but playful metaphors. Moreover, they could have either positive or negative meanings. Prince Pückler describes that "monster," the steam locomotive in a letter from London on November 23, 1827.[48] His detailed account concludes: "How else could one have obtained such a serviceable genie without the ring of Solomon, and has ever a witch burned for sorcery achieved anything like it?" Witchcraft is invoked here merely as a comparison to add weight and significance to the subject described. By contrast the poem "Natur und Menschenfleiss" (Nature and Man's Diligence) by Karl Mayer[49] contains the following verse:

> *Nicht jeder deiner Erdensöhne,*
> *Gott, fleht dich um Schutz fürs Schöne.*
> *Zu dem Gebet lass ich mich mahnen*
> *Beim Näherdrohn der Eisenbahnen.*

> (Not every one of your sons on earth,
> God, begs you to protect beauty.
> I feel urged to say this prayer
> Because of the threatened coming of the railway.)

Although the poem lacks any allusion to magic, technology is drawn completely into the shadow of demonically evil, devilish, and sinister sorcery. As an example of yet another interpretation, a poem by Justinus Kerner, *"Im Eisenbahnhofe"* (In the Railway Station), deals less with technology per se than with human hubris, which is often at its base. In Fontane's ballad "Die Brück' am Tay" (The Tay Bridge) even large-scale technical achievements are reduced to vain trumpery by demoniacal natural forces. These few examples suffice to indicate that many members of the bourgeoisie adopted at least a cautious attitude toward technology. Additionally it should be noted that the beauty of technology remains almost completely alien to the literature and plastic arts of nineteenth-century Germany.[50]

The ambivalent term *Zauber* (magic) was deliberately chosen to head this section. Just as we can recognize the demonic quality of evil, we can also see the positive magic of technology, as indicated by the words of Prince Pückler. Moreover, inventors and technicians themselves view their work in technology as something that goes beyond science or technology. Count Thun, the enlightened "seer of ghosts," asked Lavater on January 12, 1784: "What do you think of the quasi-godlike invention of Montgolfier?"[51] Wherever new inventions are pursued and applied, this consciousness of a quasi-godlike (we could also write: demigod-like) quality may surface.[52] In fact, it can be evoked as experience. Siegfried

Gerathewohl offers a modern example which the pathological fear of heights explains only in part. "During a trial flight with the Skyrocket the pilot reached a height at which more than 96% of the earth's atmosphere was below him. He attained a speed never experienced before and gasped involuntarily, 'my God!' 'Yes, my son?' a voice supposedly answered via the microphone."[53]

The same motif appears, in an amusing form, in an anecdote from the end of the last century. The following version was printed:[54]

The Voice from Above

At the end of the last century—when no one had yet thought of airplanes and Zeppelins—a balloon manned with airship officers was launched from the site at Tegel and toward evening had drifted into a lonely area of West Prussia.

When the gentlemen prepared to land they looked out for some assistants to hold the anchor rope. Finally they discovered an honest peasant in a field ploughing with a team of oxen.

The head balloonist cupped his hands and shouted down: "Hey! Hey! You, my man! Listen!"

In the fervor of his work the farmer had not noticed the approaching monster; suddenly hearing the voice from above, he sank to the ground with hair on end, put his trembling hands together and stammered: "Speak, Lord, thy servant heareth!"

This story hardly detracts from the credibility of the more recent episode. Characteristically, however, it took a very fast and new airplane to produce this experience. Just as characteristically, the fear of earlier manifestations of technology meanwhile has inspired such narrative genres as jokes and anecdotes, and the simpletons who considered the railroad a work of the devil are now thought amusing. Time defuses the mines which new technical tools first seem to hide within them.

Without doubt this process corrects what formerly was overrated and misjudged; but it also covers up the demonic power which, in fact, is part of technology. The danger inherent in this indifference is particularly obvious today. Therefore it makes sense to expose this demonic quality from time to time. Friedrich Georg Jünger, for example, has impressively compared the outward appearance of technical apparatus with the world of dinosaurs, with insects and submarine creatures.[55] It is further important to emphasize the positive "magic" of technology, as Robert Musil has done.[56] However, this literary display must not be taken to represent the view of technology held by today's "folk."

Even though the "magic" of technology is still effective here, it is no longer a darkly demonic or "demigodly" impulse, but a more threadbare, almost entirely aesthetic, category. Dazzling car bodies, artfully harmonized parts, extras like the shining "magic (!) eye" of tape recorders most visibly express the magic of technology. Such magic is commonly based on the very conscious attempt by manufacturers to make their technical appliances stand out from the usual. This all but proves that we have become used to technology. The fact that today technology presents the normal everyday environment of the common man is decisive for us and will be discussed below. This short synopsis only indicates how the process of assimilation took place.

THE "NATURALNESS" OF TECHNOLOGY

On the Saturday before Easter, the Easter fire is lit in front of Catholic churches late in the evening. The Easter candle and the sanctuary lamp are lit here, and pieces of wood are often set aglow to bring their owners luck. The fire must be produced "naturally." The outside walls of some churches contain small round cavities or longer scrape marks, traces of attempts to produce fire by friction.[57] Generally matches are excluded from this fire custom. However, in the vicinity of Weinheim the Easter fire is often started with a lighter,[58] not because traditional rules are neglected, but because making fire in this manner is considered natural. It is certainly important that the lighter merely mechanizes the oldest form of producing fire, as steel or stone are involved in either case. But it is clear that the use of the lighter does not indicate a cunning interpretation of an unwritten rule but a change in attitude toward technology.

Even the first production of fire was a "technical" act, one that may be considered an essential beginning of human technology. However, with habit it soon acquired a "natural" character. This was possible because, with few specific instruments needed, making a fire was barely different from other natural activities, and once the concept of the natural is applied to human activity, it transcends its strict limits and becomes valid in a relative sense. Matches clearly divided the old and the new way of making fire when they appeared in the second quarter of the last century. The new way pertains more obviously to technology. Custom protects itself and insists on the old practice.[59] However, by the time the lighter is introduced, man is already surrounded by technical gadgets to such an extent that he uses them without being constantly aware of technological alienation from the natural state. The apparatus itself has acquired a "natural quality" which even new inventions achieve all too soon.

Our little example might appear overstudied if this development were not substantiated by many other examples. The reserved attitude of the population toward railroads was mentioned in connection with Philipp Matthäus Hahn. To date stories are still told in many places of individual citizens or even community leaders who believed they recognized the devil or at least some kind of evil force in locomotives. These narratives indicate a distance from such attitudes. They belong to a second phase of development after the harmless quality of such technical inventions has been established, so that foolish old people, as well as defects in the new technology, can safely be made fun of. Railroads then became a familiar object of children's rhymes and humorous songs. In his "Unordnung und frühes Leid" (Disorder and Early Suffering), Thomas Mann uses the following children's verse in an ironic sense:

Eisenbahn, Eisenbahn,
Lokomotiv!

Fahrt sie fort, bleibt sie da,
Tut sie einen Pfief.

(Railroad, railroad,
Locomotive!
Whether it is setting off or standing still,
It whistles.)

With small variations these humorous lines in verse or song were popular in many regions. People of the Vogtland sang:

Eisenbâh, Eisenbâh, Lokomotiv':
wenn se net wâtter kâ,
nôch tut's an Pfiff.

(Railroad, railroad, locomotive,
when it cannot go on,
it keeps on whistling.)

In the Erzgebirge the conclusion was borrowed from another migratory verse:

Eisenbah, Eisenbah, Lokomotiv,
Wenn de mei Schätzl siehst,
Gibbst'n da'n Brief.[60]

(Railroad, railroad, locomotive,
If you see my sweetheart,
Give her/him a letter.)

In contrast to the established main lines, the later branch lines of the railroad were given ironical names. For example, the small steam line between Heidelberg and Weinheim, opened around 1890, was called "Fiery Elijah." Even today the narrow-gauge branch line between Mosbach and Mudau is known as "Bämbele" (Duck Killer) and the Härdtsfeld branch line near Aalen was named "Schättere" (in a play on sounds). Such ironical names express the same remarkable proximity to and familiarity with technical innovations as does the well-known song of the "Schwäbische Eisenbahn" (Swabian Railroad), first published in 1894 in a students' song book. The same form of playful assimilation of new technology appears in 1862 at the carnival in Brixlegg (Tyrol), where the traditional Fountain of Youth was shaped like a steam locomotive.[61] On the whole the invasion of new elements and their assimilation can be traced in carnival events. In 1910, for example, the coming of electricity is humorously announced in Neresheim, where the Committee of Jesters adopted the following theme for the carnival activities:

In Neresheim
Elektrische Kraft
Elektrisches Licht
Elektrische Strassenbahn.[62]

(In Neresheim
Electrical power
Electrical light
Electrical tramway.)

The tramway and electrical lights were imitated "by specially constructed arc-lamps."

However, all this still belongs to the assimilation-of-technology phase. Today, when this phase has been left behind and much of technology is taken for granted, stories from pioneering times no longer seem uncanny and barely cause amusement. The fact that locomotives once horrified people who considered them the work of the devil now seems merely remarkable and curious, the more curious if one considers that the railroad models of that time have meanwhile acquired the patina of romantic travel poetry. It no longer seems terrible or even essentially funny. *Today's* situation is characterized by a joke from Berlin recorded by Heinrich Lützeler in his Philosopy of the Humor of Cologne:[63] In Berlin a small Messerschmidt scooter stops at a red light next to a huge tractor-trailer. From his cab the driver benevolently bends toward the woman who is riding the small scooter and asks: "Young lady, does the little one take gas or are you still feeding him yourself?" This "humanization" of technology seems humorous only when contrasted with the utmost "objectification." Because technical phenomena have become self-evident and "natural" and are merely regarded as factual objects, the transfer into the human sphere appears so grotesquely funny. A cabaret joke circulating in America expresses this even more drastically. A man approaches the bar, points to his escort, and says to the bartender, "Fill her up!" This joke, too, is based on the fact that technology has become so self-evident that it can be transferred to man and his social relations in an ironic sense.

However, this joke, which carries inappropriate objectification to absurd lengths, is only possible because English vehicles are often referred to by the feminine pronoun not the neuter, as in German. But this careful personification represents an earlier stage. Moreover, it has been observed before that Anglo-Saxon nations in particular use technical appliances with great unconcern.[64] This lack of concern can be contrasted with our frequent German tendency to "animate" technology, as expressed in naming motor vehicles and in close emotional ties to them. Anglo-Saxons lead in the use of technology. When Martin Heidegger calls for "a detached attitude toward objects" to be adopted when dealing with technology,[65] his demand is without doubt more radical and includes the call for "contemplative" thinking. But even a detached involvement with technical objects helps to prevent man from getting completely lost in technical and mechanical thinking.

No doubt the development of technology itself makes such a detached attitude easier. "Appliance frenzy," the concept in political economy which refers to the "mania to acquire goods" generated by technology,[66] could also refer to the temporary formation and arrangement of technical implements. Julius Stettenheim, a

Berlin humorist who wrote under the name of Wippchen, gave a caricature of a report on the novelties introduced at the 1893 Chicago World's Fair. Among other things he describes the following device:

> An ingenious mind invented an apparatus to prevent the loss of canes and umbrellas, which can easily be attached to the cane or umbrella. This is a machine that weighs at most thirty pounds and fires a shot every five minutes by means of clockwork. Thus the owner of the cane or umbrella is reminded that he has placed something, which he wants to take with him when he leaves, where the powder smoke becomes visible. Expensive as the apparatus is—it costs $60 and each shot costs about 25 cents—it pays for itself in the course of time.

Incidentally, this caricature had a predecessor in the disproportionately large corkscrew of Hogarth's quack in *Marriage à la Mode*. However, it clearly shows the proliferation of gadgets, as opposed to useful objects, made only to provoke new wants and needs and to increase the mania of and for gadgets. By contrast, recent developments increasingly adopt simpler functional forms—a phenomenon which even advertising geared toward the stimulation of consumer needs has to take into account.

The detached attitude toward technology and its increasingly "natural" quality can be recognized in the fact that technical requisites and motifs have entered all areas of folk culture and exist there as a matter of course. The few songs which glorify and idealize technical achievements are not typical, i.e., Brand's "Machinist Hopkins," the song about Lindbergh's flight by Brecht and Weill, or the song of two others who flew across the ocean, "Der weisse Vogel flog über das Meer" (The White Bird Flew Across the Ocean).[67] Technical phenomena that enter preexisting forms of song and penetrate them to an increasing extent are much more common. The slow country waltzes *(Ländler)* of Upper and Lower Austria are still accompanied by *Ländler* songs, in which even new inventions may be celebrated: the threshing machine and the milk separator, the telephone and the airplane.[68] Songs specific to trades and classes now include special songs for truck drivers.[69] During carnival activities masked people roar along on motorcycles. The *schiachen Perchten*[70] (traditional masks) of Gastein as well as the *Hexen* (witches) of Gengenbach carry red flashlight bulbs, which add a wild glare to their eyes. The wooden disks of the *Funkenfeuer* (sparkling fire) now are often replaced by old tires, which are set alight and rolled downhill. Children's rhymes and play are filled with technical components and allusions.

Flieger komm runter,
Die Sonne geht unter!
Flieger geh rauf,
Die Sonne geht auf

(Pilot come down,
The sun is going down!
Pilot go up,
The sun is coming up)

is a variation of an old rhyme from Nuremberg.[71] The mechanization of children's toys is increasing. In his folklore of the *Ruhrgebiet*, Wilhelm Brepohl describes how children at all age levels adopt mechanical toys.[72] It is not only technology that has become "natural" that is being introduced; people's occupation with the small mechanical world of the toy retains much of the original delight at any kind of mechanization, which during the late Baroque era frequently resulted in mechanical plays about the nativity and Mount of Olives. The fact that enacting such themes with real persons was prohibited during the Enlightenment only partly explains the creation of these mechanical devices.[73]

The self-evident assimilation of technology into the folk world is particularly obvious in linguistic behavior. Naming practices have often given technical phenomena a folksy turn. The *Storchenauto* (stork's car) of the midwife is only one example among many. Mechanical images like "having a long circuit" (i.e., to be slow to catch on) dominate colloquial speech, and a dictionary of colloquial German cites many similar examples.[74] Even fixed figures of speech have been with us for a long time. To accuse a young man of being a rake because he would even chase a locomotive if it wore a skirt, at first seems a highly individual judgment. In reality this is a well-known formula. And the phrase "Ein alter Mann ist kein D-Zug" (an old man is no express train) appears even before the First World War in a soldiers' song:

> *Die Aufsicht hat der Leutnant,*
> *die Ruhe haben wir.*
> *Ein alter Mann ist kein D-Zug,*
> *er ist nur Passagier.*[75]

> (The second lieutenant is in command
> we can relax.
> An old man is no express train,
> he is only a passenger.)

As you leave a gas station in Southern Germany they might say to you: "Fahret Se's guat!"[76] (drive it well!). By a small shift the old phrase "Machet Se's guat!" (lit., do it well, i.e., take care of yourself!) was adapted to the new situation: "it" here is not the car, but in a sense the sum of all things that could happen to a person. At first the new phrase only makes sense as a variation of the earlier phrase. But it is quite possible that it will become detached and as distinct and self-evident as the old one.

One might object that all our examples tend to render the problem innocuous: technology is merely incidental, or at any rate the object of cultural expressions. However, the process of technology turning into a subject of folk culture is much more crucial. The real danger for folk culture is seen in film and radio, the record player, and technical mass products. Often these are used as points of reference to contrast the folk world with the technical world. However, awareness of the self-evident manner in which technology is assimilated into cultural expressions indicates that sober judgment is necessary, and this should enable us to discover the "natural" quality of technology as well as its demonic elements. In his critique of mass psychology, Peter R. Hofstätter has conjectured "that the condition of our culture diagnosed as 'massification' is much more accurately described as a condition of 'isolation.' The group is now recognizable only by the aspect of its occasional deviation, because one has become estranged from it."[77] Perhaps the alleged total disintegration of folk culture can be similarly qualified: it, too, seems to be in part the result of an "isolation" of the culture-bearing classes,who intentionally measure folk culture only according to an image to which it can no longer conform. Where all technical forms are excluded beforehand as "mass culture" or "manifestations of civilization," folk culture shrinks severely. Then contemporary *Volkskunde* is reduced to the study of relics, an occupation which nevertheless frequently leads to claims of being able to impart *Weltanschauungen*.

The fierceness with which technically mediated goods are excluded from any consideration indicates that the overused notion of *gesunkenes Kulturgut* (sunken cultural good) has only barely shaken the belief in a productive, self-creating folk culture and "folk soul." However, the oppositions of "self-reliance" and "non-self-reliance"[78] have always separated high culture from folk culture, even though precise observation proves that such oppositions are not absolute, and the process of reproduction, for example, can acquire quite self-reliant characteristics. In this context "activity" and "passivity," too, become relative terms. "Passive" human functions always contain a certain amount of activity. Quite rightly the more recent psychology of speech has placed speaking and hearing very close together. This interference in our discipline is indicated, for example, by the many spontaneous narratives inspired by a film[79] or in the fact that neither records nor broadcasting has impaired active reproduction. Popular songs are not only heard but also sung. Membership in choral societies has not decreased; on the contrary, it has vastly increased since the introduction of the radio.

This also contradicts the thesis that technology has invaded and dissolved all forms of community that support folk culture. Tacitly this thesis draws on the opposition of *Gemeinschaft* and *Gesellschaft*, which has been questioned above. Without doubt the increased mobility due to technology has made relationships more wide-ranging and has dissolved traditional groups. Old neighborhood relations, for example, are often replaced by circles of acquaintances and social contacts,[80] which also characterize the structure of societies and clubs. Overall, however, group life is no less intensive than it used to be. Occasionally even technical phenomena create or encourage new groups. Associations which cluster around types of cars and more often around motorcycles, at times with support from the specific manufacturers, very soon adopt the usual character of a club and are not at all limited to communal excursions. The Lambretta Club in Wangen, for example, regularly organizes bowling evenings.[81]

Sometimes technical devices can contribute to the revival or the creation of "communal forms" of an older type. Jointly owned freezer installations now frequently unite smaller villages and hamlets even where the prerequisites for neighborly relations and other village groups no longer exist.[82] Although the mechanization of agriculture has removed the foundation for many old customs, working with machines can spawn communal celebrations. For example, in

Danube-Swabian villages the threshing machine was decorated after threshing was completed.[83] In northern Hesse a threshing festival, to which the farmer invites all the neighbors who have assisted with the threshing, was named "Machine."[84]

A glance at social foundations similarly indicates that technology has not caused the end but rather alterations of folk culture, which permeate the folk world quite naturally. It still remains to be established whether that folk world is rooted in religious depths which are permanently opposed to the phenomena of technology. This would generally substantiate and justify the opposition. According to Ernst Jünger, no Christian priest could "doubt that, when a sanctuary lamp is replaced by an electric light bulb, we are dealing with a technical and not a sacred matter."[85] This interpretation accords the wax candle a relationship to the numinous which is denied the electric light; it is correct insofar as it applies to the self-determined law of technology, which draws all things into the transient realm and cannot acknowledge eternal values. However, it fails to recognize that technology can always be made serviceable and can fit even religious forms without disruption. Practice proves that the opposition established by Jünger is based on limited theoretical principles. The old forms of folk piety dominate the church even where electric current feeds the sanctuary lamp. Even in long railroad trains hired for pilgrims, resembling fashionable "dance expresses" (i.e., train rides for entertainment), the traditional pilgrimage prayers are still said, led over the microphone. Obviously forms have changed profoundly; but by no means does technology dissolve and destroy every form.

The interweaving of the technical world and religious folk belief is particularly evident in the blessings of motor vehicles, which are quite common in Catholic regions. St. Christopher, originally the patron saint of travelers, now protects drivers. This patronage has possibly spread from France, where St. Christopher pins were more common than in Germany, even before the war. So far the routes of dissemination have not been investigated.[86] In Germany the blessing of motor vehicles takes place more often on May 1 or on the local patron saint's day than on St. Christopher's day in July. During recent years the annual blessing of motor vehicles conducted by Daimler Benz even attracted children with their scooters. Such phenomena should not be ignored as a fashionable pastime.

In part the "St. Christopher blessing" of agricultural machinery and motor vehicles has replaced the very old and vigorous tradition of blessing horses. However, it has been observed that riding events of all types, including sacred riding festivals, have not necessarily decreased over the last few years and that the number of riders and horses did not diminish everywhere. This can partly be explained as an "amplified reaction." The modern blessing of motor vehicles has brought new meaning and participation to the old practice of blessing horses. In part, however, it is also based on a countermovement which distinguishes organic living nature from the mechanized technical environment and in sentimental fashion singles out "nature" from its surroundings. This is one reason for the increasing significance of all kinds of flower festivals—from Mother's Day to Valentine's Day[87]—which we may not entirely reduce to commercial impulses. Such countermovements should not be ignored. We shall repeatedly deal with

these movements in what follows. However, they must be understood as secondary movements and must not be identified with the relationship to the natural
environment that was characteristic of the pretechnical era. For this movement,
too, the "natural" and self-evident quality of technology provides the background, which is subsequently pierced in more or less conscious revolt.

TECHNOLOGY AS A RELEASE MECHANISM FOR REGRESSIONS

"Magical" attitudes and reactions, which appear again and again and which occasionally are considered essential expressions of folklike thinking overlaid by
technology, must be viewed against the background of the naturalness of technology. Against this background we evaluate them correctly as exceptions from a
quantitative point of view and understand them as qualitatively different from
earlier, pretechnical forms. They are not relics which have survived the strange
world of technology and mechanics in an unbroken tradition, but regressions
caused by technology itself, which go back to genetically earlier stages of development. The fundamental associations discussed in the section "Folk World and
Technical World" demonstrate that this division is more than mere playing with
concepts.

Characteristically such attitudes do not permeate all of the technical world, but
only specific sections of it. Therefore they cannot be compared to the examples
from primitive cultures and from East Asia cited above, where the technical
world with all its phenomena continues to refer to the earlier forces and values at
least for a transitional period.

While there the function and power of technology are specifically measured
against "traditional" or "magical" standards, for us regressions are most often
caused by a breakdown of technology, by disturbances and interruptions of the
technical function. When such things occur we suddenly realize that technology
seems "natural" not because we master it completely, but because of habituation
and use. Now it becomes apparent that we do not understand the technical process. A child is frightened the first time it presses a button on the radio and hears
music. Once it has become used to this response, it is just as frightened when for
some reason the response does not occur. Everyone is put into the position of this
child when a familiar technical process, which is basically not understood, is
interrupted for any reason. This demonstrates that technology with all its naturalness can be unpredictable—one might add: like nature.

The breakdown of machinery is both part and object of folk narratives to an
extent that bears no relationship to the real significance of such failures. These
narratives convey more than the fact that breakdowns are possible and that a
machine has to be repaired once in a while. Indeed, they demolish this rational
association and prove that technology has its limits, at which the reactions of
"reasonable" resignation and regressive coping divide. This has resulted in very
different narratives. The following legendary anecdote has come down from the
beginnings of motorization:

An officer of the Salvation Army who had acquired a rattling vehicle was stuck in the middle of an intersection. He got out and attempted to restart the engine with a crank handle. Soon he began to sweat with the exertion and the mocking cheers of encouragement from passersby. After some fruitless effort he took off his jacket, which unintentionally exposed the crest and mottos of the Salvation Army on his sweater. This earned him even more derisive shouts. Suddenly, in broad daylight, in the midst of an urban intersection, surrounded by a gloating crowd, he stopped cranking and kneeled down to pray at the runningboard of his obstinate car. Then he tried the crank once more, and, lo!—the engine started.[88]

A small shift in emphasis gives this narrative an amusing turn. For example, in Swabia it is said that after praying fruitlessly a priest finally uttered the "Swabian greeting,"[89] which proved successful with his engine. Lützeler reports from Cologne that a priest recommended a short fervent prayer to a swearing motorcyclist who could not start his vehicle. The motorcyclist accepted the advice, the engine started, and the priest followed him with his eyes, shaking his head: "Damn it, I wouldn't have believed it!"[90] Both the amusing and the more serious narrative indicate that incidents of mechanical failure present a provocation that demands an answer. It becomes obvious here that such an incident can induce regressions.

Various legendlike narratives simply describe a series of accidents or particularly remarkable breakdowns. They suggest questions but leave the answers to the audience. Such narratives include reports and stories of unlucky motorbikes whose successive owners became victims of a rapid series of severe accidents. Other narratives explicitly state that some witch or at least witchcraft is the cause of an inexplicable technical failure.[91] In such narratives even the repair shop is unable to identify the defect in the motorbike.

Thus the use of technical media suggests an expectation of magic. The more intensive and daring this use, the more pronounced the tendency toward magic can be. In Thomas Mann's *Zauberberg* (The Magic Mountain), Naphta says of the aviators, "most often [they] are rather ugly, questionable individuals, above all very superstitious. They would take lucky pigs or a crow along on board, they would spit three times here and there, they would wear the gloves of lucky drivers."[92] Naphta's observations about aviators during the First World War is still relevant, but it would be a mistake to search for such regressive attitudes and reactions exclusively or even mostly among people whose profession it is to deal with intricate technical appliances and machines. According to Jean Paul,

Among the nations following each other in the pursuit of education, one always takes the lead and is emulated by the others to various degrees. However, each successive nation which assimilates the self-improvements of the first among them obtains these more violently and faster because they do not emerge from within, that is, through a slow process of preparation, as was the case with the first nation. In the same manner the last divisions of an army have to follow the fastest.[93]

This remark can be applied to our question, with the exceptions already discussed. It may also be transferred from the ethnic to the social sphere. Those classes and groups which were last affected by technology must "follow the fastest." Above all this is valid for large sections of the peasantry. Regressions are confusions and breaks in this process—a stumbling or stopping during the too-rapid process of catching up.

However, it would be foolish to consider the problem of regression only in connection with the mechanization of agriculture. We only half understand regression if we fit it into the context of advance and progress. The problem here is not simply the adoption of attitudes developed earlier in history which have definitely become outdated over time, but regression is at the same time a resort to genetically older elements and thereby to deeper spiritual levels. This anchoring in depth rather then an anchoring in the past often gives regressions a dangerous power, a power which can be effective even where regression is repudiated. The unmasking of belief in witchcraft was and is a popular literary theme partly because of these circumstances; it is not entirely due to the enlightened missionary consciousness of the writers. Charlotte Birch-Pfeiffer's drama *Die Grille* (The Cricket) was as popular in her time as was the recent radio play *Die Furcht hat grosse Augen* (Fear Has Big Eyes) by Horst Mönnich. In the drama a girl is freed of the suspicion of being a witch, as is a woman in the radio play. However, both pieces are particularly fascinating because of the regressions they attack. It seems that this fascination is less harmful and somewhat weaker in the "rural character sketch" of the last century by Birch-Pfeiffer than in the modern radio play, where a former gas station attendant turns out to be a magician and where the scene of action repeatedly alternates between a freeway and a cattle barn, and between a gas station and a farm.

Apparently the images from the modern world of differentiated technology do not impede the reversion to regressive magical thinking, but rather facilitate it. This process makes sense if we consider it parallel to similar compensatory movements. Within modern poetry particularly the most extreme cerebrations provoke regressions to the unconscious—consider, for instance, the development of Gottfried Benn. The history of modern painting shows the same thing. For all that, we are not concerned here with merely individual and intellectual escapades from diversity into apparent simplemindedness, but this countermovement can be traced all the way to folk culture. Helmut Plessner has interpreted the dissemination of sport as an attempt to "oppose the excessive cultivation of thought with a new primitiveness."[94] Without a doubt this can be generalized beyond physical activities. The relatively simple preindustrial world does not necessarily have to be simplified. By contrast, the technical world, with its complex society, strongly invites simplification—and implies "short-circuit" regressions. A humorous story provides an example: Psychoanalysis is very popular in America, so much so that even children learn to interpret their fears and needs as "complexes." It is said of American children that before going to sleep they check under their beds for hidden complexes. This malicious story is probably an impudent invention. However, it is valuable and true to the extent that it refers directly to the limits of differentiated thinking and to the compulsion toward compact simplification in the face of complex elements and "complexes."

Regressions do not necessarily refer to the complete content of earlier notions; they can make use of a more modern form. "Earth rays," "death rays," and highway sites where fatal accidents have occurred are such regressive notions in technological-scientific disguise.[95] In the belief in Martians and the appearance of flying saucers archaic images blend with the outer limits of technical progress—which gives modern "myths" their penetrating power.[96] Technology is permeated with magic even in such an everyday phenomenon as film. Hans Arnold has investigated this problem thoroughly and, among other things, has pointed to the synoptic presentation of images rooted in a magical experience of the world, the exaggeration of the close-up shots, and the separate existence of the film world.[97]

The permeation of the modern with comparatively archaic ideas and forms of thinking is made easier because motifs and foundations of folklike thinking in all its simplicity have always blended and criss-crossed. The Bohemian writer Josef Leopold Wander of Grünwald gives a typical example in a report from the Passion rites about "general flagellation out of devotion and penitence," which was customary in Hohenelbe around 1770:

> I participated with the knowledge of my grandparents and remember well how the acolyte encouraged me as a newcomer to undergo this kind of penance. I should not be afraid of it at all: it would not hurt very much, as long as the first six to ten blows were struck in full seriousness to make my blood flow immediately. Yes, flagellation was even healthy and would substitute for bloodletting and cupping.[98]

Thus this dramatic imitation of the suffering of Christ is blended with the idea of hygiene. Doubtlessly this fusion represents the intellectual intersection between the late Baroque and early Enlightenment eras. However, it cannot be confined to these specific historical situations. Simple folk attitudes have always been mixed and complex. This is shown distinctly, for example, in the interplay between high religion and folk belief[99] and in the fusion of religious and magical notions. Germans from Csobánka (near Budapest) placed a leaf from a four-leaf clover into the prayer book to have it blessed by the priest without his knowledge.[100] Until quite recently East Prussian peasants on their death beds asked the priest who administered last rites "to read from the wine in the chalice how much longer it would take them to die."[101] That enlightened priest and fanatical disciple of enlightenment, Anton Bucher, ridiculed this entanglement repeatedly. For example, in an ironical catechism he poses the question "Why don't free thinkers adhere to the Catholic belief?" A boy answers, "Because they do not believe in witches and druids" and then establishes the reason why one must believe in witches: "Because the gentlemen at Scheyern are against witchcraft. Because the Capuchin monks have a special exorcist and, if there were no witches, the priests would all be impostors."[102]

This entanglement is particularly conspicuous in the forms of folk piety that proliferated during the Baroque and in the traditions of relic areas of customs. But it cannot be localized in a temporal or regional sense. The following example contrasts the existence of rural associations with the urban lack of associations: "When a thunderstorm threatens the peasant lights a consecrated candle; the city dweller merely disconnects his antenna."[103] The difference cannot and should not be ignored. However, it should be pointed out that here, too, in both cases we are dealing with ambivalent attitudes that express very complex forms of thinking. Lighting a candle during a thunderstorm, in itself a complex and devoutly religious piece of behavior, is most strongly permeated by a magical-theurgical attitude. In fact, this is often done simply out of habit, and from that point of view approaches the merely "technical" conduct of the supposedly urban precautionary measure. On the other hand, the simple switching process possibly contains a trace of "magic" beyond its technical character, as even this process is not completely understood and is partly carried out as a defense mechanism in which one simply believes. Therefore the effect of such technical processes is easily overestimated. On February 23, 1845, the Stuttgart *Neue Tageblatt* printed an article directed against superstition in which the writer asks: "How long is it since the alarm bell rang in the villages in order to drive away a threatening thunderstorm and, in fact, drew it down upon them because of the electrical attraction?"[104] The catch phrase "electrical attraction" was used then in a similarly unquestioning, believing manner and with reference to experience, as was true earlier of the ringing of the bell. Obviously here, too, "technical" and pretechnical notions and forms of thinking are blended.

These considerations should explain how different levels of images and thoughts can fuse even today. However, they should not lead to the conclusion that all has remained the same and practically nothing has changed. Even if regressions were much more frequent, to the point of taking over completely, the term "regression" itself indicates that what we are dealing with is no simple revival of former conditions but represents a backward movement from a different point of departure. This retreat can resemble the movements of a bullfighter who in stepping back seeks the strength to leap forward and to conquer. It can be a comfortable voluntary fall or a shocklike descent due to alarming events. Even if the basis has remained the same, each time the foothold is different and new. Even if the quest for origins may be an essential stimulus for many regressions, they are not to be equated with the original attitudes.

Put differently, we may ask "if genuine regression is in fact possible."[105] The recourse to magical thinking in the technical era produces different kinds of magic and is directed toward other contents than the corresponding magical thinking of the pretechnical world. "Superstition," which is rightly said to be as common in today's cities as it once was in the villages, is not a fixed but a variable quantity. For example, the belief in the unlucky connotations of the number 13 is very old and known in many parts of the world. It has not ceased today, but has received a new coloring. When encountered in older traditions, this belief is often vividly explained, or at least attempts are made to substantiate it etiologically. The fact that 13 as a prime number is excluded from the duodecimal system is almost always made clear, and the idea of "12," or more accurately a group of twelve in any form, is mentioned. Thus frequently the thirteenth appears to be "superfluous";[106] its removal reinstates the number twelve and a sense of correctness. Modern superstition, however, does not explain the unlucky meaning; the opposition to the lucky number twelve is hardly ever consciously realized. Modern society does not reduce a group of thirteen to twelve, but solves the dilemma elegantly by inviting a fourteenth guest. In Paris the profession of the *quatorzième* has or had evolved, i.e., one who was always ready to attend a dinner as number fourteen.[107] The unlucky meaning of thirteen has become blurred. It is not its link to concrete groups of any kind which contains the bad luck, but the abstract numerical value itself. Incidentally, the same indefinite quality is characteristic of the preoccupation with the popular and much sought-after horoscopes which occasionally feature headings like "Your stars—your destiny." However, while reading them practically no one thinks of the constellations. On the contrary, the horoscope is accepted as abstract data. Anyone who associates its popularity with the fact that a peasant who is close to nature would fix his working schedule according to the course and position of the stars, fails to recognize the essential ingredient of abstraction and the indefinite quality inherent in the modern belief in "stars."

Precisely this indefinite quality ensures the enormous importance of such factors. Vivid explanations offer points of departure for invalidation and moreover are always bound to their time. However, where the number 13 simply *is* an unlucky number without substantiation and without connection to more general associations and ideas, only a sort of mechanical process of wear and tear can weaken this significance. Of course it is possible to deny the special importance of that number. A very definite denial of the unlucky meaning, on the other hand, risks providing confirmation of the special character of the number and therefore participating in the realm of magic. In his *Einbahnstrasse* (One-Way Street), Walter Benjamin cites a sentence by Marcel Proust: "Treize—j'eus un plaisir cruel de m'ârreter sur ce nombre," and Benjamin himself repeatedly produces short aphoristic pieces which he divides into thirteen parts—here thirteen, so to speak, becomes a "round" number. The abstract power of the number thirteen is well illustrated in incidents some years ago in the distribution of new license plates for cars. The authorities not only had to deal with car owners who rejected the number thirteen, but also with people who asked for the number thirteen, claiming they were not superstitious and that thirteen was their lucky number.

The distribution of new license plates[108] proved furthermore that thirteen definitely is not the only number distinguished in this manner, but that it merely provides a focus for many opinions. Apparently there are many other lucky and unlucky numbers which are not substantiated by any traditional numerical magic. What is new here is not only the relatively high numerical values involved—the numbers go up to 1,000—but above all the fact that the choice of numbers is rooted exclusively in individual sentiments, experiences, and deliberations. The particular significance of these numbers is no longer based in a cultural-historical context but is the result of their being charged with magic by the individual. At most a magical conductivity can be detected in numbers containing the same numerals or decimal figures, e.g., 333, 818, or 400, which are considered superior to others.

This phenomenon of a new and often individual charging process is characteristic of magical thinking particularly in our time. To be sure, such a charging process is part of the beginning of many magical notions. A clock must have stopped once or several times immediately before the death of a person and subsequently have been associated with that death before this phenomenon became a widely acknowledged omen. The disintegration of such generally accepted notions, however, resulted in a situation where practically any phenomenon can now be "charged" and understood as foreboding. For example, after a great mining disaster people talked about a young medical assistant who had prepared bandages and splints for action two days earlier.[109] Evaluated after the disaster, this activity became endowed with the significance of an omen, which, however, does not necessarily mean that it will be remembered to the extent that other events are similarly interpreted. In two similar incidents at the 1958 soccer World Cup in Sweden, a journalist insisted before a decisive game on wearing the same jacket he had worn during previous games when his team had been victorious, and the German radio station consciously chose the same commentator who had reported on earlier crucial successful games.[110]

Certainly such phenomena are not fundamentally new. Their proliferation, however, is a characteristic of the technical world. In fact, technical appliances can enter traditional forms of magic; occasionally relatively rare mechanical objects—e.g., a red car or a silver wheel in the early stages of the automobile industry—are believed to bring good fortune.[111] However, the growing number of such objects makes it impossible for the association with good luck to remain fixed. Instead this new situation calls for the singling out and charging of more and more new objects. The very same acceleration and variety which prevents us from permanently endowing new objects with magical properties combines with social dynamics and differentiation to further question the old magical values and attributes; it calls for new charges in each case. In the nineteenth century this process affected large portions of the bourgeois culture; in the twentieth it is increasingly affecting the entire folk culture. The contrast between then and now becomes obvious, for example, when we compare the concept of magic used in the novels of Grimmelshausen with the magic elements in Friedrich Theodor Vischer's novel *Auch Einer* (Another One). The magic described by Grimmelshausen can be explained with the assistance of the *Handwörterbuch des Aberglaubens* (Dictionary of Superstitions) and sometimes even represents an enrichment of this compilation. This magic exists in traditional contexts and is generally valid except where it touches the limits of reasonable consideration. By contrast the magic contained in *Tücke des Objekts* (Malice of the Object) no longer fits the *Handwörterbuch des Aberglaubens*. The humorous prescription to let water get warm in your mouth while waiting for visitors does not add to the folklore of water. However, it is definitely related to the far-reaching detachment of magic from its traditional relation to specific objects, which has also affected folk culture.

This process is not the direct result of mechanization, i.e., the use of machinery, even though the introduction of machines can contribute to the shift. But it is a product of the technical world, an indirect result of technology, which creates not only a new world of objects but also new social and spiritual realities. This process blurs the old horizons, within which the traditional goods of folk culture found their validity.

If we trace the disintegration of certain horizons that were once valid, we seem to draw nearer to today's folk culture. This trail is pursued in three different preliminary investigations: by examining the shift of the spatial, temporal, and social horizons.

CHAPTER

2

SPATIAL EXPANSION

"UNITY OF PLACE"

The notion of the old village as a self-contained organism is still one of the essential components of folkloristic opinions. However, it is *not* exclusive to folkloristics. It may not be possible to ascertain to what extent the long dominant and uncontested interpretation of settlement history—that self-contained villages represent the original form of Germanic settlement—has contributed to this opinion. However, we may assume that the image of the self-contained village organism has added to the stabilization of this new historical theory, which is only being questioned in the most recent research. This mutual influence is the more plausible since for over a hundred years an enormous amount of rural poetry and literature has popularized that image. In such literature many motifs of earlier idyllic poetry have survived. What formerly appealed as literary play to a limited social circle is now offered to the general public as a realistic description.

By contrast scholarly *Volkskunde* together with social history endeavors to draw the real picture of the old village—or better the various villages and their past.[1] Church and land registers, inventories and divisions, proceedings of councils and church conventions contribute to this picture in an important way. Chronicles and contemporary literary evidence also provide significant references, even though they tend to draw the plot toward farce and undoubtedly prefer stories to history. Varied as the results of this research are, individual data repeatedly conflict with the traditional opinion. For example, even in villages mobility was extraordinarily high at times. Not only traveling artisans, but also farm hands and maids moved from place to place, and farms often changed owners. Above all, heavy immigration from outside followed wars and epidemics. Thus almost everywhere the population base changed repeatedly over the centuries. Furthermore it is now obvious that communication with cities, at least within the same general area, was always good enough to support an active exchange of spiritual and material goods. The close contact established between the nobility and the common folk in the small provincial territories, particularly of southwest Germany, should definitely be considered in investigations of the history of customs. A direct connection led from high culture to folk culture via the nobility, who lived in European dimensions even while tied to the province.[2]

All of this contradicts the traditional image of the self-contained village and forces us to reconsider various questions. In this sense Josef Dünninger recently scrutinized the catchword "urbanization."[3] He first established that the transfer of craft occupations to industry and the mechanization of agriculture in fact resulted in the "ruralization" of many villages. He then noted that the catchword "urbanization" needs at least "some measure of correction because of the older historical findings of continuous contacts between rural and urban culture. It is not the making of the contact in general that is decisive, but rather the degree of productive-active development of a specifically rural stylistic character from former models and from the merely passive acceptance of today's more or less masslike, formless urban models." We realize here that rural character is not primarily a question of external "containment" but a question of style which certainly has its social and historical conditions, but is not merely a function of these conditions. The concept of *Sitte* (habit, manners) again becomes the focus of folkloristic investigations concerned with "life in traditional systems."[4] *Sitte* is the shaping force behind these systems.[5]

However, historical research into villages also provides rich insights into the dissent, envy, and continual strife which seem to have dominated rural life more in former times than today. These real insights do not make the concept *Sitte* an imaginary construct. The imprinting power of *Sitte* simply has its limits. Furthermore the formal power of *Sitte* is expressed in a variety of material manifestations and may well substantiate contrary positions.[6] These insights indicate that the concept *Sitte* evidently does not entirely explain the "specifically rural stylistic character." Instead we must either relinquish the idea of village unity or substantiate it differently. However, the "unity of place" can be proven and substantiated in phenomenological terms.

No specific comment is necessary to indicate that "unity of place" is a term borrowed from dramatic theory. The comparison is unsatisfactory and would fail if we were to apply the dramatic facts consistently to our case. Nevertheless the term is carefully chosen. While the expression "village unity" involuntarily creates an association of harmony and thus approaches the image of the well-tuned, self-contained organism, the expression "unity of place" at first merely indicates a place where the action occurs. The action includes a wide variety of characters, plots, and motives for action, and includes conflicts and tensions. This is how a drama emerges on stage. But the events are interrelated and the unity of place is *one* dramaturgical device to give this interrelationship a clear horizon. By the same token the unity of place we have in mind does not in reality emerge from an ethical principle which uniformly permeates a place, but from horizons which limit the unity of the action and the possibilities of comprehension. Whatever is beyond these horizons never enters the field of vision.

Language as the essential medium of communication provides proof of the unity of place. We should not confine our research in this instance to those dialects which indeed are differentiated from all other regional dialects by individual phonological features. Certain proverbial phrases are similarly tied to specific locations and are barely, if at all, understood in the next village. The fact that

someone was "about to die"[7] was frequently indicated by euphemistically referring to the route to the cemetery by the names of local personages or sites found
along the way. In an example from Stuttgart, the proverbial saying "Er sitzt auf
dem Törle" (He is sitting on the gate) referred to a chamber above the New Gate,
where from 1547 on criminals awaited their execution.[8] A similar expression featured the name of a field, "mit dem geht's bald dem Krauchen zu" (he will soon
be headed toward the Krauchen). In Augsburg the path led to the *Hennadone*
(hen Anton), apparently named after the sacristan of a cemetery who kept
chickens.[9] In Munich the way leads to St. Stephan's cathedral.[10] People in Cologne say: "Ihr werdet mich bald nach Melaten tragen" (You will soon be car-
rying me to Melaten). The same idea is expressed in Tübingen by "Mit dem
geht's den Krummschenkel hinab" (He is headed down the *Krummschenkel*), and
in Isny the dead went "zum Sennenhof zum Hennenhüten" (to the Alpine farm
to tend the chickens).[11]

These are urban examples. But corresponding euphemisms exist in villages,
although less frequently than in cities. At times they also apply to the next village, sometimes for such a simple reason as sharing the same cemetery. One may
object that this is essentially only a play on local names, and that the various
euphemisms prove nothing but the fact that the names of small fields are not
usually known beyond the immediate vicinity. In fact, inherent in this common
occurrence is a problem that has barely been addressed in studies of field nomenclature. It is the question of how the mesh of local names reflects the awareness
of space. We must first add the qualification that each name can to a degree
substitute for the appellative description and consequently for the impressive vi-
sual description. The euphemisms cited above, particularly if used regularly, often ceased to evoke the image of the cemetery referred to by name and merely
indicated the notion of death and dying. The fact that names of locations can
evoke such nonspatial images makes possible the use of names which have no
spatial-visual connotation. Thus the kind of saying which is still typical today,
"Der gehört nach Zwiefalten (Schussenried, Stetten, Winnenden)" (He belongs
in Zwiefalten . . .) does not call for the concrete images of these places or even
their geographical locations; rather they are nonvisual euphemisms for mental
institutions. Their use is evidence of the tension between narrow and wide spaces
which also determined the spatial consciousness of earlier times. However, the
existence of linguistic formulas understood over large areas does not invalidate
the narrower horizon proven by other linguistic images and figures of speech. It
is very significant that local nomenclature was used for such a fundamental event
as death, an event which certainly had to be discussed frequently. Furthermore
these euphemisms belong to a group of many other figures of speech which are
pertinent only locally or within a small region.

The following examples are a few figures of speech from Sarata, a village of
Bessarabia colonized by Swabians.[12] Judging by dialect dictionaries and collections, their actively preserved rich store of such figures of speech corresponds
closely to the language used in our villages until the beginning of the twentieth
century. "Es brennt nach wie dem Max seine Feuerflinte" (It burns late like

Max's flintlock) was said in cases of delay. Maximilian Math from Sarata owned an old-fashioned buckshot gun that was fired by means of flints. While hunting hares, the mechanism failed. The shot went off a few minutes later and hit the toes of the hunter's boots. The same Max Math owned a windmill which almost ceased turning because he did not grease the shaft. This gave rise to a proverbial phrase indicating laziness: "Er dreht sich auch wie dem Max seine Windmühle" (It turns like Max's windmill). A fixed phrase was used in conversations of marital partners: "Gelt, Gänslein, du hast auch geheiratet" (Well, silly goose, you too got married). This is supposed to have been uttered originally by a man after a year of marriage; this man had first approached Katterfeld, the priest, with two brides, both of whom he wanted to marry. That a specific man is mentioned is no proof of the historical veracity of such a tradition. Anyone familiar with the laws of folk narrative will suspect a migratory narrative, the truth of which is supposed to be confirmed by the inclusion of a known person.[13] At the same time this process of rapprochement and local attachment of narratives that originally were disseminated more widely is indicative of the unity of place.

Some proverbial phrases are more comprehensive and include nearby localities. "Er macht's wie der Kulmer Kuhhirt" (He acts like Kulm's cowherd) was said when someone gave notice before he could be fired. This cowherd had listened at the door and overheard the decision of the parish council not to hire him again on any account. Afterwards he hurried there to say he considered it beneath his dignity to stay in Kulm and that he would leave. If some work was needlessly repeated, it was said: "Der geht auch doppelt drüber wie die Katzbacher übers Tanzen" (He does the work twice, as the Katzbacher did with the dance). Similar situations, when someone had done futile work, drew the comment: "Du pflasterst auch die Strasse nach Dennewitzer Art" (You are paving the street the way they do it in Dennewitz), where allegedly the street was paved with manure that promptly washed away in the next rain.

All of this unites a small circle of localities. Quite generally the immediate environment is included in the field of vision. To be sure, other examples illustrate the isolation and the pronounced individualism of single villages. The extremely severe protective measures against amorous nocturnal visits from neighboring villages is one such instance. Gerhard Lutz has collated these regionally diverse measures, which range from riding a wheel-barrow and plunging into a well to paying fines.[14] However, these traditional defenses, where the inhabitants of one village have it out with young lads from neighboring villages, are at the same time a form of communication and prove that the horizon extends beyond the village boundaries.

At times such proverbial phrases may migrate together with the narrative to which they belong and thus leave their original environment; it also happens that over time they are transmitted as formulas without retaining their original reference. By contrast, other linguistic expressions, similar to the euphemisms mentioned earlier, are tied so closely to the situation of a small area that they remain unintelligible elsewhere. Examples include the naming of particular winds familiar only to a native population.[15] The fishermen in the northern region of Lake Constance differentiate between the *Kluser*, which blows from the *Klause* between Linden and Bregenz, the *Mauracher Klöpfer*, which comes from Maurach, and the *Schussenklöpfer* or *Schusser* from the Schussen. Additionally there is a *Fischbacher*, a *Thurgäuer*, and a *Luxburger*.[16] The names indicate a direction, which assumes a certain spatial consciousness and in turn influences that consciousness.[17] Weather dites, too, often apply only to a limited area, since they refer to certain signs in the vicinity: "Trägt der Bleichten einen Hut, wird das Wetter morgen gut" (If the Bleichten is wearing a hat, the weather will be good tomorrow) is said in Dormettingen near Balingen, where the Plettenberg is used for orientation. The names of mountains themselves are variously determined by the sites from which they are viewed. Numerous *Mittagsspitzen* (noon peaks) can only have received their name from the viewpoint of one particular locality and often bear that name there only. Even constellations of stars have received local names, and it seems like a subsequent parody of such regional associations when a *blason populaire* is told about inhabitants of another village attempting to catch "their" moon. In Harkau near Ödenburg Ursa Major was called *Kogelwagen* (Kogel carriage) because its "shaft point" touched the peak of the Kogel mountain at 2:00 am. Generally constellations helped to establish temporal orientation.[18] Leopold Schmidt discovered specific names for constellations from the eighteenth century in the travel letters of Baron von Moll; e.g., the people of Matrei called the Pleiades *Kalser Pfannholz* (Kals Panhandle).[19]

It is perhaps no accident that this example has led us to a valley of the high mountains. Where the mountains constitute an imposing physical horizon for most localities, the horizon of mental unity seems narrower and stricter as well— though not insurmountable and not without gaps. By contrast, elsewhere larger regions are linked, as demonstrated by the proverbial phrases from Bessarabia and by the names given to the winds of northern Lake Constance. The proverbial phrase "Er tut, als hätt er's Mäkelis" (He acts as if he had the Mäkelis), which seems to be related to the once prosperous patrician family of Möttelin in Ravensburg,[20] was also common and understood in the wider surrounding area. In Neubronn the following saying was noted: "Der tut mit dem Kopf wie der Rathausmann zu Aalen" (He moves his head like the man at the Aalen City Hall).[21] The saying refers to the Spy of Aalen, a mechanical wooden figure at the old city hall. In very general terms, such proverbial phrases indicate the field of influence exerted by cities. However, according to the evidence provided by proverbial phrases larger rural areas are united as well. Everyone in the Killertal understands the statement "Da liegt der Schütz von Schlatt!" (Here lies the hunter of Schlatt!) even though the original legend is no longer known. The comparison *offen wie Afelse* (open like Afelse), current in Alsace, involves the wider environment, for the unsheltered position of Avolsheim only stands out when compared to the walled communities of the neighborhood.[22] The Suppingen song book features many songs and humorous short poems[23] which include names of alpine villages: "Mei Schatz, der isch von Scharastett ond i von Ettlschiess. . . Er hot so dicke Wada ghett ond i so dünne Füass. . ."[24] (My sweetheart hails from Scharastett and I am from Ettlschiess. . . He has such fat legs and I have such thin feet . . .). These songs often include local banter and weave it into fields of semantically related names, as demonstrated by Hugo Moser.[25]

Such local banter proves that each area delimited in this way has connections running across to the next. In his essay "Linguistic Boundaries and their Causes,"[26] Hugo Moser describes in detail the way the consciousness of larger units lies over the separate consciousness of local groups and the way circles widen until they reach the consciousness of a national character. Similarly the "zones of attachment to one's home," which determine the consciousness of the inhabitants of new housing developments, have recently been investigated.[27] These zones expand from family ties within one's own home to a worldly wise awareness which leaps even beyond national boundaries. This seems to blur the unity of place we are looking for. Consequently we have to ask ourselves whether the assumed horizons are simply arbitrary constructs which emphasize one among a number of relatively equal zones and define it as an all but impenetrable wall. In this connection we have to explain first of all that we are trying to establish a historical perspective. Without doubt, even in earlier times no absolute boundary existed. The horizon in question was neither impenetrable nor without breach. However, there seems to have been a boundary—even if we cannot, and never could, determine it precisely in a geographical sense—which represented the horizon for ordinary men. Within this boundary real knowledge and communal life was possible, even if the individual ranges varied. Aloys Weissenbach described Tyrolean peasant comedies in 1834. He commented on the jokes of the *Hanswurst* (tomfool), which are mostly in rhyme: "One must be familiar with the chronicle of scandals from the entire area, as well as with the dialect and all its peculiarities, to appreciate fully the comic flavor of this folk wit."[28] The horizon evident here generally did not and could not accommodate a newcomer from outside, who had to adapt to it slowly instead.

The technical machine and its products, too, can become part of this horizon. Thus at the beginnings of movies a "presenter" explained the course of the film and, as it were, adapted "the international subject matter to local tastes and interests."[29] Even today movies shown in a village have a local character beyond the specific setting of the projection room. On the other hand, the cinema is an example of the way those boundaries are overrun and horizons expand. Heidegger commented on the cinema, radio, and many of today's technological media: "Existence effects a rapprochement of the 'world' by way of an expansion of the everyday environment which is not yet comprehensible in its sense of existence."[30] Many of our examples—e.g., the proverbial phrases referring to wind and weather and particular jobs—showed that we were dealing with the problem of mastering the "everyday environment." They delimit the space we are familiar with. Theodor Litt has recently described *Umgang* (familiar contact) as characteristic of man's pretechnological coping with nature.[31] While theory and practice are uniformly linked in such familiar contact, they are separated in the relationship to nature determined by science and technology.[32] Thus the former horizon crumbles. Now even that is a part of our environment which cannot readily become familiar by contact: Man is transcending "the horizon of visible and immediate concerns."

The characteristic of familiar contact further explains why the often far-reaching and comprehensive experiences of individuals can only be inadequately received and digested by others. One may assume that in the preindustrial era the stranger was regarded as foreign more definitely and for a longer period; on the other hand he was generally forced to discard his foreign behavior more rapidly than is the case in today's mobile society.[33] However, the characteristic of familiar contact in the world within the horizon helps us to answer the important question of what was beyond that horizon—for we would underestimate the mental breadth of earlier generations if we were to assume that for them nothing existed beyond that horizon. Whatever was beyond was merely difficult to comprehend and became the subject of other forces and attitudes: of curiosity, belief, imagination. It could assume a quality of being playfully unreal, charmingly strange, or supernatural. However, because it could not be examined by experience and familiar contact, a binding canon evolved within the horizon concerning all that was not familiar. This explains the *Schwänke* (humorous tales) and jokes that always attach to foreign regions, tribes, and peoples before an actual familiar contact is established, which subsequently leads to a more realistic characterization. It is also the cause of exotic requisites and forms which often grotesquely distort things foreign. Above all many legends that are traditional in specific locations or small areas reveal how the environment mastered by familiar contact is surrounded by that which cannot be mastered, but which nevertheless exerts some influence. Such phenomena will be mentioned later when we investigate the paths and consequences of the explosion of the former horizon.

DISSOLUTION OF THE HORIZON: AVAILABILITY OF GOODS

The genre of travel literature attained conspicuous popularity during the last quarter of the eighteenth century. In comparison with earlier travel reports, the descriptions strove for greater accuracy; and their content and style approached those of regional statistical topography, which began at that time. Such travel reports and topographical descriptions as an important source for historical folklore studies have barely been exploited. Not only the materials collected but also the assumptions and the basic attitude underlying such presentations are revealing. They frequently claim to offer the first reliable access to regions which were formerly known through prejudices and erroneous opinions. In 1787 an anonymous volume, *Geographie und Statistik Wirtembergs* (Geography and Statistics of Württemberg), was published in Laibach, in distant Austria. In the introduction the publisher, Wilhelm Heinrich Korn, acknowledges originating from Württemberg: "The noble disposition of our great Joseph, who gave Europe the signal for tolerance, drew me to his states." Following the spirit of the Enlightenment advocated by Emperor Joseph, the author introduces the individual regions and localities, paying specific attention to the Black Forest. He believes that for this area in particular many prejudices have to be dismantled:[34] "This region is reputed to be depopulated and only inhabited by lumberjacks and charcoal-burners,

who are not considered of a much higher class than orangoutans. Even in Württemberg the word *Schwarzwälder* is used as a swear word.'' Certainly this is a
rather extreme description. We have to keep in mind that travel writers of that
period—and perhaps of any period—unintentionally tend to describe the borders
and barriers they have passed as particularly dangerous and difficult to overcome. The romantically exaggerated descriptions of comparatively innocuous
mountain chains and gorges are eloquent indicators of this fact.[35] However, we
should not dismiss the reproach of the author as shadow boxing. Apparently
"even in Württemberg," to which the Black Forest belongs in part, fantastically
erroneous notions circulated about the people of the Black Forest, which are
countered by the positive picture of the topographer: "The Black Forest man is by
no means as uncouth, raw, and uneducated as might be assumed from the wild
appearance of his region and its distance from cities. His garb is quite nice and
almost French.''

This little book confirms the existence of a relatively stable, fixed, and narrow
horizon beyond which one did not look, so that the other side was known only
via the distortions of hearsay. At the same time it indicates the path which then
begins to penetrate the horizon, a "broadening" in more senses than one, i.e., a
spreading of more exact observations beyond the regions in the immediate vicinity (even if this merely enhanced the comparative knowledge of the home territory), which was always accompanied by an enlightening "diffusion" of the
results obtained. Though only a few traveled in this manner, we find here important impulses for an expansive movement which attracted the simple folk as well,
and to which the dissolution of many territorial boundaries in the aftermath of
the Napoleonic wars gave an additional impetus.

We must again add the qualification that transgressions and an individual
broadening of locally conceived horizons have always occurred. Itinerant craftsmen roamed widely. However, it seems that what was locally considered appropriate behavior was decisive for them, too. In this case the horizon simply
changed rather than expanded. The well known song "Bin gewesen in fremden
Land, habe viel erfahren" (I Have Been in Foreign Lands, and Have Learned
Much) demonstrates to an almost programmatic degree the negligible importance
of going abroad, for it mentions as the single essential experience the familiar
perception "that young people sleep with each other."[36] Sailors and merchants
often traveled to other continents. Military expeditions, too, sometimes covered
fantastic distances. The attribute "fantastic" does not merely convey the idea of
escalation. In fact the experiences thus acquired were always generalized in fantastic form, i.e., dressed in the garb of the fairytale. Thus the nineteenth-century
development represents something essentially new, in spite of the ever-present
tension between confinement and expansion. From now on a general expansion
begins, the exact course of which can only be demonstrated by thorough specific
investigations, but which can be shown to some extent by individual examples.

From its inception the system of voluntary associations has been part of this
expansion. In the 1820s increasing numbers of choral societies evolved in Germany and some neighboring countries. In East Flanders singing competitions began among rural communities in 1834 and reached the cities in 1838. These

competitions spread from Belgium to Germany and Switzerland.[37] At first the competition merely united a small number of neighboring communities. However, distances rapidly increased, and soon national and international song festivals emerged. Needless to say an excursion to such song festivals in which half the village participated is fundamentally different from the mobility experienced earlier, when single or smaller groups changed their location but generally had to adapt to another fixed horizon.

Sports associations, which for more than a century had been seeking comparable achievements with other associations, escalated this kind of movement. Sports associations depend on the competitive principle more than do choral societies, and therefore they aim beyond the boundaries of associations and localities. However, in this case, as in others, the basis of the developing movement is factual: the common active interest in certain goods or purposes. The movement itself is no incidental trivial matter; the nearer we come to the present, the more frequently it proves to be the essential motivation for such competitions and events. This applies even more to "cultural" get-togethers than to sports contests—which, however, attract a strikingly large audience. Even the annals of associations and newspaper articles emphasize the fact that journeys into other regions and contact with "fellow singers" from other countries are of the essence. This newspaper report on the Dussling Music Association near Tübingen is typical: "The visit of the costumed musicians from Mittersill in the Salzburg mountains proves that geographical boundaries are no obstacle to the meeting of people."[38]

The expansive tendency is taken to the extreme when the meeting of two communities is justified merely by the name they have in common. The municipal council of Kilchberg near Zürich visited the community of Kilchberg near Tübingen and extended an invitation for a return visit. Many inhabitants of Herbolzheim on the Jagst traveled to the community of Herbolzheim in Breisgau. A newspaper covered the meeting as follows:

> Over the weekend the lively and busy little town of Herbolzheim in Breisgau was visited by the community of Herbolzheim on the Jagst. The people of Herbolzheim on the Jagst made this return visit by special train. They were welcomed like relatives in festively decorated Herbolzheim in Breisgau, and with such affection that during the Saturday evening festivities in the overcrowded hall, Mayor Willi Horch could say that the inhabitants of Herbolzheim on the Jagst had found a second home in Herbolzheim in Breisgau. A colorful medley of instrumental and choral performances by the associations of both guests and hosts drew much attention during the course of the evening. Speeches by mayors Jäger and Horch and an exchange of gifts emphasized the friendship between the two namesakes. Sunday morning's program included a sightseeing tour of the city, a church service, and an outdoor concert by both bands. In the afternoon the soccer players of both Herbolzheims competed against each other. With the promise of a return visit next year for the eleven hundredth anniversary of the sister community on the Jagst, the guests took their leave of Herbolzheim in Breisgau. While regretting that their visit had ended all too rapidly, they returned home on their special train, taking many pleasant memories home with them.[39]

Admittedly competitions were part of this occasion. However, the meeting as such is the essential thing, i.e., that reaching out beyond the familiar neighborhood—a small sideline of tourism which is popular today even among simple folk.[40]

Such meetings have a different flavor when a place-name from the former German territories in the East matches one in West Germany. For example, the refugees from Bartenstein in East Prussia met with the population of Bartenstein in Hohenlohe.[41] In principle, however, these meetings, like all similar "sponsorship" events, are part of the expansive movement which has been on the increase since the beginning of the nineteenth century. The mass immigration from the eastern territories after World War II was determined by completely different causes and did not involve a radical shift in folk culture, but it generally intensified and hastened the expansive tendencies which were already established.[42]

The expansive movement exerted a very strong influence on the form and function of cultural goods. Occasionally this is critically acknowledged, e.g., in 1855 Otto Elben detected a "dangerous reef" in song competitions: "prize-singing has repeatedly become the main purpose of voluntary associations. Competing for the prize and external honor have now replaced the sacred art of folk singing and consequently cause jealousy, arguments, and envy; many a celebration has therefore turned sour."[43] It must be added that the style of singing and, above all, the songs themselves have changed under the influence of such competitions. From the beginning the choral societies aimed beyond the previously existing horizons and did not limit themselves to the local singing tradition. On the contrary, that was often immediately reduced to second-class status in favor of the newer music passages arranged for several voices. This evaluation was reinforced by the singing events. What emerged here in the first half of the nineteenth century has, meanwhile, affected folk-cultural goods in general. For example, Hugo Moser has pointed out repeatedly that "relationships to the environment . . . become more and more supraregional, spacious, worldwide" and that dialects recede as as result; "the functions of a linguistically intermediate level [Umgangssprache], like those of the standard language, are growing at the expense of the dialects."[44] However, as before, language as an elementary feature remains strongly informed by everyday familiar use and clearly continues to reveal different spheres, which may be defined as various levels of dialect, as provincial and regional vernacular, etc. This almost "organic" expansion from the nearest to the close and then to the far does not apply to other cultural goods. In folk dance circles, for example, people did not simply go slowly beyond the traditions close to home by first including the dances of a neighboring region in their repertoire; instead such spatial considerations practically ceased to play a role.[45] This is the more conspicuous as folk dance societies are institutions concerned with conservation. They, too, are subject to the laws of our times and should or must accept that an "autochthonous quality" in the old sense apparently no longer exists. In this case the horizon has not steadily expanded, but rather crumbled altogether.

However, it would be foolish to relate the crumbling of the horizon merely to population movements in the widest sense, i.e., including tourism. To be sure, tourism has intruded in a decisive way into the orderly world of many remote villages and regions. But that orderly existence would not remain undisturbed even without tourism. Richard Weiss has investigated present-day life in the Alps.[46] He emphasizes that even the mountain farmer knows about life in the city, "or he believes he knows about it from the flood of advertising which appears in the most remote corners of the mountains, mostly in the form of the store catalogue, which for some of the mountain farm households has become the favorite and often only work of folk and children's literature—one that replaces the Bible, the almanac, and books of fairy tales." This quotation alludes to the fact that the world of such catalogues is to some degree experienced as a fairy-tale world. However, this is the world which confronts people with the very sober business of instalment payments. Newspapers and magazines do not merely transmit reports and factual information—and the pictures and price specifications of the store catalogue basically fall into this latter category too—but like radio broadcasts they also transmit proverbial phrases and riddles, *Märchen* and *Schwänke,* songs and customs, and thus directly influence the repertoire of spiritual folk culture.

Hör zu, the popular radio magazine with a circulation of 3.5 million, occasionally features summaries of particular customs. On one occasion nine drawings showed the wedding celebrations of various regions under the title "Young brides, old customs—Rain on the veil brings blessings—Life's most beautiful celebration in German cities and villages." The first three pictures carried the following captions:

> "Church at ten—then on to the pub!" In Baden as elsewhere in Germany, the *Hochzeitsbitter* [master of wedding ceremonies] is the village herald of future delights. He has flowers on his cane and hat, yet is already almost surrounded by the smell of the roast. Wherever he presents the invitation, he is offered bacon, bread, and wine. In some regions a bridesmaid extends the wedding invitation, or even the bridal couple themselves go from farm to farm. Weddings are preferably celebrated in the fall, when the harvest and home butchering have been completed. Then people have time for celebrating and enough to fill the pan.
>
> "I will carry you in my arms for the rest of my life!" Is that what the newly married man wants to say when he carries his wife across the threshhold? He thinks so. In reality the custom is based on a belief of our early ancestors: Evil spirits live under the threshhold of the door. When the man carries the woman over this spot, the evil brood cannot harm her. A gallant gesture. However, it should not just remain a gesture.
>
> "Who will be the next bride? The bean will bring it to light!" In Hesse the lucky one, who is soon to step before the wedding altar, invites her girlfriends to a merry coffee party. Here an oracle addresses the most burning concern of this group. A bean has been baked inside a cake. The girl who finds it in her piece should complete her trousseau quickly, for she will win the matrimonial race. Is it certain? Does anybody guarantee this? The bean doesn't!

Subsequent explanations[47] similarly indicate the local roots of certain wedding customs, and individual pictures emphasize regional costumes. They even point out contrasts which separate the customs of one region from those of another. However, the pictures are placed as a unit and appear to be an overall representation of German wedding customs. We do not want to overestimate the actual effect of such a presentation. But such presentations, together with the pronounced blending of the population, may be responsible, for example, for the general diffusion of the *Polterabend* (noisy evening, i.e., the evening before the wedding when dishes are broken at a party for the couple to be married), which was originally confined mainly to the Low German regions. In any case such a presentation contributes to a development whereby old customs lose their old functions. They need not die out. Quite the contrary, the pretty pictures may provide an additional support to sustain them—as will be discussed later. But they are no longer entirely subject to the cardinal law of older folk culture, where "traditions are received and experienced in a peculiar state of unconsciousness," as Leopold Schmidt put it.[48]

Before investigating this change more closely it is worthwhile to inquire about the sources of this magazine piece. They cannot be established with certainty in all details. However, some very precise references permit the inference that they are based on folkloristic literature. This fact must not be suppressed. When we are faced with such phenomena, comments are generally restricted to the great influence of newspapers, radio broadcasts, etc., thus relating the phenomena in question to the technical foreground. In reality, however, the line can be extended from here into the history of scholarly disciplines and cultural history. Practically the only difference between the presentation in the magazine and in folklore collections (especially of the nineteenth century) is the brevity and larger circulation of the former. In principle, however, those collections proceed similarly in that they are mainly conditioned by considerations of preservation and cultivation for which the material has, as it were, been provided. Romantic folklore scholarship on the whole was not, or not solely, concerned with scholarly collecting, but with revival; the developing collections were regarded as a means of enriching the folk culture.[49] In his review of Grimm's *Sagen*, Arnim compares his childhood with current times: "The growing generation is so much more richly endowed: may it learn to use its wealth!"[50]

This wealth assumes the dissolution of the horizons existing up to then. Perhaps today we may have to conclude that people with enlightened minds—such as the topographers—for all their critical attitude were more likely to think within the given spheres of life than were the Romantics. The latter knew well how to empathize with folk thinking as they saw it. However, the meaning of the word *volkstümlich* (folk traditional), which for Herder still connoted the popular, now characteristically took a turn toward the national: Jahn's concept was accepted. The previous horizons, which undoubtedly continued to be effective for some time, could be abandoned the more easily as the concept of the nation provided a new horizon for "folk" life. The dominant influence of the idea of the national on the folk culture of the nineteenth and early twentieth centuries can hardly be overestimated. Again this can be traced particularly well in the development of voluntary associations, a typical feature of the newer folk culture. In 1855 Otto Elben called the final chapter of his book on the history of male singing in Germany "The National Significance of Male Singing."[51] He repeatedly mentions this national significance in other parts of the book as well.[52] However, this nationalist concept did not provide a horizon in the usual sense. It contributed instead—together with the growing efforts of popular education—to the exchange of goods and to the transcendence of the limits of the comprehensible and the "familiar." This development was inevitable, and it would be foolish to make it the cause of polemics against the nationalist impulse. However, we must emphasize that many of the more recent changes in folk culture can indeed be traced to the double meaning of the word *Volk*.[53] And it must further be emphasized that the expansive impulse inherent in the extension to the level of the national could not be intercepted. It finally led to the "washed-out quality of culturally average behavior which out of complete naivety decorated itself with the feathers of all times and peoples."[54] The depreciative tone of these words, however, still needs to be examined.

Wilhelm Heinrich Riehl severely criticizes this washed-out quality of the culture of "the leveled and refined bourgeois world," to which he opposes the enduring powers of the nobility and the peasantry. However, it is obvious that the laws of that bourgeois world spread to the rural world long ago. In discussing the process of name-giving, he observes in the bourgeois world an

> escalated eclecticism leading to complete confusion. . . People reach for the names of all times and nations and base their choice merely on chance and personal preference. The name no longer characterizes the personality, the family, the class, the profession. It degenerates into a mere external label and, when a respectable tailor has his children baptized Athelstan, Jean-Noël and Oscar, or Natalie, Zaire, Olga and Iphigenia, this is basically no better than simply numbering them, for each of these names is as unalive as a dead number.[55]

This example can easily be transferred to the customs prevailing today, especially among the working class and rural folk. A survey of entries at the registry office reveals that, precisely in these circles, fashionable first names—e.g., those derived from films and popular songs—dominate, and other names really are chosen from the arsenal of "all times and peoples." Like all popular cultural goods they have become "available." When first names are chosen today with traditional, regional, or even family connections, people are still choosing more or less consciously from a large supply of what is readily available. Thus the general attitude has changed. But we have to contradict Riehl, for it is exactly this possibility of choice which prevents the name from equaling a number. The meaning of "chances and personal preferences" not only may be interpreted depreciatively when referring to the power of the suprapersonal custom, but also must be seen positively when referring to the evil of impersonal dullness.

Street names of the most recent past exhibit strikingly how insignificant clusters of names, often of animals and plants, expand the supply of names which was previously restricted to certain local and historical factors. Today we encounter in almost any place names such as Badger, Marten, Weasel, and Polecat

Street; Heather, Lilac, and Lily Avenue; and the like. In an investigation of the historical structure of the street names of Ludwigsburg, Willi Müller indicates the basic principle of association which operates even in these clusters. However, he also emphasizes the fact that this process of naming could "hardly reveal anything but a compensation for a lack of cohesion in such matters."[56] This is all the more relevant since the group of "natural street names," which mainly derive from field names, is constantly shrinking. Free availability here seems to encourage a somewhat mechanical and very impersonal nomenclature. Not only are these names linked themselves, but also they generate very specific associations and so indirectly describe concrete factual relations. Clusters like Lily Street, Rose Avenue, etc., characterize the suburban fringe settlements developed from the 1930s on. Names of poets are typical of the quarters inhabited by civil servants. Streets with (changing) names of politicians also have similar locations everywhere. Such names essentially shape the model of urban spatial structure, which now barely depends on the landscape, and therefore they do not remain mere external labels.[57] The clusters of flower and animal names and the like are by no means unpopular; they generally suit the bright and friendly new suburban quarters. At least in naming practices aesthetic and decorative impulses dominate.

This case is similar to the presentation of wedding customs mentioned earlier, where colorful costumes dominate the picture. The beautiful and the pleasant constitute one of the essential pillars of popular cultural goods, which are subject to availability and therefore threatened in their existence. In street names and even in wedding customs this development is a harmless process. The potential for aesthetic considerations is in a way inherent in the matter—to be sure, even previously many wedding customs were practiced not merely because they were considered binding traditions but because they were beautiful. However, the aesthetic point of view and the actual aestheticization of goods intrude to a high degree even into realms which in their essence allow at most for an accidental aesthetic element. Only a detailed examination of the change in forms of folk piety and folk belief can indicate the emancipation of "ceremoniousness" which threatens to turn into an end in itself.[58] Above all such an investigation must cautiously question where this modern "ceremonial" element departs from the ceremonial as a basic component of all ritual. But this change in the forms of piety seems to be related as much to the disintegration of that horizon which originally defined the religious cosmos as to the renunciation of binding religious forms. The following exceedingly superficial verse is widely disseminated today:

> *Ihr glaubt, der Jäger sei ein Sünder,*
> *Weil selten er zur Kirche geht—*
> *Im grünen Wald ein Blick zum Himmel*
> *Ist besser als ein falsch Gebet*

> (You believe the hunter is a sinner
> Because he only rarely attends Church—

A glance at the sky in the green forest
Is better than a false prayer)

The verse appears as a wall decoration even among devout families. The attribute "false" may offer an explanation: the verse seemingly objects only to *false* prayers. But perhaps availability is decisive here too, for it permits this example of the sentimental sanctification of nature to be placed next to forms of established belief.

The significance and range of this availability become obvious when we consider, for example, the transformations which folk legends have undergone since the beginning of the scientific-technological era. The legend as presented today in innumerable illustrated books of legends has been stripped of its original power. Poetic elements are emphasized, as in the old romances by Schwab or Uhland. The spatial relations have practically lost their importance. This development may not be compared to the migration of legends, in which—morphologically speaking—motifs and narrative schemes are introduced from outside but seek a new position within a firm horizon. Legends of subterranean beings or evil sorcerers exist or existed in many places. But in each case they were at home there and filled and animated the space of the familiar environment. By contrast, in many of the newer legend collections, place-names are reduced to meaningless requisites and hence make just as little sense as in a *Märchen*. That some localities cultivate the memory of their legend tradition carefully, is only the other side of the same coin. When motifs from the world of Pfullingen legend are displayed on the fountain at Pfullingen Town Hall, this too indicates the loss of power and the displacement of the legend figures.

But the essential folk legend of today is not the legend of the legend books. More typically it is represented, for example, in the technological-utopian legend. Jung emphasizes that flying saucers appear above all earthly horizons: "Given the threatening nature of the global situation today, as one begins to realize that all may be at stake, the projection of fantasy reaches beyond the realm of earthly organizations and powers into the sky, i.e., into the cosmic space of the stars, where once the rulers of destiny, the Gods, had their seat among the planets."[59] On the other hand, the fact that fantasy reaches less predictably than ever into the everyday world is proven by any survey of current narratives which avoids prejudice and does not focus on relics.[60] We may state paradoxically: ghosts have become more dangerous ever since they have ceased to exist, i.e., since they no longer occupy their place within the horizon.

This example proves that availability may have multiple meanings: loss of power, aestheticization, banishment, unleashing. The dissolution of the horizon does not equal the end of folk culture but carries with it transformations which are different for each individual cultural good and which must be examined precisely. Only in this way can we arrive at a safe evaluation, for the availability of a song has to be evaluated differently from the availability of a religious form. However, the concept "availability" seems to be a guide toward the understanding of the transformations.

THE EXOTIC AS A CONTRIBUTION
TO EXPANSION

Dissolution of the horizon and great mobility do not entirely characterize the movement of spatial expansion within folk culture. At least one further important trend has to be identified: the strong effect of the "exotic." We have mentioned before that the horizon expands not so much in organic circles, i.e., by transferring the concept of neighborhood, without changing its essence, from the everyday to more distant realms, but that the aspect of neighborliness diminishes altogether. Now we must recognize that what is very distant often enters the living environment of the simple folk much more strongly than what is nearby in the extended sense. Willy Hellpach has referred to the fact that "the average man is either interested in that which pertains practically to the sphere of his everyday life and which affects it, or in that which is completely strange, the 'exotic'—the neighbor or the stranger."[61] In this form Hellpach's statement is certainly not limited to the present age, and it somehow still assumes the firm horizon. But where the horizon has remained intact, the exotic may suddenly turn into the miraculous—not only in the sense that a certain magic adheres to all that is strange, but also in the sense that it is completely stripped of its other reality and is placed into a dimension alongside folktale-like and supernatural elements. Apparently it is necessary that that which is strange should come into close range, but should not yet have become commonplace, in order to be specifically experienced as something exotic or enjoyed because of its exotic traits.

The scientific-technological era, however, has brought the whole world into close range without making large parts of it commonplace. This explains the special significance and the special scope of the exotic nowadays and hardly needs illustration. Corresponding to Hellpach's notion, comic strips and serial novels take their plots either from "everyday life" or from the exotic, or sometimes from both in a more or less artful blend.[62] The most financially profitable and stable genres of the German cinema are the *Heimatfilm* (sentimental films glorifying one's native area), the Western, and the thriller. However, even thrillers and many other entertaining movies make use of exotic attractions. How many exotic elements have entered even the remotest village is evident in observations and reports of carnival events. In Bad Waldsee in Upper Swabia a ball is typically announced to the visitors in the following fashion: "We present original Waldsee customs according to our theme: 'Prince George the Hopeful in his magnificent oriental palace, surrounded by his court and his guard of princes, receives the caliph with his vizier and the women of his harem, his conjurers, clowns, and magicians.' "[63] Two years later the ball is held "in Venetian style," and even the smallest hamlets announce themes such as "Jungle Secrets," "A Night on the Lagoons," or "Nights in Hawaii."

It is precisely in carnival customs that we cannot avoid the *history* of the exotic, which may provide us with information on its essential nature. In the cities exotic themes appear by the nineteenth century. The *Fasnet* (carnival) of 1885 in Riedlingen featured the arrival of the "Shah of Persia"; and in 1903 the "Adven-

tures of the Prince Carnival on his Voyage around the World" were presented.[64]
At the *Fasnacht* (carnival) of 1890 in Villingen, "The German Expedition to East
Africa" was performed with the prelude "Shelling and assault of a rebellious
Negro village by the warship *Carola,* then entry of Wissmann's army into
Bagamoyo."[65] The 1896 celebration featured "The Japanese-Chinese war with
the assault on Port-Arthur." In the following year "The Turks standing before
Vienna" was presented, with the prelude "The siege and defense of the city of
Vienna."[66] This demonstrates how exotic elements blend with history and even
more importantly with contemporary political and national issues. The acquisi-
tion of the German colonies and the battles in these colonies provided particularly strong stimuli for such presentations. Perhaps the most extreme example was
the enormous drama of 1911 about the rebellion of the Hereros, which was staged
outdoors in the small village of Diepoldshofen in the Allgäu by a former member
of the colonial troops of German Southwest Africa. About 400 people fought
before a huge audience on the hills around the village.[67] In Schwyz a whole class
of *Fasnacht* plays received the name "Japanese plays" after a drama society,
henceforth known as the Japanese Society, had performed a play in 1863 that
parodied the recently established relations between Switzerland and Japan.[68]
These examples show that it is precisely a first fleeting contact which gives impetus to the representation of the exotic.

However, it is not only the political and economic opening-up of the continents
which is decisive. To some degree older impulses from high culture continued to
influence such performances. Thus in 1857 "The five continents" were represented at the *Fasnacht* in Donaueschingen.[69] This motif is familiar to us from
Baroque paintings and is splendidly realized, for example, in the frescos of the
stairs in Würzburg Castle. We also encounter it in religious representations of the
eighteenth century: "The order of procession for Good Friday 1745 from Meran
indicates that the four continents were represented before the Heart of Jesus as
figure 144 and as the 15th carried stage (Ferculum)."[70] However, even this is not
a new invention, but an adaptation of secular courtly forms to the sacred realm.
The *Brauchkunst* (consciously staged customs) of the courts[71] was particularly
rich at the time of the great voyages during the Renaissance, when the foreign
continents were often represented. To be sure, the "inventions" at German
courts, late descendants of the "Trionfi," show that the attraction of the exotic
must be understood mainly as an aspect of escapism: noble society hides in the
dress of foreign peoples, for the same reasons that it conceals itself in the mythological dress of wild men and bacchants or, in the so-called inns, in the simple
costume of peasantry.[72] Such courtly mumming and masquerading was common
all over Europe, and a comprehensive investigation should provide fine insights
into cultural history. It occurred earlier in southern and western Europe than in
the central part,[73] even though the parade of exotic figures of Middle High German epic poetry already resembled masked processions. In any case, these masquerades remained popular at German courts for a very long period. Even as late
as February 16, 1810 a masked procession took place in Weimar under the title
"mass migration," headed by the wife of President von Frisch as Schamanka, a
Tartar fortune teller.[74]

Even though the styles and themes of such performances differ widely, exotic elements are almost always included as essential components. Their use is not merely fanciful; foreign countries and peoples must first have entered the field of vision before they can inspire imaginative representations. Occasionally attempts are even made to portray the character of different nations. Thus the carnival of 1510 at the English court featured Turkish, Russian, and Prussian costumes. At times the depiction closely approaches reality. It has been said of Ben Jonson's masque *Gipsies Metamorphosed* that "one could almost use the fiction as an ethnographic source for the life and language of seventeenth-century English gypsies."[75] But this does not dissolve the exotic element, for additional motifs are involved. Pictures and descriptions of courtly masquerades include allusions to biblical figures as well. Characteristically it is the three Magi who are portrayed, frequently accompanied by a large entourage in blackface. Subsequently the latter participate in religious processions as well and, in a process of reversal, carry courtly elements into the sacred sphere.[76] Religious aspects are incorporated in the *Brauchkunst* at the courts as long as they are picturesque—often meaning "exotic." The most diverse elements meet in the figure of the Moor. When a fourteenth-century decree by the council of Regensburg forbade " 'all *schemen* and all *mörinne*,' the second term certainly referred to black masks."[77] The appearance of Moors at the Nuremberg *Schembartläufen* (procession of bearded masks) has been interpreted as deriving from vegetation-demonic origins because a summery white dress is often part of these masks.[78] However, for a large city like Nuremberg courtly parades should be considered a possible influence as well as a contact with religious representations.[79]

The special significance of the "Black Madonnas" for pilgrimages even in our age strikingly proves the essential connection between the exotic and religious realms. The image of the picturesque and peculiar alien captures the completely different and foreign aspects of the world of religion. Even in secular times, perhaps particularly in secular times, transcendence is expected in what is particularly beautiful and foreign. Exotic music, unless distinctly humorous and dance oriented, very often creates the impression of being of a sacred nature, even in cases where this is not based on fact. However, this essential connection between the exotic and the religious is augmented by factual and historical associations. Biblical stories lead into the strange, mysterious orient, with which at least a fleeting contact has been established since the Crusades. During the fifteenth century the "curiosity cabinets" of European princes, often precursors of museums, were filled with whale ribs, ostrich eggs, corals, and other peculiar objects. In the late Renaissance, so-called ostrich egg goblets achieved popularity.[80] It may be assumed that exotic elements also play an essential role in the medieval, above all late medieval, and then again in the Baroque cult of relics. Characteristically a sixteenth-century inventory of the "aristocratic pilgrimages" of the principality of Württemberg not only contains references to saints' relics—such as the fist-sized piece from the tooth of St. Christopher displayed by the nuns on the Böselsberg—but also a "griffin's egg" on the Engelberg near Neuffen, which was visited from far and near.[81]

All these historical impulses do not necessarily continue to affect us at the present, nor are the exotic aspects now diffusing to any great degree within folk culture. We might assume that the growing potential for real communication and encounters, and above all the dissemination of scientifically based knowledge of foreign peoples and countries of the world, would at least have intercepted the exotic and provided it with a frame. From this point of view the exotic would at most add a subtle charm to the knowledge gained without being able to falsify it any longer: political encounters and scholarly anthropology are replacing the exotic. This is how Ernst Jünger viewed the process, i.e., a shrinking of the number of "romantic regions" due to the victorious advance of technology: "Yesterday perhaps they still existed 'far away in Turkey' or in Spain and Greece; today in the jungle belt around the Equator or on the ice caps of the poles, but tomorrow the last white spots of this peculiar map of human yearning will have disappeared."[82] In reality he is voicing an appeal rather than a scientific observation. Romantic regions persist in real life in spite of the technological conquest of the world, and the exotic thrives in spite of actual discoveries and knowledge.

This is observable before our time. In part the intellectual discovery of faraway peoples was supported so strongly by the exotic impulse that scholarship could easily turn into an escapist idyll. Thus the discovery of foreign peoples much resembles the discovery of the simple folk at home. It was not by accident that an interest in folk song was first aroused by Montaigne's Brazilian song "Out of the Virgin Forest."[83] Kant wrote in 1785: "The knowledge disseminated by the new voyages about the diversity of the human species so far has contributed more to stimulate the mind to investigate this matter rather than to satisfy it."[84] In the travel letters of the eighteenth century, which follow upon Montesquieu's *Persian Letters,* delight in the exotic blends with the urge to acquire exact knowledge.[85] Finally the exotic had the stronger effect. Friedrich Heer has repeatedly indicated how the ruling class of Europe failed when confronted with the "challenge of world communication":

> The court of Louis XIV in Versailles celebrated the beginning of "modern times," the eighteenth century, with a New Year festival in "Chinese style." What alert minds of that time, such as the Jesuits around Ricci and the Protestants around Leibnitz, understood to be an invitation for a fundamental rethinking to prepare Europeans for the challenge of world communication was understood here as "Chinoiserie": as garland, as masquerade, as an outlandishly beautiful piece of jewelry, which was incorporated into the feudal palace in a Chinese room in the form of furniture, silk tapestry, jade vase.[86]

It was not the "rethinking" which spread in the nineteenth century, but the "Chinoiserie" and parallel phenomena. Cooper's Leatherstocking novels had a far greater effect than the "factual poetry" of Charles Sealsfield. Likewise the undemanding, idealizing exoticism of Friedrich Gerstäcker and Karl May has determined and continues to determine the image of countries and peoples outside of Europe for an extremely wide circle of readers.[87] In a survey of nineteenth-century detective novels Walter Benjamin notes the "oriental landscape" next to "that voluptuous orient in their interiors: the Persian carpet and the ottoman, the hanging lamp and the noble Caucasian dagger.[88] The limitation to "beautifully foreign" elements becomes obvious in our relationship to the colonies. During the era of the German colonies the theme "Night in Samoa" replaced "Nights in Venice,"[89] and the generic term *Kolonialwaren* (colonial goods) was typically adopted as a sign by almost all grocery stores, to be replaced recently by the similarly typical term *Feinkost* (delicatessen).

The study "Über Physiognomik" (On Physiognomy), written by Lichtenberg in 1777, directs biting sarcasm against the physiognomists who directly infer stupidity and obstinacy from a physiognomy resembling that of a Negro. This study includes some remarkable comments about Negroes, for example, one in which the author "had even heard them chatting coherently about book titles at bookstores in London, and more is hardly to be expected of a Bel-Esprit in Germany." Such an attitude indicates the start of the dismantling of the merely exotic and a real appreciation of the stranger. However, this attitude is isolated and the general humanitarian movement of that time continues to include the exotic, for it mostly calls for loving devotion rather than clear recognition; in the spirit of Rousseau the strange reality is reinterpreted as a natural condition. The story *Paul et Virginie* by Bernardin de Saint-Pierre, which was very popular at that time, expresses this particularly well. In 1781 Lessing's *Nathan* was first performed on stage. Even though this drama is certainly superior to any earlier works of a similar type, it can nevertheless be considered in a common historical context together with the dramas of the Baroque period, which stressed the exotic and were still performed in Lessing's time in monasteries, among other locations. So *Die kindliche Liebe in Japan* (Children's Love in Japan) was performed in 1762 at the convent of Wengen in Ulm, followed in 1777 by the operetta *Etwas aus China*, composed by Canon Lederer of the Augustinian order at Wengen.[90] With all due qualifications, a line may also be drawn from Lessing's *Nathan* to Theodor Körner's drama *Toni*, which was performed by many theatrical associations and amateur theatres during the nineteenth century. The equally popular Boer plays succeeded this drama at the turn of the century: *Die Heldin von Transvaal* (The Heroine of Transvaal) seems to have generated an enthusiasm in which exotic and nationalist impulses were mutually encouraging.

The Magic Flute also was first performed at the time of Lichtenberg and Lessing. An amorous Negro has to sing:

> *Alles fühlt der Liebe Freuden,*
> *Schnäbelt, tänzelt, herzet, küsst,—*
> *Und ich soll die Liebe meiden,*
> *Weil ein Schwarzer hässlich ist.*

> (Everyone feels the pleasures of love
> Cooing, skipping, cuddling, kissing—
> And I must shun love
> Because a Negro is ugly.)

Friedrich Karl Baron of Erlach included this song in his collection *Die Volkslieder der Deutschen* (German Folk Songs),[91] along with other pieces "from operettas and dramas of German composers." He chose those "which have most become part of oral folk tradition." His was the last sizable folk song collection which followed such guidelines. Later a more rigorous conceptual interpretation excluded such songs from the treasury of folk songs, though not from the most popular singing traditions of simple folk. A boarding school pupils' magazine of 1855[92] includes a revealing article on "The opera and its significance for the folk in musical terms." The unnamed author first points out that about nine-tenths of all music books sitting on pianos contain opera music. He leads the reader through the town and lets him listen to a female rendition of a song from *Robert le Diable* then a flute version of an aria from *Der Freischütz*. This is followed by a band marching to an arrangement from Flotow's *Martha*. The barrel organs on the fairgrounds play opera tunes, and in a faraway corner a little old woman grinds the organ to coax out a Lortzing melody.

> We want to go home, for the song of the czar has made us feel sad. Even at our door we can hear the rhythm of the inevitable Sunday polka, played more or less flawlessly by our neighbor, and—guess, dear reader, what this description was all about? To prove to you our first sentence, i.e., that today's opera has a tremendous influence on the musical education of the folk and that, if you are interested in the latter, you also have to consider the nature and the fate of opera music.

Taking this admonition to heart, a line can again be drawn from the amorous Negro of *The Magic Flute* to the colonial song of the "Negro Sweetheart," which in some areas "has become a real folk song."[93] The first verse reads:

> *Wer kennt in Europa die Schönen?*
> *Nach Afrika möcht ich gern ziehn,*
> *Und ich will mich an die Schwarzen gewöhnen,*
> *Die Schwarzen und Braunen sein schön;*
>
> (Who in Europe knows the beautiful ones?
> I would like to go to Africa,
> And I want to get to know the blacks,
> Black and brown people are beautiful;)

Here the original character of a couplet has been changed into that of "a yearning love song."

During the last decades of the nineteenth century and in the early twentieth the operetta strongly influenced the actual repertoire of songs current among the folk, as did the earlier folk opera. From the operetta it is only a short step to the *Schlager* (popular hit song). It is obvious that the exotic dominates both operetta and the modern popular song.[94] All these songs—from the *Land des Lächelns* (Land of Smiles) to *Sonniges Sorrent* (Sunny Sorrento)—demonstrate that the possibility and often the actuality of real encounters and comprehension do not destroy the exotic appeal. Many popular songs sing of places most affected by tourism and thus are experienced as real. However, the places in the songs are interchangeable and serve only as pegs on which to hang the same old familiar-exotic requisites. The author of the successful popular song *Rote Rosen, rote Lippen, roter Wein* (Red Roses, Red Lips, Red Wine) admitted characteristically: "In Venice I fed pigeons, in Rome I admired antiquities, in Capri I went out on the sea. Nothing helped. Then, one evening last spring on a rainy Bavarian village road I saw a garish poster: alluring grapes, blue sea, sky and—between the lips of a beautiful woman—a red rose. And lo and behold, I suddenly had both melody and text in my head."[95] Primitive as the assumption is that inspiration naturally occurs in the face of the object, the paper stimulus for this hit song and its exotic elements is nevertheless characteristic.

Not only the locations of the songs but also to a certain extent the destinations of tourism are interchangeable. To be sure, canonical sights are sought in each case. However, beyond that it is often just the exotic atmosphere conjured up in the popular songs which people crave. After the horizon has dissolved and faraway places have become accessible, a permanent contest takes place between the experience of reality and exotic ideals: the exotic is the playground of expansion. On the one hand the idea of the exotic now determines real experiences to a high degree. On the other, the exotic often reveals itself as the precursor of impartial knowledge. In the village of Eisenharz in the Allgäu in 1958 the *Sternsingen* (Procession of the Three Magi) was particularly noteworthy because "besides King Caspar a real representative of the dark continent dwelled in the community and gave testimony of the great force of the Christian faith and western culture," i.e., an African medical student happened to be staying in the village.[96] This little example shows how the exotic elements of custom and theater pave the way for a real understanding and meeting with the foreign, which finally is no longer considered exotic. It is not an isolated example, but part of a very widespread encounter with the strange or foreign, the most representative perhaps being the penetrating power of jazz, some of which has to be considered an element of contemporary folk culture. At first surrounded by the full appeal of the exotic, it became so strongly assimilated that the exotic element has partly evaporated. Esoteric lovers of "genuine" jazz complain that it has reached a dead end—this is one view of the process.

HEIMAT—FORCE FIELD AND BACKDROP

To mention jazz, popular songs, and "the everyday-world manifestations" of carnival under the heading of folk culture is indeed at variance with the conventional tacit or explicit definitions of this term. After all, isn't the culture of the *Heimat* (native area) the only genuine and proper folk culture?

Until now we have deliberately avoided the concept *Heimat*, even where we described "unity of place" and the protective effect of relatively firm horizons. In fact the concept of *Heimat* as it is generally understood approximately corresponds to the spiritual force field which has developed within these horizons so that each point and each good in this force field is also assigned a "native" value.[97] We have not spoken of *Heimat,* in order that the concept would not be defined prematurely and, more importantly, because this concept originally did not belong to that world, but was made to fit into it later on. No doubt the characteristics of *Heimat* are very pronounced in earlier folk songs. But typically the word *Heimat* hardly ever appears in songs before the nineteenth century. Consequently Walter Wiora explains: "Songs of *Heimat* are not only those poems which distinctly sing about *Heimat* and idolize it, but also deeply rooted, homely songs which remind us of *Heimat* because their characteristics resemble the *Heimat* style."[98] It might seem peculiar that the settlers from a Danube-Swabian village should define as a *Heimat* song a variant of a narrative song about a peasant who sleeps with the maidservant.[99] Nevertheless this description fits the circumstances for such an intimate, familiar native song.

In fact, the word *Heimat* seems to have been generally very rare and most often had a different meaning from today's. In individual dialects *Heimat* still primarily indicates the parental home or the farm property; and correspondingly up to about 1800 the term *Ausland* (foreign countries, abroad) mainly described the fields beyond the farm boundaries. Finally the word *Heimweh* (homesickness) only became really popular in the nineteenth century, but soon thereafter came to dominate popular songs and dialect poetry.[100] The dissemination of the current concept *Heimat* thus directly coincides with the dissolution of the horizon. Only in the course of the nineteenth century is *Heimat* increasingly the theme of songs, and it becomes an explicitly recognized and acknowledged value. Since then the concern with *Heimat* has noticeably increased while the dissolution of the former horizons and the force field delimited by them went on at the same time, as did the reaching out far into foreign realms.[101] The two movements must be seen both as running in opposite directions and as connected. Because the whole world, as it were, had turned into a stage, the backdrop of what pertains to *Heimat* was erected in place of the former horizons to counter the demolition of the force field. Even the more expanded situation has, without doubt, retained many native "fixed points," goods, and social relations which are of a familiar and therefore also of a *Heimat*-like character. *Volkskunde* should not neglect this everyday structure of relations[102] in favor of the conscious "*Heimat* movement";[103] the fact that today *Heimat* is called for and proclaimed with great emphasis and frequency makes even such sentimental concerns important objects of folkloristic contemplations.

In West Germany a pronounced consciousness and feeling about *Heimat* is often found among refugees and those expelled from the former East German and Sudeten territories. In the last few years Alfred Karasek has counted a total of 260 different *Sudetendeutsche Heimatblätter* (regional papers of the Sudeten Germans) which appear at shorter or longer intervals.[104] This is merely one example among many others. But it is not only the old *Heimat* which plays a special role for these displaced persons. At times they explicitly turn toward the new *Heimat,* which is eagerly "conquered" and whose specific goods and characteristics are assimilated.[105] The special emphasis on all that relates to *Heimat* among those who are at least temporarily without a *Heimat* is commonly explained by the proverbial truth that man only learns to cherish something after it has been lost. Beyond this we must emphasize the fact that even the concept *Heimat* is characterized by sentimentality, that anything pertaining to *Heimat* when explicitly mentioned and brought to consciousness is always of a compensatory nature, i.e., it is not the unnamed essence of a barely disturbed force field. This is precisely the reason why the concept proves to be so enduring in the face of shocks to the external and internal systems. In his published research on German refugee families, Helmut Schelsky writes that the opposition of *Heimat* and *Fremde* (foreign realm) belongs "to the dualisms of the nineteenth century," for "the law of the *Fremde* has long affected our whole society."[106] When we look beyond the social facts to the dominant spiritual attitudes, we have to supplement this statement with the assertion that it is precisely "the law of the *Fremde*" which provokes the resort to *Heimat*. The particular esteem in which *Heimat*-like things are held can even be considered as a parallel to the stabilizing of the family observed by Schelsky; in fact, it may be assumed that the need for a native place and for feeling at home lead to the "defensive position of the family."

The pedagogical "principle of *Heimat*,"[107] too, will have to be considered against the background of spatial expansion. Only after the educational institutions have participated in dissolving the original horizons does this principle consciously lead back to the space once defined by these horizons. This applies today to rural education, where the principle was developed. In practical terms the traditional goods on which education according to the *Heimat* principle is based no longer belong to any great degree to the child's environment. Instead the child now experiences former folk goods almost exclusively in the form of educational goods. This creates extremely difficult, apparently barely acknowledged, problems for both pedagogy and *Volkskunde*. In any case the nature of the *Heimat* principle, which in a certain sense not only leads "from the narrow to the wide" but also from the wide to the narrow, must be viewed more comprehensively. Perhaps its value no longer lies so much in an organic expansion of knowledge as in the transmission of regionally specific historical values. Permanent as the experience of *Heimat* is for the child, education can no longer build on a vigorous, undisturbed sense of *Heimat* confined to the immediate environment. However, education can help to provide points of orientation for the "creation of a *Heimat*"[108] and to develop an active consciousness of *Heimat*.

A conscious, indeed didactic attitude is characteristic of a large part of the *Heimat* movement. Although *Heimat* dramas, which have increasingly been invading the folk theatre since the end of the last century, tend to use "romantic" requisites, as a rule they attempt to dramatize a piece of real history. Perhaps this *Heimat* theatre can be considered the most characteristic new form of folk theatre of our time. Thus a curious development leads from the far-ranging Christian-Western Baroque drama to the historical-national folk theatre of the nineteenth century and to the narrowly confined *Heimat* drama.[109] The reasons many local anniversaries are celebrated also have to do with local history. Often the celebrations include a performance of a historical *Heimat* play, an exhibition of museum pieces, and the publication of research on local history. However, the present environment is as much of interest as the past. Thus the public "picture puzzles," first adopted by larger organizations, are becoming increasingly common. A report from a village in Upper Swabia reads:

> To conclude the hiking season the local group of the Swabian Alb club orga-
> nized a public slide show. For the first part of the carefully designed program
> Albert Weishaupt of Grünkraut presented the beauties of our Upper Swabian
> *Heimat* in gorgeous color slides. The picture puzzle: "Do you know your
> *Heimat?*" created much intense pondering. It often proved difficult to identify
> correctly the sixteen photographs typical of the village. Nevertheless all the
> participants thoroughly enjoyed the competition. The locally knowledgeable
> winners will receive small prizes—calendars with the themes of hiking and
> *Heimat*—in the next few days.[110]

Realistic components involving historical and topographical data have even found their way into various *Heimat* songs. Thus the Härtsfeld-Heimat song mentions the convent at Neresheim: "Artists, monks, townsmen's compulsory labor built it to the glory of God."[111]

On the other hand the clichés permeating these songs demonstrate that the affirmation of *Heimat*, too, is subject to the law of expansion:

> *Härtsfeldheimat! Deine Wälder*
> *Rauschen weit und tief hinaus,*
> *Vätermüh rang um die Felder,*
> *Enkeltreu beschirmt das Haus.*
>
> (*Härtsfeldheimat!* The rustling
> Of your forests is heard far and wide,
> Fathers toiled in the fields,
> Faithful progeny protect the home.)

The introductory cry of "Härtsfeldheimat!" in this verse is interchangeable, not so much because of a poetic shortcoming of being unable to portray the unique aspects of that landscape, but because the sense of *Heimat* is satisfied with the prefabricated contents of clichés rather than being informed by real life. The "*Heimat*-addicted songs of the Tyrol"[112] would be considered a type of *Heimat* song even deep in the flat country. *Heimat* festivals, too, often prove to be clearly tied to this general sense of *Heimat*, as well as to a consciousness of the actual local past, and therefore include the larger environment. During the *Heimat* festival at Laupen in 1957, over 200 carrier pigeons were released "to deliver the message of the festive joy of Laupenheim to their respective home-towns of Crailsheim, Munich, Frankfurt, and Augsburg."[113] The brass band of the village of Eintürnen in the Vorallgäu went on an excursion to Stuttgart in order to greet their fellow countrymen, join them on their way to the vintners' festival at Schnaiten, and provide entertainment there along with people from Remstal.[114] Even in the vicinity of Bremen, in northern Germany, a small com-munity organizes a *Heimat* evening styled after a "vintners' festival," complete with artificial vines and songs from the Rhine.[115] In 1956 a Tyrolean "*Heimat* poet" organized "Tyrolean *Heimat* evenings" in several villages of the Allgäu.[116] In this case, too, the desire to inform people about a different region and its inhabitants seems to have been transformed into the enjoyment of the sense of *Heimat* in general. The same idea is particularly clearly realized among people in the mountains, perhaps because of the natural horizons, among other reasons. However, *Gebirgstrachtenvereine* (mountain costume societies) thrive even in the subalpine mountain ranges and in the flat country. Generally their members do not hail from mountainous regions or even from Bavaria; nevertheless they consider themselves workers for the preservation of *Heimat* traditions. A spring celebration of the mountain and folk costume society *Almenrausch* in Aalen in Württemberg was entitled "Let's preserve the customs and habits of our elders."[117]

Such observations result in the paradoxical fact that the confession-like commitments to the *Heimat* brought out here are clearly subject to the "law of the foreign realm." The rather common *Heimat* festival designed exclusively to serve the tourist industry characterizes the situation most quickly, if not completely. It may even be said that in this case standardization has progressed farther than with many material goods which are determined directly by technology, even though the spread of technology is considered decidedly dangerous by participants in the *Heimat* movement. Indeed, distinct differences often persist in the spread of technology, at least in the case of larger regions. For example, the Society for Consumer Research in Nuremberg found preferences for particular kinds of kitchens in the various German states. While 30% of the women in the Rhenish Palatinate and 7% in Bavaria wanted a kitchenette, the women of Schleswig-Holstein and Württemberg favored a normal working kitchen.[118] This is only one example of the regional differentiation of technical commodities still to be worked out in detail,[119] in contrast to the much more standardized, undifferentiated phenomenon of the *Heimat* sentiment. To be sure, even here we find differences; for example, it seems that the Bavarian and Swiss sense of *Heimat* is more influential than that of other regions, and in northern Germany the sentimental kind of *Heimat* feeling seems to be less developed than in southern Germany.[120] However, on the whole similar phenomena dominate the entire German linguistic area.

In addition to the *Heimat* plays with their concrete consciousness of *Heimat*, the folk theatre includes many sentimental plays designed around a yearning for the *Heimat* and a final homecoming. The author of one such play reported proudly:

> The song in the second act, "Heimat deine Sterne!" [You stars of home!, a song that was very popular in West Germany in the 1950s], was not sung by the actress who played Birgit Steffen, but by the piano player M.H. The audience was completely reduced to tears. The second song of the same act, "Nach der Heimat möcht ich wieder" (I want to go home again), was sung by twelve men of the choral section of the "Harmony" Club.[121]

The *Heimatfilm*, notwithstanding various picturesque backdrops, in a sense also portrays the generic *Heimat*. Even the very first German films after the turn of the century attempted to reproduce the poetry of native folk songs by filming prearranged pictures. Again in 1924 a number of films centered around folk song themes were produced,[122] and newer *Heimat* films also often focus on common folk and *Heimat* songs. Alongside the *Heimat* song, which celebrates the real *Heimat* at least in reminiscences, we find popular songs with an extreme *Heimat* orientation which often directly transform exotic elements into a nostalgic longing for the *Heimat*—even *Wanderlust* and nostalgia have become all but interchangeable.

The current sense of *Heimat* is most closely related to the dominant feeling for nature, which again is often less informed by real facts than by the requisite images. A recent newspaper item from Hindelang near Sonthofen read: "Unknown artists and mountain enthusiasts have inserted a copper cassette into a rock at the end of the Eisenbrecheklamm [a mountain] near Hinterstein. When the viewer turns a knob, he is shown beautiful pictures of life in the Allgäu Alps and of the forestry industry."[123] This is the extreme escalation of a general state of affairs: even in the midst of nature "beautiful pictures" of a more universal kind of nature accompany us, and even in the face of a very concrete *Heimat* we do not escape more general *Heimat*-like notions and sentiments. As the "picturesque," the beautiful aspects of the *Heimat* are pushed into the foreground, the exotic and *Heimat*-like elements move closer together. As for pilgrimages, journeys to faraway destinations used to dominate the scene. They provided the opportunity to meet the world, and they enhanced cult objects with the appeal of the exotic. In spite of the great pilgrimages to distant places, the small pilgrimage sites, which are nearer or even very close to home, have become more important today. In this case the cult objects seem enhanced by the living, native proximity. Probably this indicates a substitution of *Heimat* for the exotic: in the era of the great expansion concentration on the narrow area of the *Heimat* results in a more enhanced appeal than reaching out for the distantly exotic.

In other, more significant cases native elements meet with the exotic. In the fall of 1957 it was reported that the costume group of the *Heimatverein* in Thalkirchendorf in the Allgäu participated "in the famous orange festival in Catania in Sicily."[124] The shepherds dance group of Markgröningen went to Brest for the international *Trachtentreffen* (meeting of costume enthusiasts).[125] A *Trachtentreffen* of the *Almfrieden* mountain society in Schwenningen on the Neckar attracted "more than 3,000 costumed participants from America, France, the Netherlands, Switzerland, Austria, and Germany."[126] One could cite many other instances of such *Trachtentreffen*, which demonstrate the blending of exotic and native elements particularly well. Because the exotic no longer exists beyond a fixed horizon but is experienced in the midst of a discoverable world, and because conversely the quality of *Heimat* is no longer confined to the original area of the *Heimat*, the formerly opposite tendencies blend in a sort of *Binnenexotik* (inland exotic), as this form could be called, which is informed by the picturesque and combines the conservation of *Heimat* with a meeting of the world.

The fact that such a hybrid form can become dangerous, especially when its *Heimat* message is emphasized in fake pathos, hardly needs to be pointed out. On the other hand, the "inland exotic" is an example of the "concrete," i.e., that which has evolved from manifold impulses and roots, which is even more characteristic of folk culture than of high culture. Most often the features and directions we have isolated appear jointly in reality.[127] Therefore we have had to mention the historicizing permeation of the *Heimat* repeatedly. This touches on the question of the diffusion of modern folk culture over time, which will be investigated more closely in the following chapter.

CHAPTER

3

TEMPORAL EXPANSION

ACCELERATION AND STEADY STATE

Processes across both space and time are subject to their own laws. It is impossible to determine a parallelism whereby temporal horizons would be overrun by a deep penetration into the historical sphere and whereby such an expansion would be opposed by a movement corresponding to the spatial concentration on the *Heimat*, a movement which would be situated entirely in the present and refrain from any historical infringement. Instead a cross-over seems to take place: the spatial concentration on the *Heimat* generally seeks to reach out in time, into the past, while great spatial expansion as a rule is of an ahistorical nature. In any case, conservationist attitudes—with their historical aims—are specifically influenced by the law of temporal expansion. Perhaps it is for this reason that the historicizing movement is generally much more vigorous and effective than any attempt at spatial concentration, which in the *Heimat* movement is accompanied by a historical dimension.

Important as the historicizing impulse is for contemporary *Volkskunde*, we must first acknowledge that it is perpetuated in an "era of the most intensive de-historicizing of the old cultural society."[1] Vertical relations and processes are largely replaced by horizontal ones. Florence Kluckhohn's systematic categories of values for classifying human societies clearly distinguish between vertical, hortizontal, and individual (i.e., autonomous) interhuman relations.[2] Everywhere in contemporary society hierarchical and patriarchal relations are being replaced by cooperative relations. The process of horizontalization can thus be traced in the social as well as in the cultural sphere. It is substantiated by unprecedented spatial expansion; many goods of folk culture are no longer transmitted over long periods of time, but are exchanged or adopted across great distances.

The essence of this temporal process can be comprehended in the concept "acceleration." In the narrow sense this concept describes the quickening of bodily development during youth and the increase in average body size, an anthropological problem for which Walter Hävernick has given important folkloristic explanations.[3] However, according to Willy Hellpach this problem can be defined in a wider sense as "the acceleration of experiential time measures,"[4] i.e., a "psycho-physical" phenomenon observed mainly among urban people. Hellpach divides this phenomenon into sensory, psycho-motor, and endo-psychic processes. The rapid change of impressions in the city is paralleled and partly caused by the rapid change in cultural goods which are available in abundance in the technical world. The acceleration of the experiential time measure also influences cultural behavior, so that the concept of acceleration can be transferred directly to processes of the objective culture and to certain kinds of cultural behavior.

As an example Hellpach points out that the ready wit of the urban citizen "is not merely a greater glibness, but a more skillful adaptability to any change in situation."[5] This ready wit has found an objective form in the joke. And though ready wit and joke cannot be limited to the urban context, both are characteristic of the technological age. Even the mode of everyday speech reveals accelerative moments. Thus dialect speakers are increasingly adopting an "attitude of reaction"[6] and adjust very rapidly, either consciously or unconsciously, to interlocutors in terms of dialect "level" and speaking style. Such an orientation is not entirely new. Examples of linguistic adjustment in conversations can be found in Middle High German literature—they are particularly noticeable in *Meier Helmbrecht!*—and these should be researched and examined comprehensively for their sociocultural bases. Such sections should not merely be considered poetic conventions, even though they certainly do not describe a universal talent. Dialect passages, which began to appear in sixteenth-century High German dramas, are partly indicative of burlesque interpolations, but nevertheless they are also relevant in sociological and psychological terms.[7] Characteristically, a Thomas-Münzer tragedy by Martin Rinkhart of 1625 shows the mayor of Orlamünd startled into speaking dialect by the arrival of Martin Luther. The possibility of using a variety of linguistic levels has been exploited repeatedly by playwrights, including Gerhart Hauptmann. In his *Biberpelz* (Beaver Pelt) the court clerk uses High German with the head of the court and vernacular speech with the washerwoman; and in *Die Weber* (The Weavers) cashier Neumann addresses the workers in Silesian dialect and the boss in High German. While the earlier examples show conversational adaptations to the interlocutor, the newer ones indicate a ubiquitous tendency to make rapid and frequent code switches. The extent, variety, and speed of linguistic code switching constitute a distinct change from earlier periods. An increase in absolute speech tempo can be observed, but the loudness of dialect speech is diminishing. Combining these with other observations, we may conclude that somewhat more is being said than before, but that individual remarks are no longer given their former emphasis. This linguistic observation conforms to the larger context; for the production, supply, and consumption of folk cultural goods, too, is vaster than ever, while the emphasis, weight, and effect of each specific cultural good have diminished.

Acceleration must be viewed in relation to a sociopsychological phenomenon alluded to by Hellpach in his statement that "the kind of observation used by urban man [is] rapid and keen, but it cannot, for it must not, be either deep or intimate."[8] Following the work of Georg Simmel, urban sociology has acknowledged that the social life of urban man is broken up into numerous partial encounters to which he cannot and must not surrender entirely.[9] Thus the pronounced transitoriness and, as it were, the lowered volume in the assimilation and reproduction of the cultural good must in part be understood as necessary protective measures. And just as we have to amend the sociological findings by noting that forces remain free for occasional strong and binding social encounters precisely because of the generally practiced reserve, so we have to add that the distinction and emphatic comprehension of specific cultural goods is only possible because many others are touched upon only fleetingly. This potential contains both an educational opportunity and a difficult educational problem, for that which is emphasized prominently may at times serve to provoke more intense "protective measures" and barriers. After all, that which we comprehend emphatically also uses up the strength we need for the fleeting encounter with the acceleration of the goods.

Transitoriness is the general signature of many of the current goods of folk culture. "Horizontalization" may even be observed in the phenomenon of obsolescence: obsolescence somehow no longer sets in mainly over time, but rather over space. A hit song dies away not because it has been sung and heard too often, but because it is heard and sung "everywhere."[10] This might seem like a linguistic game, a mere transference from temporal to spatial categories. However, it is indicative of the characteristic process whereby a song, morphologically speaking, is hardly allowed enough time any more to unfold, develop, and die away within a limited space or group, but transcends such limits and compresses its development into the most fleeting time span. When we observe phenomena like the popular hit song and honestly admit that they contribute importantly to the shaping of modern folk culture, the historical element appears totally lost. Contemporary folk culture seems entirely bound to the present.

However, when the historical element is examined more carefully, the dehistoricization we have established must be qualified in several respects, even without pointing to specific historicizing forms and tendencies. To begin with, fashion often reverts to past forms. "Fashion" in the narrower sense of clothing offers the clearest example. However, furniture styles also obviously repeat themselves. Lucius Burckhardt recognizes even in contemporary modernistic furniture the continuation of the opposition between Baroque and Classical traditions which permeates the nineteenth century.[11] The "availability" of goods relates not only to broad areas but also to long time periods.[12] Secondly, even the most fashionable cultural goods are subject to historical traditions. Gottfried Benn once said that under certain circumstances "a first-class hit song [encompasses] more centuries than a motet."[13] This should not be cast aside as the comment of a writer who has no nose for such matters. The beautiful comparison Benn used for Büchner's *Woyzeck* in his speech at Darmstadt in 1951 proves the opposite: "But when you read it today it has the peace of a cornfield and like a folksong comes with the heartfelt grief and sorrow common to all."[14] However, that incidental comment has two sides to it. "To encompass more centuries" may indicate powerful historical foundations, impulses, and ties; it may also mean that our own century reveals itself as pure and unadulterated. It is no accident that these meanings, which seem so far apart, can be combined in an aphorism: in reality even "modern" is a historical category.

Whenever we search emphatically for the new, the current, the fashionable, our thinking has already become historicized. However, in such cases we are dealing neither with pronounced individual historical knowledge nor with familiar knowledge of "the image of the structure"[15] out of which historical education grows. Instead present concerns are more or less consciously contrasted with all of the past, i.e., a past that is not investigated in terms of its individual data or its supporting forces. The acceleration of goods and experiences not only means a more rapid depreciation of goods and therefore a narrowing of the cultural "horizon of expectation,"[16] but generally also establishes a tight border with the past, even if fashion is penetrated by historical forms. However, it would be an indication of bias if we were to contrast this fact with an image of former folk culture that indicated a wide-open temporal horizon and the conscious use of the resources of the past. At earlier stages of folk culture, tradition did not amount to a conscious searching for and excavation of the past, but constituted a continuous process of transmission and handing down. The binding character of tradition was not due to the long periods of transmission; on the contrary, the long periods of transmission resulted from the binding character of that which was always newly traditionalized. This means that particularly in earlier times only a short period was surveyed into which traditions projected; in the concept of tradition the historical dimension is dissolved. We may even assume that the spatial and social core of binding custom was as essential as the temporal-historical core: what was customary in a particular place and what everyone did was just as important as the fact that it had "always" been done. In the concept *man* (the pronoun *one*), called by Heidegger the "subject" of the world,[17] these various aspects of binding custom are united. This "one" essentially determines the realm of *Volkskunde*.[18]

"One," however, is also the subject of fashion, as overall these considerations bring custom and fashion closer together. This runs contrary to traditional definitions of *Volkskunde,* which tend to distinguish the subject in principle from more general cultural sciences on the basis of the opposition between old custom and new fashion. However, such boundaries can hardly be substantiated by the actual facts of folk culture, or even by its historical facts. The opposition hardly mattered for the folk itself. Erk's collection of songs, *Deutscher Liederhort,* includes a song from the eighteenth century, "Es ist die Mode so" (Fashion is like that),[19] which attacks fashionable weaknesses. However, as the publishers already suspected, the song was inspired by an aria from the opera *Lottchen am Hofe* (Lottchen at Court), by C. F. Weisse, and therefore implicitly by the tradition of songs aimed at the follies of fashion of the critique-á-la-mode of the seventeenth and eighteenth centuries. The culture of the upper classes generated not only fashion but also the opposition between fashion and custom. Most dialects make no distinction in principle between the two. In a folkloristic investigation in Hamborn the researcher concluded that neither *Sitte* (usage) nor *Brauch* (custom) was part of the active vocabulary of the informants: "That which all do is described as *"Mode"* [fashion], no matter whether it happens in Hamborn or in the countryside."[20] In southwest Germany the expressions *Mode* and *Brauch* are interchangeable, while *Sitte* is not normally mentioned in everyday speech.

Even if such linguistic observations do not provide hard and fast evidence, they suggest that the word *Mode* would not have become as popular if fashion and fashionable impulses had not always played a role in the folk world. In his archival studies, Hans Moser has repeatedly observed that new fashions have always simultaneously been obligatory components of that world.[21] The more we turn to the present, the more dominant the significance of fashion becomes. A section of Leopold Schmidt's *Volkskunde* of Vienna is headed "The Role of Fashion."[22] In any case, the difference between custom and fashion is not entirely due to principle. Exaggerating somewhat, we could even state that custom is the manifestation of fashion in times of perseverance, whereas fashion is the manifestation of custom in times of acceleration.

Further, it seems that many of the images of steadfast and stubborn custom derive from an optical illusion: viewed from a larger temporal distance movement and change recede in favor of a unified, static, firmly set picture. Leopold Schmidt has indicated for the study of folk drama how "the seemingly static" quality of folk drama dissolves "more and more into a steady dynamic under the influence of history."[23] This observation may be transferred to all other fields of folklore. However, the optical illusion, favored by predetermined opinions that consider tradition a rigid entity, also has objective causes: despite the fact that tradition consists of separate, basically different manifestations, the latter are easily combined into a uniform, seemingly invariable phenomenon by a historical retrospective that is not clearly focused because often such manifestations are, so to speak, variations on a theme. For example, sixteenth-century folk songs were constantly in a state of flux, mostly because of the dissemination of printed songs. However, the small number of song categories and the uniform style, which is dominant within these categories despite any changes in theme, produce an equilibrium among the large number of songs which results in a standardized appearance. This point addresses a fundamental problem of scholarly research and comprehension. The term "steady state" comes to mind; in biochemistry it refers to the formal preservation of cells and organisms while the material is in a constant state of turn-over.[24]

The steady state of the phenomena of folk culture applies not only to the past. The whirl of acceleration caught in this steady state serves to clarify the concept. Just as gears rotating at a certain speed appear as a uniformly moving body and finally even as a body at rest, so the complete picture of the steady state is produced by acceleration. Each hit song which moves youthful souls for a short time tries to be new and, in fact, presents something new. But constant change congeals the image to *the* hit song or at least certain types of hit songs. Similarly, characteristics and components that are different and even extravagant in their details combine to produce the image of *the* amateur theatre, *the* local anniversary, *the* Heimat festival, *the* musical gathering, to mention just a few examples.

In such cases we are not necessarily dealing with an illusion, but with the real dissolution of the merely fashionable aspect of what is commonly called custom. This fact obliges contemporary folklore studies to advance beyond the specific to the typical forms of folk culture and folk spirituality. Wilhelm Brepohl concludes his observations on "Das Soziologische in der Volkskunde" (The Sociological Aspects of *Volkskunde*) as follows: "In the dynamic society the characteristics of folk tradition *[Volkstum]* are no longer the forms, but the norms."[25] These norms are defined in ever so fleeting cultural forms, which *Volkskunde* should not scorn if it wants to participate in discussions of the contemporary culture and spirituality of the simple folk.

The fact that these newer forms, which constitute an essential part of folk culture in general, are hardly noticed and most often pushed aside all too easily as "nonculture" is primarily due to the temporal expansion, to the historicizing of science and life. Not only is scholarly folkloristics often informed by past forms and images of folk culture, but also these historical forms actively intrude into contemporary folk culture. The rapidly passing, acceleration-prone goods are contrasted with others which seem ennobled by a long past and which are cultivated and preserved because of their historical character. Clear insight into contemporary folk culture is as impossible where these historical forms are considered the only ones related to the folk, as where they are considered secondary and are completely ignored in favor of more modern forms. Today's folk culture encompasses rock and roll *and* folk dance, hit song *and* folk song. The "Pandora's box of historicism," as it was once called by Friedrich Meinecke,[26] has not remained completely closed even for the simple folk. It is necessary that we evaluate correctly the extent and type of historical influence, the essence and effect of historicizing within folk culture.

REVIVAL AND CONSERVATION OF FOLK CULTURE

The first edition of the *Zupfgeigenhansl* (a folk song collection that became all but a cult book, aimed at encouraging an active singing tradition), completed for Christmas 1908, includes a few empty pages the purpose of which was described in the introduction:

> Write here what you have heard on sunny heaths, or in the lowly huts of the folk, for we all, all must help to rescue what yet can be saved from the decline of living folk poetry. The old folk song is still alive; what our fathers have loved, dreamed, and suffered still exists fresh and joyful in our midst. Freya, who was pronounced dead, still whispers today from under the leafy robe of the hazel bush and Tannhuser's plaintive song sounds as it did a thousand years ago from inside of Vreneli's mountain.

It is tempting to analyze these sentences linguistically to show how the vitality of the youth movement conquers and outplays the allegation of decline. However, we will merely point out the daring arc which is stretched from the modern era to remote antiquity. The murmuring of mythical figures is coordinated with "what our fathers have loved, dreamed, and suffered"—thus the tradition seems to be extended into prehistory as a continuous stream that must be captured and carried forward. But everyone knows that the youth movement was in an important sense a revolt against the fathers, against their social and cultural forms. The "fathers" invoked in the introduction of the *Zupfgeigenhansl* were not contemporary men between the ages of forty and fifty, but their elders, ancestors, and forefathers, whose ideals and forms were now to be restored after having recently been denied by the generation of the fathers.

Consequently the major source of the folk songs of the *Zupfgeigenhansl* was not living tradition, but the *Erk-Böhmesche Liederhort*, "whose three volumes at Heidelberg were scoured for songs that could be revived."[27] A detailed investigation of the literary sources for the songbook leads to the conclusion that each entry seemed to have been painstakingly prepared "to give the impression that these were old versions."[28] Thus the historicizing tendency also determined the aesthetic ideal in a decisive way. The folk song of the fifteenth and sixteenth centuries, often considered "classic," provided the standards of evaluation. The "classic" folk song also furnished a large part of the collection. In this sense "classic" as a concept indicating historical periods is overlaid by the ahistorical concept of value. Generally the efforts of the youth movement were not primarily directed at the rational penetration of past eras and the revival of their specific goods, but at a revival of that which at least allegedly has proven its worth over long periods of time—"What has survived the test of time simply must be good"[29]—or simply at the prehistoric, the venerably old. Revolutionary as many of its social goals were, the youth movement was part of a long tradition, with its "historical regression in an ahistorical sense."[30] This tradition began when antiquity became the focus of literature in the sixteenth century and reached its climax in the Romantic period. In an illuminating essay[31] Karl Schultze-Jahde shows that in the sixteenth century people were occupied with Germanic antiquity and all but ignored the much closer Middle High German era, and that, correspondingly, Middle High German literature has moved into the foreground since Bodmer, while the more recent literature of the sixteenth century recedes. All these regressions and renaissances are subject to a three-stage time process starting from an exalted primordial era, passing through historical eras of decline, toward a final era that is again exalted. This three-stage time process exerts such a great influence on our world view and philosophy of history that we cannot pursue all of its ramifications in the context of this study.

For our purposes the evidence that this tradition of historical regressions became popular during the course of the nineteenth century and has since influenced essential areas of folk culture is more important than any detailed insights into the philosophical and literary sources of this attitude. Such evidence is provided by the *Zupfgeigenhansl*, which was influential far beyond the academic core areas, as was the youth movement in general. This attitude is even more obvious when we also note these tendencies in the song books of the choral societies. In 1906, two years before the *Zupfgeigenhansl* was published, two volumes appeared in Leipzig under the title *Volksliederbuch für Männerchor* . . . (Folk song book for male choirs, published at the request of His Majesty, Wilhelm II, Emperor of Germany). It contains many old songs, especially from the sixteenth and seventeenth centuries, most of which were later included in the *Zupfgeigenhansl.*[32]

It may appear odd that we should place the fiery youth movement alongside the sober aspirations of the choral societies. It seems right, however, for it is the identification of common points of view in what appear to be widely divergent movements of a specific era that may reveal how important and characteristic these points of view are for the era under consideration. In this connection we must point out that the activities of the choral societies, whose choice of songs was influenced by strongly historicizing tendencies, touch very closely on the efforts of folk song scholarship and scholarly *Volkskunde* in general, which were disseminated in numerous *Heimat* societies and the like. This relationship was obscured because of the many critical remarks folklorists tended to direct against the activities of the choral societies. For example, Alfred Götze wrote:

> When educational societies adopt folk songs, have them printed with artistic scores and edited texts and then quite tidily feed all of it back to the folk, or when male choirs and female quartets sing 'folksongs' in four voices, this unfortunately can no longer be considered folksong. Instead the opposite is true: it succeeds in making the plain old folksong appear artless and contemptible compared to the young and proud sister, feeble like a harebell flower next to the proud, cast-iron bell.[33]

For Götze and many others the "folk song" of the choral societies lacks the spontaneous quality of singing. Justinus Kerner, according to a report by his son Theobald, listened to the *Liederkränze* (choral societies) which performed his songs for him with mixed feelings:

> Much as my father enjoyed such recitals, he nevertheless believed that genuine folk singing would be doomed because of the choral societies. Just as beer has deteriorated since learned chemists have been taking care of its preparation, so the folk song loses its original quality by virtue of the pedantic drilling of songs and the anxious arranging and raising of voices. Everywhere one notices the conductor's baton and the desire to emulate the townspeople. The songs, too, are most often no longer folk songs; because of the choral societies free larks have been turned into bullfinches which adjust their singing to the organ pipes.[34]

Undoubtedly the regimentation of singing has essentially transformed the "biology" of songs. The regulations of some choral societies explicitly prohibit their members from singing outside the singing practices of the society. From the beginning the choral societies acted against the tradition, actually popular among the folk. According to its regulations, the Stuttgart Liederkranz, which was established as one of the first German choral societies in 1824, pursued the objective "of uniting the many admirers of song among the population of Stuttgart, of arousing and developing choral talent, of gradually replacing the somewhat tasteless poetry and melodies of the folk with better ones, and thus giving an increasingly general and nobler direction to interest in the musical arts, which is so pronounced in southern Germany."[35] It is precisely the idea of revival and conservation which brings the choral societies into close proximity with the goals of *Volkskunde*. Even when folk song scholars recorded songs directly from the folk, they compared the body of songs they made available to the public with the songs that were popular at the time. Song festivals might be seen as the characteristic festive form of the nineteenth century, as indeed Otto Elben regarded them a hundred years ago.[36] Because song festivals did not primarily feature popular songs, which were available anyway, they did not evolve from existing traditional systems, but flourished under the banner of revival and conservation and featured songs that had become submerged, which were performed in strict adherence to traditional or newly arranged texts and melodies.

In emphasizing the song festivals and comparing them to gymnastics displays and shooting competitions, Otto Elben explicitly rejects "mere entertainments," such as *Schäferlauf* (Shepherds' Race), *Metzgersprung* (Butchers' Jump), *Schäfflertanz* (Coopers' Dance), *Schifferstechen* (Sailors' Joust), and the *Kirchweihen* (annual celebrations of the consecration day of the local church): "Even where the custom has been preserved, probably most such festivals are antiquated and no longer rooted in the living consciousness of the folk." Without doubt this situation is influenced by the nationalist concept of folk. The festivals mentioned existed in narrow professional, judicial, or church contexts which did not allow a wider national interpretation. Moreover, such festivals remained outside the dominant trend of the time, for they took place as obvious continuations of old customs rather than under the auspices of revival and conscious conservation.

However, it is striking that such festivals are still alive and did not wither away under the pressure of new events. It would be wrong to consider this to be evidence for the almost plant-like survival of an "essential" folk culture, untouched by the vicissitudes of history. Instead precisely *such festivals* continue to exist under the influence of revival and conservation. While festivals organized around songs, gymnastics, and shooting competitions continue within a self-evident, if not very old, tradition—almost completely neglected by folklorists—specific festivities, such as a *Schäferlauf*, a *Schäfflertanz*, and the like are cultivated from the point of view of historical revival. In this case "tradition" is specifically invoked, although interest is not focused so much on what is handed down directly from one's forebears as on aspects of the ancient that are endangered by recent developments and are valued precisely because of that fact. At the Hessian *Schäfertag* (Shepherds' Day) in Hungen in 1922 a master shepherd recited a festive poem, which read in part:

> *Schaut zurück auf die Germanen,*
> *Auf das Volk ein Mann, ein Wort.*
> *Und Ihr werdet leise ahnen—*
> *Lange geht's so nicht mehr fort.*

> (Look backwards to the Teutons,
> To the folk true and honest
> And you will slowly begin to suspect
> That this cannot continue much longer in the same manner.)[37]

This single, isolated piece of evidence is nevertheless characteristic of the decisive ideals of revival and conservation, which incidentally have not quite disappeared from the choral societies. During a meeting of the Schwäbische Sängerbund (Association of Swabian Singers) in 1953, the president explicitly described the singers' purpose as "the renaissance of the German folk song and the conservation of genuine cultural creations."[38]

Recently Ernst Topitsch pointed to the "problem complex of the reflexivity of theories in the cultural sciences,"[39] which certainly should not be overlooked here. The folk culture of recent times is most strongly influenced by the science and culture of the folk, the more so since this science has been understood to be of a pragmatic nature during both the Enlightenment and the Romantic era. Within *Volkskunde* the catch phrase "problem of continuity" even today still refers to the question of the survival of pre-Christian, above all Germanic, forms during Christian times. This has contributed to the fact that within folk culture, too, the search has focused on allegedly ancient forms, so that any more recent continuity has often been interrupted. While forms that are at least pretechnical have repeatedly been sought for and selected, later developments have been neglected. However, technical resources are at times used in the process. Earlier folk costumes are "revived" on the basis of old photographs, radio programs bring old dances back to life—e.g., a sung version of the *Zwiefache* (a dance of alternating measure) became popular again after it was broadcast by Bavarian Radio—and records provide the basis for folk dance performances. These restorative movements should not be underestimated. Under the title "Great Interest in Folk Dance," the *Stuttgarter Zeitung* reported on February 7, 1957 that "At the invitation of the Stadtjugendring Fellbach [Fellbach City Youth Club] 300 young people from Stuttgart and Waiblingen, some of them in beautiful costumes, met in the townhall to practice folk dances. The event proved that folk dancing is attracting increasing numbers of followers even in the city." Many other similar reports could be cited. It is striking that they come almost exclusively from towns and cities. The statement that folk dancing is attracting increasing numbers of followers even in the city, should be amended to read: it is *precisely* in the city that folk dance is cultivated. This was definitely established at the last special conference of the Arbeitskreis für Tanz im Bundesgebiet (Working Group for Dance in the Federal Republic) in November 1958.[40] The same observation can be made at so-called folk singing events, which also are popular in large towns and cities. This situation indicates that such events do not emerge from a continuous tradition but represent compensatory attempts at revival.

The fact that they are nevertheless frequently proclaimed to be and misunderstood as being a continuous tradition is directly due to spatial expansion. The traditions of foreign places are not usually familiar to the observer, who in general is ready to regard any expression of folk culture as an element of local tradition, even if it is really a newly introduced feature. When the community council of the Swiss town of Kilchberg, near Zürich, visited the community of the same name near Tübingen in October 1956, the young people of the local section of the Schwäbische Albverein (Swabian Mountaineering Club) performed a difficult ribbon dance in honor of the guests, the kind of dance that is taught and learned in special folk dance classes. The Swiss council president specifically mentioned the dance in his speech, and in addition to the bugle corps, the school choir, and the choral society he thanked the youths of the Albverein for their performance of "an exquisite round-dance unknown in our area, a dance born out of the soul of the folk and preserved down through the ages." And just as this Swiss gentleman assumes a naturally evolved tradition, so we in turn almost always perceive in the manifestations of Swiss folk culture an expression of unbroken tradition—often more justifiably so, but at times erroneously, too.[41]

Without doubt the concept of tradition should not be limited to that which exists in entirely unbroken, continuous transmission. Man as "the time-binding animal"[42] can adopt the experiences of the generation directly preceding him, but he can also choose to refer to history. Almost all traditionalist movements do not consider it their primary task to preserve what pertains to yesterday, but rather to renounce yesterday's traditions in favor of older, more historical, more substantial ones. However, the expansion of the concept of tradition must be understood and thought through as such if we are to avoid the danger of short-circuiting by equating original and historical elements with the results of revival and conservation.[43] Above all we must expose the error contained in the belief that the adoption of old forms also completely restores the old system of meaning and content. This error becomes obvious when even the short definition of amateur theatre in that great dictionary, *Der Grosse Brockhaus*,[44] states that they continued the tradition of "the old mystery plays." The terminology of the amateur theatre movement indicates that its members believed they would be able to recreate in a secular context the unconditional commitment that characterized the religious mystery plays. Thus "the play community of the future" is mentioned, where "everyone is conscious of being a pillar in the cathedral of communal yearning."[45]

This no longer refers just to a historic ideal which is to be newly realized, but to a belief in a kind of return to nature or at least to an ahistoric natural state. In his critique of the "noble amateur," as he calls the representative of the amateur theatre movement, Artur Kutscher focuses precisely on that point by stating that nothing appears "more easily artificial than nature acted out."[46] To be sure the striving for a natural quality by the amateur theatre movement is based on very definite historical and dramaturgical preconditions. But it is also associated with historical recourse and the general idea of revival and conservation. Where tradition is not tied to the immediate past but reaches far back in time, the historic element easily turns into timelessness: that which in reality had been influenced by history and society now appears as permanently valid, as nature. This seems to happen particularly easily in Germany; here, in contrast to other Western European nations, organology prevails over sociologism.[47] This misunderstanding seems to be the more violent and the more general the farther the alienation from the real or apparently natural state progresses in reality: "The more the administered world spreads, the more events are appreciated which offer the consolation that things are not quite so bad. The yearning for that which has remained undamaged by the process of socialization is mistaken for the very existence of the same and even for some supra-aesthetic essence."[48] Within the sphere of influence of the social and technical apparatus the yearning grows for nature untouched by technology; but what can be supplied is, so to speak, only "social greenery," which is then misinterpreted as natural wild growth.

There is an assumption that what occurs early in history and still projects into the present in the form of survivals is at the same time ahistoric, is nature. Even the simple folk have adopted this assumption in the course of the last century. Leopold Schmidt writes: "What nineteenth-century *Volkskunde*, internally fertilized by Rousseau and Romanticism, disseminated in the form of the 'peasant romantic' entered the store of ideas at virtually all social levels. The youth movement at the beginning of the new century also contributed to this store."[49] The broad strata of the folk eagerly seized upon that interpretation, as it seemed to ennoble their own culture and life styles. Richard Weiss has pointed out that the mountain dweller experienced through songs of cows and cowherding "an unrealistic, but beneficial self-glorification of his own hard existence."[50] We can generalize from this observation and say that the common folk on the whole experienced and accepted such an "unrealistic but beneficial self-glorification." And just as the alpine people generally are believed to possess a "sort of timeless unchanging" quality, so the simple folk often view their present festivities and customs as an expression of "ancient" tradition and therefore as "so to speak timelessly unchanging," as natural phenomena. This matter will be discussed again in another context.

This conceptualization has mainly been encouraged by so-called applied folklore, which in turn has been confirmed and enhanced specifically by this very conceptualization in a process that is still going on. Where a folk dance, a half-forgotten custom, and an old game are not only investigated in a scholarly manner but also are reintroduced and revived in actual practice, they easily appear divorced from historic ties, as if they did indeed belong to timeless nature. But where, by contrast, such customary forms are adopted and reproduced with the pathos of timeless validity, "applied folklore" seems to be confirmed by the folk itself. However, it is this which mainly provokes attacks on *Volkskunde* by related scholarly disciplines: "It is philistine, to put it mildly, to expect that the folk could be revived by folk dances or a return to folk art. Such applications of folkloristic efforts should definitely be stopped," wrote Heinz Maus in 1946.[51] Though academic folklore per se has repeatedly distanced itself from "applied folklore," this was most often done without any previous theoretical discussion. One of the few examples of such a discussion is contained in Leopold Schmidt's fundamental study *Die Volkskunde als Geisteswissenschaft* (*Volkskunde* as a Branch of Humanities).[52] He states that popular "traditions are received and lived out in a peculiar state of unconsciousness" and then goes on to infer

that the tenet of the unconscious quality of tradition also provides the basis for the essential differentiation of *Volkskunde* as a science from all efforts which attempt to make use of its scientific foundation, i.e., above all so-called applied folklore. The latter, in fact, is based on the conscious application, conservation, revival, etc., of certain culture goods. However, because folk life, on the contrary, functions—i.e., continuously interacts in all its traditions—in relations that remain unconscious, a distinct opposition results. *Volkskunde* as a science can basically only make such matters its object, but cannot participate as an active subject.

This inference is correct and the argumentation is convincing as long as the assumption of the tenet is valid. However, it is characteristic of the folk culture of the age of technology that this tenet has to be qualified substantially: not only the academic folklorist but also the common man now understand tradition in part consciously *as* tradition. In more recent times the tenet of the unconscious quality of tradition does not question applied folklore; on the contrary, the existence of applied folklore—in the widest sense—serves to qualify that tenet.

This is by no means intended to encourage the careless application of scholarly work. If *Volkskunde* did not conceive of other tasks beyond providing material for folk dances, customs, festivals, and perhaps handicrafts, it would truly forfeit its right to be considered a scholarly discipline. Friedrich Meinecke once wrote:

> Science must serve life not directly, but indirectly and often will achieve this the more effectively, the more carefully and strictly it remains isolated in itself. . . . Of course, when he feels the urge in himself and the time demands it, even the pure scholar and thinker will engage actively in life and will not shun the dangers thus incurred for his discipline. That is even desirable in the interest of cultural work. Thus, however, an antinomy develops between the demands of science and those of life in general which cannot be solved logically.

Accordingly the folklorist cannot and should not avoid the problems of practical "conservation." Even if that antinomy remains insoluble, he must attempt to assess the theoretical provisions for the "application" of his subject.[53]

The common comparison, which likens *Volkskunde* and the conservation of folklore to the natural sciences and the conservation of nature, is insufficient in this case. Even if we take into account the usual "uncertainty principle," this comparison still implies that folklore grows naturally; actually it is always determined by historical and social factors. Belief in natural growth easily leads to uncritical and complete commitment to the tradition,[54] i.e., in the sense of the revival of old forms which are believed to be endowed with natural permanence or to have developed naturally, while in reality outdated historic forms are being mummified. By contrast Max Frisch once answered the question "What is tradition?" as follows: "I would think: to tackle the problems of one's time with the same courage one's ancestors showed in their time. Everything else is imitation, mummification, and if they still consider their *Heimat* to be a living entity, why do they not resist when they see mummification masquerading as protection of the *Heimat?*"[55] Such a statement is not primarily directed against the preservation of historic values, which is self-evident in a time of historic awareness, but against the transfer of a museum-like style to the living culture, which, in fact, ignores the power of the historic.

The conservation of folklore which compares itself to the protection of nature moreover ignores the fact that folk culture never exists in isolation but is a function of the high culture of the time. This does not mean that it could not influence high culture; however, while high culture is able to detach itself to a large degree from folk culture, folk culture by contrast is always dependent on high culture to a very marked extent. No matter how definitely we are able to acknowledge the justification for and individuality of a folk culture, we must also recognize that our era of increasingly democratic education and culture confronts practically everyone with the highest cultural goods, and that any retreat to what exclusively pertains to the "folk" threatens to increase the "cultural lag."[56] From this point of view Theodor Adorno has attacked the musical orientation of the Youth Movement, which considered music only "for its didactic, cultlike collective suitability," thus damaging its artistic integrity. It is precisely this damage to the autonomy of a cultural good which gets in the way of its socially proper existence—an existence corresponding to today's social conditions—and encourages objectification.[57] By contrast we could distinguish—with Simmel—between cultural goods in their autonomous reality and in their function as cultural values. However, we have to admit that each instance of the glorification of cultural backwardness as the only natural, healthy state is dangerous in an era when the former horizons have dissolved. It is difficult to decide to what extent extreme measures must now become generally valid, i.e., how far backwardness must be addressed as such and to what extent, by contrast, it is necessary to point to old horizons or to establish new ones.[58] Each attempt to "apply" scholarly *Volkskunde* must be subjected to such questions.

But even if unequivocal clarification were possible in this case, it would not result in the entire conservational effort being redirected. After all, this effort has long transcended the realm of *Volkskunde*. To a certain extent revival and conservation have become popular approaches, and "applied folklore" in the wider sense has for a long time and in many ways characteristically been changing the attitude of the folk itself toward tradition and inherited cultural goods.

NARROWING THE SCOPE FOR ACTION

In Gerhart Hauptmann's drama *Die versunkene Glocke* (The Sunken Bell) the forest hobgoblin takes out a small pipe and lights it with a match. John A. Waltz, who has examined the folkloristic elements of the drama,[59] devotes a particularly long section to this phenomenon. Quite justifiably he emphasizes the strange— one could almost say alienating—impression this scene creates: "This grotesque scene is apt to strike one as very original." But then he proceeds to document with many examples the fact that Hauptmann is actually following German traditions: in the *Deutsche Sagen* (German Legends) of the Brothers Grimm tobacco-smoking spirits and ghosts are as common as in the collections of Mannhardt, Vernaleken, Rochholz, and Alpenburg. Nevertheless even a German reader or member of a theatre audience would be startled by this scene, and such a reaction indicates that historical distance is assumed not only for legend traditions, but for any folk good at all, as we shall see. This is not only a misconception affecting intellectuals but a fairly general modern-day attitude, which contrasts with the formerly self-evident, continuous adaptation of folklore to contemporary conditions.

Many legends contain elements from the period when they were told and written down. Even the folktale has long been in the habit of transferring its plot to the environment and to a large extent also to the era of the narrator. Hans Ulrich Sareyko has shown that in East Prussian fairy tales "the king is not conceived of as an urban king, but as a landowner," the dramatis personae correspond to persons in rural life, and the "courtly" elements of the narratives derive from the manors and the peasant economy.[60] In regions with vigorous narrative traditions we almost always find this adaptation to the contemporary environment. Lutz Röhrich has collected many such examples: fairy tale heroes who take airplanes and read newspapers; a revenant who uses a bomb; the Valiant Little Tailor, who kills the bears by spraying them with "petrol"; women who paint their fingernails.[61] In the Hungarian tale of the snake king the unhappy mother telephones her husband, the king, after the birth of her snake son.[62] Greek immigrants in America tell a fantastically funny story of how the Americans—and before them the Greeks—invented the game of baseball.[63]

The African animal tale is entirely at home in the modern everyday world: "The magician brings his notebook in order to practice his magic correctly, children attend school, two rivals play chess and accompany the individual moves with threatening allusions. The antelope plays the harp; the leopard knows how to weave and even visits the bathroom; the hyena instructs its children to tell visitors that mother is not home." Friedrich von der Leyen, who noted these African examples,[64] justifiably adds: 'Our Grimms' *Märchen* do not wear such modern dress." Grimms' *Märchen* thus differ not only from exotic narratives but also from the folktales collected later in many German regions. The brothers Grimm themselves tended to add the glow of the good old days, and therefore historical distance, to their narratives. However, it would take a separate, careful investigation to ascertain how closely the world of their *Märchen* resembled the world at the turn of the nineteenth century. It is more important that Grimms' *Märchen* lasted for the next century and a half without any changes and during this period dwarfed any other German narrative tradition. The many later folklore collections from various German regions barely changed this situation: such is the poetic power of Grimms' *Märchen*. However, their endurance would not have been possible without a growing tendency toward the historicizing preservation of forms. Several years ago the Ministry of Culture, Education and Church Affairs for Baden-Württemberg appointed a full-time "storyteller," who had a repertoire of 300 tales from 65 countries. She did not tell them spontaneously, but "spoke" them as memorized texts.[65] Here any shift of motifs or even decorative features, any adaptation to the present, becomes quite impossible.

The blatant case of this "story speaker" fits in with a more general historicizing tendency. The law of *Requisitenverschiebung* (requisite shift) established by Leopold Schmidt by analogy with Schultz's *Zahlenverschiebung* (number shift) and other shifts in the transmission of myths[66] is increasingly being obstructed by the historical attitude. Leopold Schmidt has shown, for example, how at various cultural levels musical instruments and other *Märchen* requisites are exchanged and adapted to contemporary practices. However, *Märchen* today are generally expected to feature old-fashioned requisites: costumes worn in earlier times, instruments which are no longer played, even social conditions as they existed in the past. In part it is precisely because Grimms' *Märchen* cater to this need for antiquated requisites and forms that they have remained the representative form of the *Märchen* for more than a century. The law of requisite shift has largely been replaced by the law of *Requisitenerstarrung* (requisite freezing).[67]

If characteristic shifts of former times were projected into the present, it would seem odd not just to (or even primarily to) educated people. Museums feature many works of folk art which represent biblical scenes in contemporary costumes. For example, a sampler of embroidery patterns from Brunswick dated 1775 shows a crucifixion scene with John and Mary wearing rococo costumes.[68] This kind of adaptation was no longer evident in the fine arts of that time,[69] but folk art continued its attempts to adapt costumes and requisites to its own time far into the nineteenth century. Gradually, however, the awareness of historical distance spread and the reluctance to shift grew, particularly in religious representations. This situation has become almost general today. In another instance, in a letter dated February 17, 1521, Martin Luther described the *Winteraustreiben* (custom of Driving Out Winter) in Wittenberg, where instead of the figure of Winter a figure of the Pope was driven into the river. "Luther calls the spectacle a clever invention of the students."[70] In 1525 at the *Bautzener Todaustreiben* (custom of Driving Out Death at Bautzen), a stick with letters of indulgence was burned; and the following year a paper effigy of the Pope was thrown into the fire at the marketplace.[71] On the opposite side, in some localities in the Unterinnen Valley the custom of *Lutherverbrennen* (Burning Luther) at the time of the solstice was retained up to the nineteenth century. In some areas "Kathai," Luther's wife, Katharina, was burned as well.[72] Any uneasiness in the face of such shifts and changes in customs is largely due to today's belief in the overall integrity of religion, including the various confessions. However, in addition we also tend to believe in the integrity and unchanging quality of old traditions. While today traditional forms are to be kept as pure and unaltered as possible, formerly the enduring power of tradition was countered by the explicit intent to include contemporary impulses in the tradition and to transform it accordingly.

Popular old pastoral plays almost always contain anachronistic elements. "The shepherds are probably represented just as shepherds are commonly known at the time and in the area of the performance"; at most somewhat "older types" are preferred.[73] But where amateur plays proceed similarly today, they do so on the basis of different assumptions. Instead of a naive shifting of requisites, biblical scenes are subjected to the alienating influence of historicizing and are represented sentimentally. In the earlier pastoral play the anachronism was unconscious; in the more recent plays the puzzled reaction to the anachronism is presumed and made use of: it is meant to create an awareness of the spiritual presence of the scenes.

In such a case anachronisms come in measured doses—when compared with the earlier nativity play, which uses requisite shifts that must appear in bad taste to the ostensibly similar amateur theatricals. Leopold Kretzenbacher describes the enduring pastoral play from Obermurtal in the Steiermark, Baroque in its essential features, in which the scribe Simeon nervously leafs through a fat telephone book to find the birthplace of Christ.[74] In Lassnitz the three wise men themselves consult an address book for the same place. At what was probably the last performance of the Herod play from Radantz, in Bukowina, one of the Magi had covered his gown with small glued-on pictures such as have been sold for some decades now for *Poesiealben* (album for edifying poems from friends and relatives).[75] At the performance of the play of the Three Wise Men from Etyek (Ofener Bergland) on January 6, 1953 at Abstatt (near Heilbronn), the girl who had performed as the Christ child in the nativity play proceeded to play "Silent Night, Holy Night" on the accordion during the silent scene of adoration. She had received the instrument for Christmas and was now expected (and wanted) to put it to use.[76] A few years ago, when future elementary school teachers listened to a tape recording of this play of the Three Wise Men, criticism not unexpectedly focused on the musical accompaniment. Some of the listeners defended the addition, others attacked it, but both sides characteristically argued from the point of view of preserving tradition. While some accepted the play without reservation in the form that had evolved, the others considered the newfangled instrument a deviation from tradition. Thus both parties basically attempted to limit the scope for action in favor of being faithful to historical tradition. Without doubt such fidelity to history has other redundant meanings beyond requisite freezing. However, requisite freezing is both an essential form of expression and a result of such attitudes.

The fact that the participants in this discussion were future teachers should not lead us to the conclusion that requisite freezing and faithful adherence to history are concerns and demands exclusive to a small educated class. Even though the simple folk accept many a shift more easily, and at times simply interpret what is meant to be an alienating effect in an amateur theatrical performance as a naive anachronism, the usual goal is to preserve the old, historic form as exactly as possible. However, it may be significant that at least in rural areas much of the folk culture passes through the hands or at least the silent censorship of the local teacher. Some years ago the Volksbildungswerk (Institute of Folk Education) in Burgenland published 40 folk songs on loose leaves: "Within a single school year it was possible to distribute 250,000 of these sheets."[77] As characteristic as measuring by school years is in this context, the results of that action are nevertheless very impressive. We may assume that it succeeded so well in part because the songs were printed on loose leaves not only for economic reasons but also because this seemed to revive the old form of the broadside ballad. If this assumption is correct, then it could be considered parallel to Hans Naumann's observation that the overall style of broadside ballads during the nineteenth century strikingly retained the tone of the eighteenth century.[78] Quite likely this, too, is not only a consequence of the premise that "the folk taste in general lags about 100 years behind the taste of educated people" as well as the fact that the street ballad was in its heyday in the eighteenth century, but also a result of the historicizing tendencies of the previous century, expressed in a language that is frozen in form and a style that is inspired by archaisms. Again we find a surprising parallel: the later editions of the *Zupfgeigenhansl* returned to the historical forms of songs in cases where the first editions had preferred other texts and melodies because of more recent singing practices.[79] While earlier folk tradition often merely insisted on a few elements as fixed formulas and therefore allowed for a playful rearranging of the remaining parts, now the whole form became fixed and was valued precisely because of its frozen state.

We have previously indicated that this freezing of requisites can be provoked directly by technological developments; the Easter flame is not to be lit with matches but with "natural" fire.[80] Thus Birlinger and Buck report from the region of Riedlingen: "If one wants to kindle a flame for the poor souls, the light must derive from the sanctuary lamp in the church, as a profane light would possess no power. In an emergency one produced by steel and stone will do, but never one produced by modern matches."[81] The explicit mention of "modern" matches translates the opposition between the "natural" and the technical into the temporal opposition between old and modern. The old is to be preserved unaltered even in the peripheral forms of a custom. Such a narrowing of the scope for action must also be understood in part as a reaction to the dissolution of the spatial horizon and to the availability and acceleration of the goods of folk culture. Where very different goods are offered in rapid succession, faithfulness to tradition seems possible only when forms are allowed to freeze and the frozen forms are accepted with the utmost fidelity.[82]

Obviously such a freezing is a sign of weakness; the letter of the law must be heeded more carefully the more brittle the spirit of the law has become. Wherever tradition was the true life-determining force, it allowed for a wide enough scope to be enriched by the latest impulses. A verse introducing the *Schwäbisch-Haller Siedertanz* (dance of the salt-boiler workers of Schwäbisch-Hall) says: "The custom is old and that's how it should be—and it's a serious form of entertainment." A serious entertainment—this dual character of play, the fecundity of which has been described in detail by Johan Huizinga—is very often abandoned in "preserved" traditions in favor of a process of increasing rigidity; these traditions are frozen out of an anxious aversion to damaging historical forms, and what existed in continuous evolution is misunderstood as a completed process. This is even obvious in customs which by nature involve fun. Three years ago two *Narrenzünfte* (guilds of jesters) engaged in an intense quarrel because at one of their meetings one guild had performed a humorous song which the other considered its property.[83] The quarrel was a direct result of spatial expansion: jesting customs, too, move beyond the immediate environment and become part of organized events which resemble singing competitions and the like. However, a serious quarrel was only possible because each guild insisted on its own tradition remaining fixed in form and thus did not perceive that similar or identical elements could become part of customs of other places.

Other quarrels have centered on the priority of certain types of masks. In all such cases the condemnation of similar types in other guilds goes hand in hand with people's own adherence to a form that has grown rigid and is generally no longer allowed to develop further.[84] The course of carnival customs as well is often relatively strictly regulated. Thus the annual parades frequently follow the same route at the same time and in the same order. Such strict order can produce an impressive image, as proven by the *Rottweiler Narrensprung* (Rottweil Jester's Jump), in the form in which it has been customary since the beginning of this century. This order is not *only* the result of a historicizing freezing process; it also derives from a basic inclination toward everything which constitutes proper and ritual behavior. Nevertheless the *Narrensprung* differs from similar customary events of earlier times specifically because of the strictness of its order and arrangement. Year after year at carnival time a shop window in Rottweil displays an artifact constructed of enlarged photographs, some of which date back to *Narrensprünge* before the First World War. This paper *Narrensprung* includes references to individual personalities who once participated. Overall, however, it conforms completely to the picture currently presented to the visitor during the *Fasnacht* in Rottweil. By contrast the *Schembart* (bearded masks) manuscripts of Nuremberg indicate a colorful and changing wealth of very different figures and presentations. Characteristically the point of departure each year was designated as *Schempart* because it changed from year to year.[85] The difference between these urban forms of customs of the fifteenth and sixteenth centuries and what is customary in Rottweil today should not be considered merely sociogeographic. To be sure, the town of Rottweil was always more committed to the rural customs of its environment than was Nuremberg, which was more open to the world. But that basic difference is mainly due to the intense modern effort to be faithful to tradition and the narrowing of the scope for action which almost inevitably accompanies this process.

However, it is precisely in Rottweil that the carnival mood and activities are so vigorous that the external fixation of forms does not necessarily indicate internal rigidity. Now and again the strict framework is transcended, for a growing number of women are wearing masks, and children are increasingly participating in the *Narrenhäs* (jester's costume). Closer investigation should confirm that the word *Narrensamen* (jester's seeds) is partly responsible. This indicated at first the sweets and confetti thrown into the crowd by the jesters, later small dolls, and finally the children, who started accompanying or preceding the *Narrensprung*. Even though the masks are limited to a few types, a more individualistic arrangement within the type is possible. Gowns of the same type are composed of various colors; and the pants of the so-called *Gschellnarren* feature a variety of painted decorations: pictures of animals, people, stars, and plants. Thus the narrowing of the scope for action could perhaps be understood here as a kind of container for the bubbling spirits and the bright colors. Nevertheless a restriction exists; it is new in this form, the result of a consciously historical outlook.

The narrowing of the scope for action becomes even clearer in the many attempts to preserve old costumes or to revive the old ways of wearing costumes. In his essay on the research tasks of folklore collections, Leopold Schmidt observes that it is above all the "range of variation" which imparts life to folk culture.[86] No doubt this is true specifically for folk costumes too. In an investigation of the town of Mardorf, where costumes are still worn, Mathilde Hain has shown that a "scope for individual achievement" lies mainly in the handmade production of specific costume parts and the way the "supply of forms available within the community" is reshaped and unfolded.[87] However, the "range of variation" and the "scope for action" are evident not only in the production and external appearance of costumes but also in their function. The women of Deronje, formerly a German village of the Batschka, owned six different church dresses: brown, green, blue, grey, red, and black. "It was not prescribed on which Sundays they had to wear certain colors for church, but they had to change their dresses so that they wore a different one for each visit until the sequence had been completed, and only then were they allowed to start over again."[88] This is evidence for the contrast between freedom and obligation which once characterized folk culture. However, the realm of freedom proves to be relatively large in true relic areas, where so far the culture has not been influenced by transfiguration and self-glorification and has remained untouched by efforts to historicize the *Heimat*.

Folk costume scholarship recognized the existence of variation in the appearance of costumes relatively early,[89] and the conservers of folk costumes have repeatedly attempted to do justice to this situation by suggesting small variations in the arrangement of costumes. Nevertheless the conservation of costumes has narrowed the range of possibilities, particularly in terms of function, as the conservers constantly had to organize and regulate all public appearance in costume. Essentially the costumes of specific *Trachtenvereine* (costume societies) do not differ from those of other voluntary assocations; such costumes closely resemble uniforms. This seems inevitable, particularly in cases where even the last remnants of the folk costume had disappeared before the attempts at revival began. For example, the great energy devoted to costume revival in the Allgäu has so far been successful mainly with music bands: by the fall of 1958 101 of them were already wearing costumes.[90]

While the current conservation of folk costumes most often attempts to simplify and therefore to adapt old costumes to today's circumstances, until recently the conservation of folk costumes meant little more than the preservation of the existing condition and cut—again a fixing and freezing of forms. When people bring the past into the present as a result of historicizing tendencies, looking at it as if through a telescope, the holistic view is lost and the viewer instead focuses on details of the frozen form. Perhaps this image may explain the frequently observed phenomenon of "degeneration through size" (*Degeneration über die Grösse hinweg*), e.g., in some areas the *Schappel* (bonnet) was constantly enlarged and was even decorated with Christmas tree ornaments before it died out. If this explanation is correct, then what is generally interpreted as divergence from the fixed form would to some extent be revealed as too strict a focus on an individual form. Such an interpretation is suggested by the scrupulous adherence to certain old details in costume revival.

Such insight into the definite restriction of the scope for action inherent in the current "preserved" folk culture no longer merely teaches us to understand many of the more or less recent developments; at the same time it allows us to recognize the diversity and the freedom of the former folk culture. This is not just a banal circular argument. The narrowing of the scope for action is the result of an amplified reaction between scholarly premises and practical realities. Similar to the historicizing view, which frequently led to a virtual freezing of forms, this reaction in turn strengthened the theoretical view of tradition as a fixed, unchanging entity. Today therefore the view of the past is often more self-conscious than it was even a century ago. Folklore collections of that time combine data from the whole range of folk history—if often very colorful and devoted to one-sided mythological interpretations—while today an all too severe process of selection tends to choose only the "bound" forms. This is illustrated by the example of folk drama scholarship, where a limitation to a few plays and play types which have been transmitted down through the centuries in barely altered form easily leads to the notion that these traditional series were the only dramatic expressions, occurring in strict succession and not allowing of any deviation. However, in reality this strictly contained system of plays most often exists in the midst of a wide range of theatrical possibilities. The passion plays of Waal, in Bavarian Swabia, have an important tradition, as the oldest copy dates to 1792 and performances have hardly changed since then. Despite the close ties of the passion play to religious factors—even today the performances are followed by public worship in the local church—the play grew within the sphere of the Theatergesellschaft Waal (Waal Theatrical Society), which also staged numerous secular plays. Eleven different plays were produced after the local ruler had constructed a theatre in 1813, before the society attempted the "Great Passion" in 1815:

Die Hussiten vor Naumburg mit Chören (The Hussites before Naumburg, with Choirs)
Die Huldigung der Musen, ein Drama auf das Geburtstagsfest des Grafen (The Homage of the Muses, a Drama on the Occasion of the Count's Birthday)
Der Kerkermeister von Norwich (The Jailer of Norwich)
Brudersinn und Vaterlandsliebe (Fraternity and Patriotism)
Der betrogene Geizhals, eine Operette (The Miser Deceived, an Operetta)
Die Schulfrüchte, eine Operette (The Fruits of the School, an Operetta)
Opfer des Dankes, zum Geburtsfest des Grafen (Offering of Thanks, Celebrating the Birth of the Count)
Fridolin, oder der Gang nach dem Eisenhammer (Fridolin, or the Way to the Iron Hammer)
Johann von Nepomuk
Die kindliche Liebe nebst einem Melodrama (The Love of a Child along with a Melodrama)
Die Brandschatzung und die Kinder an der Krippe zu Bethlehem, Ein Weihnachtsstück mit mimischen Darstellungen und Gesang vermischt (The Levy and the Children at the Manger in Bethlehem, a Christmas Play with Mime and Song)[91]

Leopold Kretzenbacher writes that many of the actors in the essentially Baroque procession and chamber plays in Steiermark also perform "on the amateur stages of village life in all the plays about romantic poachers and sentimental hunters and peasants."[92] This, too, is probably not so much a case of present-day degeneration as an expression of the formerly generally rich variety and breadth of folk culture.

These comments are not meant to question the individuality and the special status of plays which are part of custom and cult. They are intended to indicate the scope for activity within folk culture of which even the most rigorous historical tradition is a part. Only the very real narrowing of the scope for action in modern folk culture has obstructed our view of the freedom of earlier forms.

PRESENTATION OF THE HISTORICAL

The freezing of cultural forms and the narrowing of the scope for action are a result of historicizing. However, "historicizing" is a broad concept; formulated more precisely, that process assumes the adjustment to an accepted or established, allegedly rigid, historical form. This process must be distinguished from another one which is also part of the concept of historicizing, i.e., the historical substantiation of contemporary cultural forms. This process reaches a first climax during the Enlightenment, when the forms opposed by the upper classes were partly supported with the help of historicizing, and customs, the original function of which had been lost or was no longer understood, were newly validated. Gregor Römer[93] has examined many such processes and has shown how customs, which once were *practiced* as the simple realization of specific functions, are later in a sense *performed* because of the influence of historicizing. Consequently spring and summer customs become memorial festivities; customs of agrarian cults, e.g., the parade of ploughs, are retained and extended to celebrate the memory of certain historical dates, such as the troubled period of the Thirty Years War.

Precisely those festivities, which often evolve from meagre remnants of customs, became increasingly popular during the nineteenth century. The sense of history had grown; existing forms of customs were no longer merely historically substantiated but were used to depict history. The historicizing of the present to some extent turned into a presentation of history. As the historicizing process did not adhere to exact historical methods and standards but frequently offered half-learned, fantastic etiologies, so the presentation of "history" combined more strictly historical elements with legendary and mythical motifs. In the eighteenth century the cherry festival of Naumburg was explained in pseudo-historical terms, with the appeasement of the Hussites by a group of children. Kotzebue used this plot in the drama *Die Hussiten vor Naumburg* (The Hussites before Naumburg). In 1812 Lepsius countered this erroneous interpretation with a learned treatise, but to no avail: The people of Naumburg clung to their "historical" explanation.[94]

Any representation of the "historical" origins of a festival generally made use of the same combination of results of historical research, fantastic inventions, and migratory motifs, which were peculiar to historicizing. No doubt people were not aware of any "deficiency," especially as these were clearly playful representations. Even before folk theatre groups adopted the historical drama and elaborated it in local festivals at the end of the nineteenth century, historical materials were commonly used in carnival presentations. In 1847 an association founded for "the benefit of the local poor" in Villingen (in the Black Forest) performed a sequence of historical scenes: the Swiss confederation at the *Rütli*, "Tell's shot," Mary Stuart's prostration before Elizabeth, and finally a meeting between Napoleon and Frederick the Great in Elysium.[95] Over and over in the following years historical themes slipped in between exotic and comic presentations. Even local history was used, when in 1882 and 1883 the siege of the town of Villingen by the French in 1704 was presented in grand style. The carnival parade of 1885 adopted a particularly characteristic theme: "Costumes and Scenes from Villingen's Prehistory," which featured the old Teutons, Charlemagne, Duke Berthold, the legendary giant Romäus, guilds and magistrates, patrician gentlemen and ladies, Swedish warriors and German mercenaries. A "medieval German spinning-room" and a "medieval German drinking parlor" were also presented.

It is quite possible that individual figures in such scenes subsequently became permanent features of the carnival. The fact that in Villingen and elsewhere girls and women have made the old urban costume their carnival outfit may be due to such historical presentations. The 1842 "Parade of Masks with Costumes from the Fifteenth to the Nineteenth Centuries" in Rottweil[96] should also be examined from this point of view. That witches "already" participate in the 1859 carnival parade of Saulgau[97] probably indicates not so much a continuity of mythical notions as a recourse to local history: many witches were burned in Saulgau from 1650 to 1680, and a witch was tried as late as 1731.[98] It is much more plausible that an enlightened and historic attitude ironically included such historic subjects in the carnival parades than that the old superstition underwent a last escalation in this representation. Finally in Säckingen at the end of the 1920s three carnival figures were created by referring to sources from "history": the figure of the "Roman" was reproduced from a stone mask from Kaiseraugst, now preserved in the *Heimat* museum of Säckingen. The *Siechenmännlein* was adapted from the town's coat-of-arms, and the figure of the *Maisenhardtjoggli* derived from a work of the poet Johann Viktor von Scheffel.[99]

A detailed investigation of all the local sources of *Fasnacht* customs for about the last 120 years could provide essential information on the development and limitations of the folk's consciousness of history. Certainly we are dealing with something new here, something that did not exist quite like that before. In 1775 the students of the Benedictine monastery in Villingen organized the first carnival parade in this town. It represented "The folly of the world, the flesh, and the devil in its terrible consequences, as a wholesome warning."[100] They chose a universal theme rather than a unique and historic one relating to their own time. This carnival parade more closely resembles the religious processions of the Baroque period than the *Fasnacht* events of the nineteenth century. However, even these processions of a generally very colorful composition included historical representations. But here, as in Baroque drama, the historic element is merely a prefiguration of the ahistorical, a depiction of eternal values and truths, rather than a representation of what is unique and historical.[101] Similarly the contemporaneous aspect of different historical levels should not be confused with historic representations. For example, when a study of the *Schembartzüge* (Procession of

Bearded Masks) of Nuremberg emphasizes "a colorful blend of the oldest and newest components,"[102] this indicates the "synchronization" which each cultural system must achieve and which is evident in the specific manifestations of a culture. However, it is not the expression of an awareness of history.

Perhaps "political" representations documented at the turn of the nineteenth century are preliminary stages of historical representation. The *Fasnacht* parade of Schwäbisch-Gmünd of 1802 presented, among other scenes: the birth of the French Revolution; Bonaparte; the retreating Russians. At that time, before the Continental blockade, sugar loaves and coffee bags were featured as well. The procession was headed by the "desire to remain a free city," which was probably symbolized in pictures.[103] These are all contemporary political allusions, influenced by the vivid awareness of being a *Reichsstadt* (free city). They should be understood as definite expressions of self-determination. Such political representations have not disappeared. A few years ago, when the German Federal Armed Forces began their fiercely disputed existence, soldiers marched in just about every carnival parade; recently most of the larger parades featured space travel. However, such components are generally mere ironic comments. Characteristically, in the nineteenth century contemporary political representations were overlaid by "historic" and exotic ones.

Today the representation of historical events, mainly those of local history, may be more common than ever, as is indicated by the many theatrical performances at local "festivals." In 1956 the *Hornberger Schiessen* (Hornberg Shooting Play) was performed six times on an outdoor stage; the "natural" theatre of Hayingen kept the play *Der Orgelmacher* (The Organ Builder) on its program for two years (this "*Heimat* play" projects the internal trials and external successes of an organ builder from Hayingen); the Historical Festival of Breisach featured the historic drama *Peter von Hagenbach*; in 1954 a master hairdresser and native of Flochberg near Aalen wrote a play based on the legend of the origin of the local pilgrimage; in Viechtach, in the Upper Palatinate, the birthplace of the historic Doctor Eisenbarth, "Dr. Eisenbarth Festivals" were organized in 1958; and the *Meistertrunk* (Master's Toast) is staged each year in Rothenburg.[104]

Parades of all kinds are dominated by historical elements. At the fourteenth festival of the Deutscher Sängerbund (German Singers' Alliance) in Stuttgart, August 1956, a pageant of two kilometers length presented "The historical development of song since the time of the Teutons and the history of the German song." An additional kilometer of pageantry under the slogan "Hearken, Singing Heart" was omitted because of various objections primarily directed against "the pretentious treatment of history," i.e., the representation of a Viking ship, a cart of camp followers, *Eberhart im Bart*, Vienna classics, and the Swabian circle of poets. The pageant at the 1957 *Rutenfest* (Switches Festival) in Ravensburg featured the trade expeditions of the Ravensburg Trading Company; an old paper mill; Henry the Lion; schoolmasters and mercenary drummers, "a colorful military review from the eminent past of Ravensburg." The same year saw a pageant celebrating the 950th anniversary of the community of Holzgerlingen which began with twenty pictures "from the history of the community" and "250 heralds and Celts, Romans, Allemannen and Franconians, noblemen, serfs, and mercenaries paraded through the town in colorful costumes." In Biberach "costumed groups from Biberach's past" dominated the picture of the *Schützenfest* (Riflemen's Festival). "The Gigelberg turned into a shady bivouac area for Swedes and imperial and town soldiers in authentic costumes, who took part in the pageant commemorating the Thirty Years War. Dances with old songs and verses of the tanners and weavers guilds, who are credited with the economic rise of Biberach in the Middle Ages, were part of the varied festival program." The description of the 1956 *Vaihinger Maientag* (May Day at Vaihingen) emphasizes the fact that "the raftsmen performed their colorful dance"; such historic presentations in general seek out picturesque and attractive elements. This even applies to the *Bürgerwehren* (Civic Guards), who have been revived in many places. A report of a large gathering of Civic Guards in Saulgau in July 1956 describes a "review of history" and makes a typical comparison: "It seemed as if two thousand soldiers with their shakos, spiked helmets, dragon-crested helmets, field service caps, and feather hats . . . had jumped out of the frames of the numerous prints in the local *Ratskeller* [Town Hall Pub] and led us back to the so-called good old days for a weekend."[105]

A few years ago the newly founded *Lützowsches Jägerdetachment* from Constance appeared in public at a meeting of Civic Guards in black uniforms and shakos with fixed bayonets.[106] However, the ancestors of the current members of the Detachment had fought on the side of Napoleon, i.e., against the *Lützowsche Jäger*, whose deeds are glorified in Körner's poem. In this case national impulses are transferred to local history. Such a blunder is possible mainly because the "historic" aspects in all of the above presentations from history are not subjected to strict standards. Rather than historic facts, picturesque, attractive, and interesting motifs from history in general are presented, and that even martial elements can be considered picturesque needs no proof. Even in the carnival parades of the nineteenth century, the primary object was not a faithful reproduction of historic events. This does not preclude the fact that they opened the temporal horizon or assumed its opening and brought the historical past into the field of vision. However, the "historicity" of such presentations is generally unemcumbered by scruples of faithfulness and accuracy. In his historic sketch of the *Fasnacht* at Villingen, Albert Fischer regrets that no books of council proceedings exist for the seventeenth century. He then speculates that these had been used to stuff the mortars for the *Fasnacht* play performed in 1882 and 1883, "The Siege of the Town of Villingen by Marshal Tallard," i.e., that they were squandered.[107] Consequently important historical evidence would have been sacrificed to the "historical" play. We may well consider this grotesque incident as symbolic and generalize from there. Even though the playful representation of historic aspects produces scenes of the past, if sacrifices essential historic facts by removing the historic distance.

So it happens that history finally is "presented" in more than one sense: it is performed and frequently shifted entirely into the present, removed from the dimension of time. The turn toward the "good old days" is not primarily historical at all. Presenting the picturesque from the past often means not only an escape from the historic moment of the present but paradoxically also from history as a whole. In Fischer's investigation of the *Fasnacht* of Villingen, the word *historical*, a truly magic word, appears on every second page. The *Narro* of Villingen is "fully and totally of a historical nature"; "the most historic part of the *Narro* is probably the mask," but "no less historic than the masks are the *Narro* rolls." If a *Narro* does not know well how to *strehlen* (address individual onlookers humorously), he should remain silent, "for he nevertheless fulfils his purpose by personifying a historic subject." Even the *Butzesel* (donkey) represents "a history." And it is said of the *Katzenmusik* (charivari) that "although barely more than 50 years old, it nevertheless incorporates a small piece of old grey history."[108] The paradox in this last statement is resolved by a typical reference to the din accompanying the "Saturnalia and the Ostara festivals." This additional explanation is necessary because all these expressions use the word "historic" only conditionally, as a temporal concept; it further connotes an evaluation, a designation for that which is right.

During the preparation for the 1956 *Grosselfinger Narrengericht* (Grosselfingen Jester's Court) the *Narrenvogt* (Jester's Provost) reprimanded one of the speakers with the remark that his subject was worthless, for it was "not historical." In this case, as frequently in modern folk culture, to be historical does not indicate that an object originated at a certain established time and was handed down from then on, but it primarily indicates what is right, orderly, what has "always" been like this, the old and good. This concept of history makes possible a certain neglect of actual history. The *Narrenzünfte* provide a further example: their association in the Swabian-Allemannic region, which essentially watches over the preservation of old traditions, nevertheless makes "no class difference between the individual guilds"[109] and admits even very new guilds if they adapt to the image of the regionally specific *Fasnet*. Since the old is considered good *eo ipso*, what is considered good in a sense is old or at least "historic." The names *Historische Narrenzunft* (Historical Jesters' Guild) and *Althistorische Narrenzunft* (Old Historical Jesters' Guild) have become all but universal.

Nowadays the historicizing of newer customs is rarely achieved by establishing or assuming a certain point of origin in history, but rather by postulating an ancient age and therefore validity. Certainly this process is not entirely new. For example, in 1785 the refiners of Halle wrote "rules" for their *Brunnenzug* (Parade to the Fountain) and *Kuchenfest* (Cake Festival). They began with the statement that the refiners had possessed their privilege "since time immemorial."[110] Certainly this formulaic invocation of tradition was no isolated instance even then. Each custom, to be perceived as such, must have a kind of archetypal component. The historicizing view aims at this, i.e., the original, archetypal aspect, which in a sense forms the integral part of the historical and must generally be expressed in historic terms.[111] This still applies today. But while in the context of the narrower horizon, that formula once merely indicated that a good had been introduced and had entered tradition, today any claim about the old age and "historical" character of a custom simultaneously suggests the notion of long periods of fulfilled history. The lighted tree at Christmas not only is experienced as something transmitted and to that extent as an old good, but is tacitly shifted into the vaguely known eras of the past. In his *Ekkehard,* Scheffel described a medieval Christmas tree celebration, which hardly startles the reader, and the sentimental pictures of the Luther family under the lighted tree rarely provoke consternation. Even the very recent appearance of the *Adventskranz* (advent wreath) has acquired interpretations that point back deep into history. The situation is similar for Mother's Day and the custom of giving flowers on Valentine's Day, which for several years has been timidly spreading to Germany from the neighboring countries to the west. In their advertisements for this day, flower shops and international supply organizations mention again and again that this is a "very old custom." Typically it is even called a "600 year old custom," with no more details being given.[112] "Ancient" now implies a number of centuries of concrete fulfilled history, not just an anchorage within the abstract past beyond the temporal horizon.

In practical terms the difference vis-à-vis former times seems small, as the notion of accurate history held by the simple folk tends to be very vague. Even today more definite standards tend to apply merely to one's own lifetime. Occasionally we observe older people describing certain phenomena as "ancient" because they existed in their childhood. It is important to understand that formerly the historical as such did not really enter into the field of vision, though historical traditions and even traditions from history (i.e., historical legends and the like) obviously transcended the horizon. Today, by contrast, the historic is given a new meaning and is in a sense de-historicized. This de-historicizing of what is historic results in a timeless "historical" quality and represents a paradox similar to the one we observed in the phenomenon of *Binnenexotik.*

The "presentation" of the historic in more than one sense is an attempt by the simple folk to deal with the profusion of historic elements. However, the result must not be glorified as "the ahistoric," which Nietzsche recommended as an antidote to the overly alert historical sense.[113] Unclear though its historical notions are, the consciousness of history and what pertains to it is no longer foreign to the folk; and the "limited horizon" in which, according to Nietzsche, forgetting would be possible, has finally crumbled for the folk, too.

CHAPTER

4

SOCIAL EXPANSION

CLASS CULTURE AND UNIFORM CULTURE

In his *Ästhetik* (Aesthetics) Friedrich Theodor Vischer asks "What is considered 'folk' when we refer to folk song?" His answer is:

> Originally it is the entire nation, before that education is introduced which separates the classes not only by property, power, privilege, trade, rank but also according to the form of consciousness. There is no difference of poetic opinion; the same song enchants peasants, craftsmen, noblemen, clerics, and princes. After this separation has taken place, however, a part of the nation is labeled the folk, i.e., the part which is excluded from the intellectual means which lead to education and thus to the more conscious and mediated comprehension of oneself and the world. Only this part is still what the whole once was, it is the substance and the Mother Earth which the educated classes have outgrown but from which they come.[1]

Certainly Vischer cannot be suspected of unrealistic enthusiasm. But in this case he draws a picture that only partly conforms to historical facts. Perhaps he is strongly influenced by the reality of his time, when the appearance of the fourth class emphasized class differences and when the desire for national unity turned to history for support. However, the class differences in education were probably greater during the Latinity of the Middle Ages than in the nineteenth century, and nowadays the ideal image of an intact folk culture is typically influenced by class consciousness. Class culture, which was still evident in the "bourgeois society"[2] of the nineteenth century, now often seems to us the natural and organic prerequisite for a structured culture, the recent dismantling of which is viewed as directly associated with the dismantling of the class system. Hugo Moser has traced a "tendency toward a uniform culture" mainly in such linguistic processes as the decline of dialects in favor of regional standard languages.[3] What he recorded as fact based on linguistic evidence all too often appears as a complaint about the "mass culture" of the industrial era, which destroys the old structures and has leveled the old differences.

Class boundaries were beginning to blur even at the time of Vischer and Riehl. In his work on German male singing, Otto Elben emphasizes its "social significance": he sees the common interest in singing as a force in breaking down the "senseless" barriers between the classes in favor of a uniform, nationally determined culture.[4] Today we have to qualify this by noting that neither Elben nor Riehl recognized the significance of the industrial workers as a new autonomous class. However, in the meantime the idea of a national unity of culture, such as is expressed in singing the same songs, has also influenced large sections of this new class. Above all political and economic developments have largely removed the class stigma from certain professional and social groups. Numerous contemporary sociological studies teach us how the criteria for judging social prestige, which are obviously always present, are now largely detached from the class structure, how the suspension of class boundaries—at first merely theoretically proclaimed—has in many ways now become fact. Occasionally folklorists explain the fading of a custom by appealing to economic circumstances. Thus *Heischebräuche* (customs which involve the expectation of some kind of remuneration) have disappeared since "there are no more poor people," as an old woman once said.[5] However, the fact that "there are no more poor people," and the overall economic development, influence not only specific folkloristic phenomena but folk culture as a whole. To a large extent economic developments, together with the means of technology, have made the "availability" of goods a reality even in social terms.

Rudolf Tartler observes that nowadays the professional affiliation of young people can no longer be deduced "from dress and other external signs."[6] The same commodities determine work and leisure time of entirely different professions and social classes. Where formerly the differentiated interplay between higher and lower social levels was essentially defined by the downward movement of *gesunkenes Kulturgut,* today new forms and goods, which as "industrial designs" draw their power of influence from general standards rather than from social structure, are frequently offered to all classes simultaneously.

However, class differences in mental attitudes do not merely disappear because of standardized cultural commodities; the process began with an earlier adjustment. Though the professions are more diverse and less uniform than ever, the age of technology nevertheless renders them similar to each other:

> The application of like forms of thinking and working is more important than any dissimilarity in the areas of application and work; the uniformity of working time and duration of leisure time is more important than any distinction in working place; the equivalence of incomes is more decisive than any disparity in the sources from which they derive.[7]

However, the similarity of forms of thinking is by no means limited to technical thinking of any kind or to mechanical notions of life. Even notions which explicitly oppose such a transfer of technical principles to life in general are nevertheless uniform and are not exclusive to certain classes or social levels. This is apparent, for example, in the very general appreciation of nature which has now spread to town and country, to hiking clubs and travel agencies. Sports, which can be considered a means of naively enjoying nature,[8] now barely indicate class distinctions. Sentimental nature worship, too, has long reached most social levels and groups and has not even spared the tangible realities of specific professions. The *Biedermeier* (early Victorian period) poems of Karl Mayer ask a shepherd:

> *Schäfer, dort an deinem Stabe*
> *Blickst du müssig durch das Feld;*
> *Ahnst du auch die reiche Gabe*
> *Solchen Blicks in Gottes Welt?*[9]

(Shepherd, while leaning on your staff
You glance idly across the field;
Do you divine the rich gift
Of such a glance into God's World?)

It is worth dwelling on the answer to this harmlessly rhetorical question. Until the writing of this poem, such a "positive view of country life"[10] and, even more, the appreciation of rural professions based on a love of nature were sure signs of educated authors and a like-minded public, who themselves were generally quite remote from all things rural; it is a literary role-playing which does not influence reality itself, even though the bearers of such poetry frequently experienced these categories as reality. However, since the last century even the previous objects of such poetry have become increasingly familiar with it. Their acceptance and adoption of this poetry results in the self-glorification we have mentioned before. Today the shepherd certainly "divines the rich gift" of his glance into nature. The sentimental attitude as *gesunkenes Kulturgut* is one of the most fundamental themes of a *Volkskunde* of the nineteenth and twentieth centuries, which so far has barely been dealt with. However, we have to reestablish that we are no longer dealing with a gradual descent of specific goods to other levels but with the compact offer of notions that were once socially restricted to all levels and groups, i.e., we are again faced with a standardization of culture.

The "tendencies toward a uniform culture" are most closely connected with the unlimited offer of knowledge and education aimed at all population groups. The democratization of education,[11] proclaimed in principle by the Enlightenment, was finally made possible because of the progress of technology, so that in our time a clearly acknowledged "second Enlightenment" could occur.[12] Even though this "Enlightenment" in reality did not reach the entire population, it changed the general attitude toward science and education, which are no longer seen as belonging exclusively to the socially privileged.[13] Above all, this socialization of knowledge, more decisively than political eschatology, has removed the pressure of irrevocable destiny from the working class. To put it differently: it has contributed importantly to the fact that even the working population can no longer be considered a separate social class.

Recent sociological investigations have repeatedly emphasized this fact, which is also evident in the development of *Volkskunde*. However, folklore collections and research of the last century express a strong reserve toward the fourth estate

even in some details. For example, Anton Birlinger added the following remark
to his description of the *Fasnachtsnarren* (carnival figure of the jester) of Rottweil: "Incidentally, the '*Narr*' is quite vain; if he belongs to one of the better
families, he unfailingly wears new kid gloves; if he lacks these, it is advisable to
get out of his way, for a proletarian or servant must be wearing his costume."[14]
Even this short detail substantiates what Riehl's outline of a *Volkskunde* oriented
along class lines spells out: that the traditionalistic bourgeois culture as well as
the traditionalistic cultural science of *Volkskunde* see themselves in opposition to
the newly developing industrial working class. In fact, first attempts to form a
bourgeois-revolutionary movement were relinquished in favor of that class-
oriented traditionalism because a new "force of mobility" had risen with the
fourth estate.[15] Thus *Volkskunde* turned into peasant lore pursued in a bourgeois
spirit. The first volume of *Volkskunde des Proletariats* (Folklore of the Proletariat), written by Will-Erich Peuckert, appeared as late as 1931. No further volumes were produced partly because of the political development in Germany and
partly because of the dissolution of the "proletariat." When Wilhelm Brepohl
summarized his folklore research in the Ruhr territory after the Second World
War,[16] he did not present "workmen's folklore" but spoke more neutrally of the
"industrial folk" of the Ruhr. On the one hand this resulted from a painstaking
process of dismantling prejudices attributed to the working class; on the other
hand this change in terms acknowledged a change which had evolved within the
working class itself. If in its former situation of distress the working class had
found support—often more or less pathetically—essentially in itself, it later as-
pired beyond those limits and assimilated bourgeois lifestyles; it had, in fact,
become emancipated.

More recent descriptions of the working man clarify this process. They emphasize that the worker's furnishings follow bourgeois standards,[17] that the taste of
older workers "is even a shade more conservative than that of the
bourgeoisie,"[18] that on the other hand the cultural situation for everyone, not
only for working people, merely allows for the possibility of "culture by the
hour."[19] Brepohl includes a variety of examples showing how their rural origin
clings to the workers of the Ruhr territory, how after the daily work is done, and
above all after their dismissal from industrial work, they tend to "regress to the
rural being which still hides under the urban get-up of industrial man."[20] All
these examples indicate how fluid class limits have become, how much the lifestyles of different social levels and large groups are approaching each other. What
we have pointed out in the case of the worker could be shown *mutatis mutandis* to
apply to the farmer also. On the one hand the farmer has subjected his former life
rhythm to the strict beat of mechanics, and on the other he has sacrificed his
independent lifestyle in favor of bourgeois forms: nowadays we find "bourgeois"
furniture not only in the worker's home but also in the farmhouse. It could similarly be demonstrated that in the course of industrialization the "bourgeois middle class" is pushed ever closer to the positions and attitudes of "workers." The
"scope of values" has been reduced when compared to the class structure of the
preindustrial class society; "the mass of the population belongs to the middle
class."[21] Without doubt the sociological finding of stratification can be extended

in a rough sense to the statement of a "uniform society"—primarily contradicting the thesis of the two-strata society established by Marx.

The examples cited above nevertheless indicate that the old class concepts are necessary to describe the movements and processes within this uniform society. In this case we are not merely dealing with a purely terminological "delay"; rather, this delay indicates that class ideals are still alive and still partly determine the culture of the classless society. The many romantic dramas of chivalry, which continue to be extremely popular on small village stages, are vivid examples. Until the beginning of the twentieth century *Hedwig* by Theodor Körner was one of the most frequently performed plays. The subtitle *Die Banditenbraut* (The Brigand's Bride) may have contributed to this success. However, the fact that the piece kept the old class society alive and led the heroine to the top of that society was probably more important.

Even inconspicuous everyday forms of thinking and ideas present in the industrial working world are subject to lingering impulses from the class society. Thus it may be observed that industrial workers at times are disproportionately well disposed toward factory owners and by contrast disproportionately ill disposed toward supervisors and other managerial personnel.[22] No doubt this attitude derives in part from the fact that the latter sometimes have to defend unpleasant innovations to the workers. However, it would certainly be too superficial and shallow to call this the sole reason for such an evaluation. Instead influences from preindustrial society seem to linger, when the social structure was regarded as sacrosanct and to a certain degree ordained by God. This type of evaluation has its own history, which should be investigated separately; here we can only suggest that according to folk legend the damning judgment of the folk generally does not affect true sovereigns but applies to the castellan, the cellarer—the seigneurial fiscal officer of bourgeois origin—and other representatives of sovereigns who are not of noble birth. At the same time many princes were thought to have supernatural powers and thus were clearly considered superior to the other classes.[23] This attempt to elevate "leaders" even more or to justify their eminence by special distinctions is still found today. Although such solid magical notions no longer enter the process, distinctions are expressed, for example, in many short narratives which describe how the owners of large companies rose from very humble circumstances: When he took his leave to go on his journey, the future owner of the company was so excited that he dropped the coin his father had placed into his hand. A carpenter had to come to saw a piece out of the floor in order to retrieve the coin, for it was the only one in the house. Similar stories are told of many great industrialists.[24] This does not primarily arise from a need for realistic biography. Rather these stories are part of a different, unrealistic context: Such a narrative confirms the exceptional ability and the exceptional luck of the man whose position becomes about as incontestable as that of a feudal lord. However, no detailed investigations of such matters have been made so far.

Thinking along the lines of class concepts does not continue merely in subconscious, underlying ways. Mainly it is more-or-less conscious regressions to the class system that seem to provide the boundaries for the uniform culture. This seems most obvious in the manifold efforts directed at a "village-specific" peasant culture, as promoted today primarily by agricultural colleges and rural youth organizations. The "revived" costume is generally part of the image of rural youth, as is the cultivation of folk dances, folk songs, and other cultural goods which are considered specific to the peasantry. Reports of events organized by rural youth associations prove that besides the style typical of general club festivities, many influences from the Youth Movement continue to be influential: Speaking choruses provide introductions; folk songs from the fifteenth century are presented, others are sung together with the public; folk dances are performed.[25] This further proves that rural youth associations, rather than representing the ideal of their own peasant class, are really participating in the general movement of revival and conservation, which includes the restoration of class images. We cannot ignore the fact that such associations also contribute to the professional education of young farmers and to that extent retain their own character; nevertheless the cultivated cultural goods are part of a larger context.

Characteristically these are the same goods which are also "cultivated" in the cities by special groups—the section "Revival and Conservation of Folk Culture" in chapter 3 provides some examples. A walk through Stuttgart shows that the exteriors of a surprisingly large number of businesses and industrial companies feature the symbol of the sower as a decoration. Certainly this cannot be explained by the tangible association that Stuttgart is still a garden city. These are compensatory phenomena which seem to be provoked particularly in large cities: Just as there is a concentrating movement toward a *Heimat*-like condition which attempts to respond to the spatial expansion, so we find regressions to a classlike condition which attempt to obliterate the social expansion. In part such attempts can be explained by what could be called dread of "social fallowness" (*Sozialbrache*). The concept *Sozialbrache,* introduced to geography by Wolfgang Hartke,[26] refers to the neglect of the common land resulting from the social upheaval caused by industrialization. Because of recent changes a fallowness could quite naturally evolve in the cultural sphere as well. Often the population seems to fight this problem in many ways; specifically "middle men," i.e., teachers and heads of associations, leaders of youth groups and communal representatives, are strongly influenced by the notion of cultivation and conservation. They "cultivate" primarily the real or alleged cultural goods of the peasantry, as the distance from the peasantry is most obvious; typically, however, the cultural good of other social groups may equally become the focus of general interest: for instance, the *Heimatverein* of a village on the Dutch border has chosen the conservation of the secret language formerly used by the merchants of this village, the *Krämerlatein* (merchants' jargon) as its primary goal,[27] and in nearby localities the merchants' language is even taught at school.

Thus the regression to the class system does not stop social expansion, but confirms it; the recourse to goods of the class culture is not limited by class, but is quite general and therefore is assimilated into the uniform culture, which is carried by the uniform society. The uniform culture is not intrinsically limited by instances of "lagging behind," as these cannot be confined to specific groups, but in the cultural advances in which only few participate. To put it differently: The concept of uniform culture becomes questionable when confronted with the division between high culture and folk culture, which today appears more decisive and drastic than in former times.

Contrary to Friedrich Theodor Vischer's opinion, doubtless in former times the same song did not enchant peasants, craftsmen, nobility, clerics, and princes alike; doubtless even then cultural forms existed which were only accessible and understandable to a small educated elite. At the same time, however, this educated elite was generally class-determined and thus fit into the overall culture, which was structured by the class cultures, which did not exist independently from each other but clearly set cultural horizons. This structure has broken down; today high culture is not carried by any definite sociologically determinable class, but by individuals who belong to flexible groups.[28] As long as the social classes determine the structure of culture it is neither necessary nor even possible to distinguish between high culture and folk culture; sociological terminology, i.e., courtly culture, spiritual culture, peasant culture, etc., is more exact in this case. The division becomes necessary only where such a sociological terminology has become impossible because of social expansion. What this means for the folk culture will be investigated in the following section.

FOLK CULTURE AS "A SYSTEM OF IMITATION"

The antithesis of high and low certainly also existed within class culture; in fact, it was more securely established there than was possible after the dissolution of class society. Courtly culture was regarded as superior to that of the bourgeoisie and of the peasantry, and peasants knew that their culture ranked lower than both bourgeois and courtly culture. This unequivocal awareness of rank led to the movement which since Hans Naumann has been named *gesunkenes Kulturgut* (sunken cultural goods). However, scholars discussing Naumann's views have frequently pointed out that the lower cultures are not merely defined by the process of sinking, but that the cultural good is transformed in characteristic ways. In fact, it is crucial that the goods—regardless of how "far" they have fallen— were completely recast within the relevant class horizon. Even where they were not subject to any material changes, they tended to acquire new functions. Above all they "became customary" and thus were elevated beyond mere imitation. The social and spatial horizons together caused even the lower cultures to acquire their own image, a definite character, despite the fact that they incorporated much that derived from the culture of the upper classes. The classes not only regarded themselves as part of a hierarchy of high and low, but at the same time as being in a securely autonomous position, which was ultimately ordained by God. What Hildegard von Bingen had already formulated in the twelfth century—that God divides his folk on earth into different classes, all of whom he loves, and that therefore the higher class must not be brought down to the level of the lower class[29]—remained influential far beyond the Middle Ages.

The disintegration of class horizons did not eliminate the natural difference in the evaluation between high and low; however, it eliminated that secure social confidence which had created cultural entities on different levels of culture and thus offered the possibility of respecting the differences between higher and lower cultural levels *and* of disdaining them.[30] The far-reaching dissolution of class horizons has radicalized the tension between high and low. Attempts made throughout the nineteenth century to comprehend folk culture as a system superior in many respects to higher culture and in any case autonomous are the result of the historical orientation on the basis of the old class culture. However, this attempt must also be understood as a sometimes short-circuited answer to that radicalized tension.

Together with the theoretical revalorization of folk culture there occurred in practice a decline. Folk culture could not be sustained and kept alive from historical impulses alone, but took directions from the forms and contents offered by high culture, which were supplied faster and in greater numbers than ever because of technology. As binding horizons were missing, such offers were often accepted without criticism; cultural goods no longer tended to be actively transformed, but were merely "thinned out" on their way to the "folk," so that "folk culture" frequently turned into a tepid imitation of upper-class culture. Peasant and bourgeois furnishing styles constitute an extreme example, for they not only adopted historical "forms of placement"[31]—such as the representative central table of the Renaissance, which replaced the corner table—but frequently included a kind of salon in imitation of the genteel world.

Arguments against such furnishings are often limited to the observation that they lack any practical function and merely serve representative purposes. Here we must suggest caution and recognize above all that representation is a fundamental and by no means basically a decadent need. The playful demonstration of one's wealth and fortune is common even on a very low cultural level, as the *potlatch* concept summarizes for ethnology. Johan Huizinga has shown that the inclination for potlatches has also played a part in higher civilizations, such as the Roman Empire.[32] Folklore museums too occasionally feature old bridal spinning wheels and similar objects, which were never used but just playfully portrayed a functional object in a particularly beautiful form and color. Costumes as well generally revealed or demonstrated the wealth of their wearers. According to reports, in Danubian Swabian villages, which in many respects have retained the level of traditions of the eighteenth century, i.e., the time of emigration, for *Kirchweih* (celebration of the consecration of their church) mothers hauled their daughters' entire wardrobes to the inn and the girls changed dresses after almost every dance; and the great farmhouses featured large "garment racks," where garments and shoes were not only stored but also displayed.[33] If we consider the lack of an immediate purpose as degeneration we fail to recognize this need for representation—we could also call it the preoccupation with status—and the playful nature of all culture.

However, the salon of the petit bourgeoisie not only lacks an immediate purpose but also does not make any sense, for it basically does not stand for anything; it merely represents, as it were, representation and is nothing but a façade.

The salon provides the preliminary stage for the *Paradezimmer* (literally, display room, i.e., parlor), which nowadays is customary in many circles, especially among working people. However, the parlor is basically different from the salon. The difference becomes clear in the nomenclature: While the salon merely imitates a genteel interior, the *Paradezimmer* is a form of representation which relates to one's own world and is measured against the other rooms. Thus the *Paradezimmer* pertains to the normalization and equalization of tension between high culture and basic culture, which will be discussed in the last section. However, the furniture frequently retains the imitative character of the earlier salon interior. The concept *Kitsch* comes to mind, which is difficult to define and whose etymology is not clearly established.[34]

An unsparing description of real folk culture since the last century can hardly avoid the concept *Kitsch,* not merely because the goods of high culture and genteel society were simply imitated without the power of transformation and inner assimilation, but primarily because these higher culture goods themselves frequently approached the borderline of *Kitsch.* Hermann Broch, who addressed the question of the nature and origin of *Kitsch* in two weighty essays,[35] advocates the thesis that *Kitsch* derives "to a large extent from that attitude of mind which we recognize as Romantic." This attitude of mind is said to have "introduced worldly and the most perishable elements directly into eternity and the realm that conquers death"; it had elevated beauty to a goddess and thus prepared the way for the *Kitsch* of "aestheticism as well as of the entertainment industry." A thorough discussion of Broch's specific conclusions and inferences is not possible here; however, the Romantic period certainly brought an ecstasy of sentiment which could only be mastered by a few but which many think themselves able to master and thus becomes a temptation and standard for many. The result is sentimentality, which is as far removed from the real sensitivity experienced by small circles in the eighteenth century as it is from the actual emotional exuberance of the Romantic. Friedrich Theodor Vischer translated this as *Empfindseligkeit* (blissfulness of feeling).[36] In the nineteenth century it began to spread to all levels of the folk as a fractured attitude, which no longer experiences nature and all that is "original" directly but rather via a sequence of stereotyped feelings that are inserted, screenlike, before the reception.[37] The influence of the sentimental on today's folk culture and folk mentality can hardly be exaggerated. Melodrama remains a constant part of folk theatre despite all attempts at renewal; even today it is often considered the highest compliment for a play or a performance if it reduces spectators to tears. "Edifying" literature, which indicates "how beautiful life would be, if people were good," according to Hedwig Courths-Mahler, a popular producer of such materials,[38] blossoms forth in many books and unbound serial novels as well as in booklets "for the Christian home." Like many films, they show the "*kitschy* image of people," the image of "the undisturbed, unpressured human being."[39] Among folk songs mawkish songs of mountain meadows and the like are most popular, and even the once powerful miner's song was eventually infiltrated by sentimental forms.[40] Any attempts by choral societies to repress the sentimental nineteenth-century songs at competitive singing events met with firm resistance from the singers; even today a Swabian choral society expects at least for the encore a *Silcherle*, as the songs composed by Friedrich Silcher and his imitators are called.

However, the intensity of sentimental attitudes—as shown specifically by this example—appears to vary from region to region; in Germany sentimentality seems more pronounced in the southwest than in the north. Even the origin of the northern German *Liedertafel* (lit., song table) differed from that of the southern German *Liederkranz* (lit., song circle); while the *Liedertafeln* consist of educated people with clear artistic goals, the *Liederkränze* attract the middle class and lower middle class who take up impulses from popular singing and blend artistic endeavors with emotional sentimentality.[41] This specific example is typical of the whole problem insofar as it touches on the social basis of the sentimentalization of cultural goods: the intensive weave of the classes and the dominant influence of the petit bourgeoisie in the south—particularly in the southwest—is contrasted with the more pronounced limits between specific social and educational levels and a receding "middle class" in northern Germany. However, it is precisely the middle classes who assimilated both the goods of high culture and the sentimental cultural goods of the peasantry. Beyond this, it is possible that the expansive quality of northern Germany, as determined by historic and geographic factors, may be important; in addition, differences in the development of tourism and the concomitant self-glorification may be responsible for differences in degrees of sentimentality.

Meanwhile we have enough evidence to prove that sentimentality is no longer peculiar to specific German regions. The German hit song gives even those songs which have an everyday, realistic quality in the American original, an extremely sentimental Sunday mood; and even when the song keeps close to the original at first, it most often flounders on the *Sentimentalitätsklippe* (reef of sentimentality) of the last lines.[42] Significantly an entirely new German word was created for the sentimental hit song: *Schnulze,* which is said to have been coined when a radio commentator used it on the spur of the moment, quite by accident, during a discussion of the *schmalzige* (greasy) and *schmachtende* (pining) quality of such songs.[43] In any case, this usage has become established and is now generally understood. In this context we should also mention the *Schlafzimmerbilder* (lit., bedroom pictures, i.e., sentimental paintings), which emphasize idyllic and emotional subjects, including religious motifs, such as the "Guardian Angel," by Bernhard Plockhorst. Since the 1880s, when new methods of color reproduction were developed, these pictures have spread in large numbers to all regions. Even today they are still sold mainly at fairs by itinerant merchants, together with wall plaques of verses and flat landscape paintings; similar items are offered in many furniture stores and by large mail order firms.[44]

The sentimental has even entered our language. Everyday communication, with its immediate back and forth, is generally safe from sentimental excess because of the controlling influence of the interlocutor. Excess blossoms the more sumptuously in the *Vereinsdeutsch* (German of voluntary associations), customarily used in speeches at club festivities and similar occasions, which also determines the style of club newsletters and popular descriptions.[45] Primarily the encounter with nature—for which the German language has developed particularly rich resources[46]—exhibits the insertion of emotional stereotypes. The following report was printed word for word in a small daily newspaper:

> Joy! turns the wheels. On the morning of July 11 at 5:30 am the 1887 age group left by bus from Linden Square to proceed first along the river Echaz, then along the Neckar. The sun was in competition with the fog, but the former proved victorious. Under a clear blue sky, illuminated by the queen of the day, we drove via Ludwigsburg to Heilbronn. There we went on board a steamboat and sailed to Wimpfen. The steamboat voyage was very interesting, we saw how the locks opened and closed again. We watched a variety of steamboats coming up the valley, laden with coal, oil, and similar important, economic things. A magnificent landscape made our eyes drunk. Like a broad silver ribbon the Neckar went on, bordered by beautiful forests, castles and ruins. Who may have lived there a hundred years ago?
>
> Accompanied by the sound of many cheerful folk songs we arrived in beautiful Schriesheim, where we partook of a first-rate copious dinner in the *Kaiser* inn. We enjoyed drinking white Kuhberg wine, for it was good and sparkled in the *Römer* glasses. While sitting thus cozily together, we sang the song of the Echaz valley in all keys.
>
> Afterwards we went to Strahlenburg castle where the splendid view into the magnificent, blessed Neckar valley was well worth our while. Vines along the valleys on both sides. Small wonder that even before our time the large cask at Heidelberg held 22,000 liters of wine. People then knew how to value wine and that wine, enjoyed in moderation, is medicine.
>
> Old Heidelberg, you beautiful, you much-honored city! These words about this magnificent city stand confirmed. So much beauty just about surprised us. We received a beautiful, lasting impression of beautiful Heidelberg Castle on the drive there. Here the art of architecture has been invested with sight. Hearts filled with joy, we journeyed up the valley via Bruchsaal and fortified ourselves at the inn. Full of songs, our hearts cheerful and free, we drove back to the beloved *Heimat*.
>
> What magnificent, emotional ties the dear, old folk songs give us, ties that can never be bought with money. We celebrate them in brotherly fashion. Safe and sound we returned to our city of Echaz around 11:00 pm. The magnificent impressions will remain a cheerful memory in the grey everyday world.[47]

This, of course, is a grotesque example—amusing because it is extreme. However, it merely exposes in the form of an unintentional caricature what is part, if in smaller dosages, of many of the goods of recent folk culture: the overloading with emotional clichés, the premature harmonizing, the striving for unlimited loveliness, innocence, emotion.

In any case, the appearance of this sentimentality is much more massive and important than can be deduced from discussions on "forms of production" in the arts and crafts, which tend to limit the *Kitsch* problem to certain phenomena. The coffeepot in the form of a cat is *kitschig* not only because it grossly insults the simple functional form but also because its decorative additions aim to evoke a sense of cuteness, i.e., sentimentality. Likewise the souvenir industry, which often produces popular vacation emblems and then simply changes the inscription—so that, for example, a mountain hut, a chamois, an *Edelweiss,* and a cow bell, as well as a sailor are all supposed to remind one of the city of Heidelberg[48]—reflects in motifs which are per se unrelated those clichéd, sham feelings that are kindled by these motifs. The fact that even a skull with greenish glass eyes is sold as a travel souvenir shows to what extent things can be sweetened sentimentally.[49] It is precisely this wide sphere of influence of sentimentality which makes it a dominant force, a force that any modern cultural science must come to terms with. Above all we must examine exactly how much collective sentimentality binds and liberates even genuine personal feelings; religious *Kitsch,* which at least does not prevent genuine religious experiences, proves that this is basically possible.[50] However, in its essence sentimentality is sham and remains questionable in its illusory quality.

All the forces explicitly concerned with the historical "revival" of folk life turn against these cultural manifestations of sentimentality—against sentimental theatre and dime novels, against mawkish hit songs and "bedroom pictures," and much more. They call for the reconsideration of the "essential" folk culture, which they assume to be merely overlaid by such fashionable, sentimental forms. However, this "essential" folk culture in the deeper sense proves to be as well, and to an even larger extent, a "system of imitation." This concept, too, derives from the work of Hermann Broch.[51] He interprets it as a closed system that is self-sufficient and does not point beyond itself, where therefore the "aesthetic demand" replaces the ethical one.

The application of the concept to our case is as promising as it is difficult. A concrete example best illustrates the circumstances as we perceive them. The author Wilfried Wroost concludes a "speech in defense of the folk play" with the demand "Folk theatre associations, put on folk dramas for the folk!"[52] This formulation conveys an impression of the circle in which this "essential" folk culture in particular moves; the "popular" or the "folklike" is often the standard by which the folk good is measured. This in itself is not as much a sociological as an aesthetic category; beyond this, however, the aesthetic element decidedly comes to the foreground within the closed system—here folk culture is not primarily realized correctly and well, but is shaped to be beautiful. Because the system is closed and hardly refers to high culture or at best considers it as opposition, the system depends on its given components, on that which "was." The "aesthetic demand" is no longer informed by the scope of values superimposed on the open system, but is based—in Broch's words—"on the realization of the system, on the previously existing formation." Thus indirectly the historicizing of "cultivated" folk culture proves to be another consequence of the social expansion, the dissolution of class horizons, which led to the opposition between folk culture and high culture and to the closing of the system of folk culture.[53]

These thoughts do not imply a total negation of revival attempts within folk culture. Here, too, a certain "intentio recta" exists which ignores the limitations (be it in the sense of *perspiere* or *neglegere*) and uses the system of imitation merely to go beyond imitation. In a similar way Erwin Ackerknecht has addressed the question of "*Kitsch* as a transitional cultural value."[54] It is significant that the concept *Kitsch* appears even in this environment. The fact of the "imitation system" explains why today beautiful folk dances sometimes seem almost as embarassing as sentimental hit songs, beautiful costumes almost as embarassing as the all-too-lovely bedroom paintings.

ATTEMPTS AT RENDERING THE SENTIMENTAL IRONIC

What can or may be done to stem the flood of sentimental imitation goods without surrendering the simple folk to the seemingly fruitless system of imitating the "folklike," the "past" folk culture, is a difficult pedagogical question. To begin with we should observe to what extent simple people themselves are capable of overcoming this imitation—or at least of keeping a distance from it. While the more passive form of renunciation is common and general, the active generation and assimilation of unsentimental, not imitated, goods are still rare in contemporary folk culture. A sign of this renunciation is the popular use of the word *Kitsch* (sentimental trash) and its adjective form *kitschig;* today these terms are readily available so that everyone may quickly label natural scenes, works of art, commodities. At times this resembles a sort of entertainment tax paid to convention—by calling something *kitschig* people protect themselves from the suspicion of outmoded taste; after this verbal sacrifice is made, one can safely engage in the private enjoyment of *Kitsch.* Frequently the verdict of *Kitsch* is pronounced on objects belonging to others, the same objects which in one's own private environment are easily tolerated and even treasured. This situation reminds us of the concept "mass," which is always applied to others and naturally excludes those social constructs in which we participate ourselves.[55] However, even if the convention which demands that we distance ourselves from *Kitsch* does not reach into all private spheres, it is important and influential; and it could only evolve because the consciousness of imitation and the desire for distance from it—even if diluted—have penetrated the world of the simple people.

However, more important than this terminological evidence is the fact that for specific goods the simple folk at least temporarily definitely rejects the imitation. For a long time such parodistic features of the folk culture were all but ignored, for they did not fit the notion of the prelogical-associative mentality of the lower classes, which was supposed to resemble the mentality of primitive peoples—a notion which its originator, Levy-Brühl, has meanwhile retracted in his *Carnets,* including his view of primitive peoples. Johan Huizinga asked pointedly "if the savage did not from the beginning combine a certain element of humor with his belief in most sacred myths"; moreover Huizinga has revealed elements of parody in cultures everywhere.[56] The notion of prelogical associative thinking seems to be a product of the nineteenth century, of which Huizinga has said: "If ever a century has taken itself and all of existence seriously, it was the nineteenth century."[57] During this century the possibilities of ironic distancing from sentimentality largely seem to have been sacrificed to a sentimentality which most often throws in the towel when confronted with humor, and which is completely destroyed once it opens itself to playful irony.

The former strength of the parodistic element in the more naive eras of folk culture can be demonstrated by a few examples. The fact that many forms of parodies have been preserved in the realm of carnival customs is hardly astonishing. *Narren* in Oberndorf on the Neckar honor prominent personalities in a ceremony which culminates in calling the honored person a *Sauhund* (swineherd's dog).[58] Similar events are customary in other Swabian localities. At the Imsten *Schemenlauf* (masked procession) the genteel figures of the *Roller* and *Scheller* are followed by the grotesquely costumed pair of the *Laggescheller* and the *Laggeroller*, who carry, instead of the chimes made from forged cowbells worn by the former, chimes of hollow rattling wooden kegs which originally were probably made from small *Laggen* (butter tubs). The *Lagge* pair's duty is to "tease and mock their precursors."[59] Rites of burying the *Fasnacht* which imitate Christian burials are widespread. However, other allusions to ecclesiastical customs occur as well: At Neumarkt in the Tauchental of Burgenland, "until very recently" a special *Faschings* picture was fastened to the church—"apparently a parody of the worship image of the 40-hour prayer."[60]

That parody does not spare even sacred objects is no new phenomenon. During the Middle Ages in particular parodies directed against the Church and religious notions were very widespread.[61] Medieval preachers and writers occasionally clad their polemic against the vices of the time in the form of mock masses, i.e., parodies of the mass text.[62] Burlesque is an important part of the religious dramas of the Middle Ages; "solemn and comical scenes follow each other not in strict succession but with some regularity."[63] Likewise the religious play of the Baroque period does not shy away from changing biblical plots and figures to make them appear comical; thus Joseph often assumes the type of the "comical old man."[64] Songs that ask for shelter at the inns at times resemble secular *Kilt* songs (songs of nocturnal visits) in form and content, and finally the scene of the good shepherd knocking at the shepherdess's door often turned into a regular *Kilt* scene.[65] It is difficult to determine, and will have to be decided from case to case, how much this represents a naive approximation of religious matters to our own world and how much it represents distancing, i.e., a parody.

In many cases it is obvious that religious plots and above all liturgical forms are used for secular purposes. In Westfalia the *haböcken Evangelium* (clumsy Gospel), a "Protestant Litany," a "Jewish Vespers," a "Vespers of Stadtlohn," a "Vespers of Hülsten," and the "Vespers of Baowendörp,: all parodies of sermons, are still widely performed at secular festivities.[66] A deacon of Markgröningen reported to the Church Council of Stuttgart in 1662 a custom of the carpenters' guild which imitated the church baptism. During this "Carpenter's Baptism" the journeyman, after passing his exam, was splashed three times with water while the following words were pronounced: "I baptize you in the name of the *Schirpfhobel*, in the name of the *Schlichthobel* [different kinds of planes], in the name of the *Rauh(hobel)bank* [rough joiner's bench]. Previously your name was Hans-below-the-bench, now your name is Hans-above-the-bench. Remain an honest fellow throughout your life."[67] In the year 1556 Count Christoph opened the "vine" in Güglingen in Zabergäu, a spring festival where "all citizens in procession carried a wine bottle attached to a pole into the vineyards, and after each citizen had decorated his hat with vine leaves, they brought the bottle, likewise decorated, back to the city hall for a public drinking bout."[68] Gerhard Lutz has pointed out the striking similarity of the "infamous processions" of folk justice to the forms of devotional processions. Furthermore, he sees the essential inspiration for the widespread scattering of chaff when morals have been offended in the positive forms of scattering, as is customary, for example, at Corpus Christi festivals and at weddings.[69]

Most of these parodistic forms basically leave the subject of the parody untouched. The infamous procession does not denigrate the devotional procession, the clumsy Gospel does not attack the real Gospel, and the solemn burial of the *Fasching* is at least not done with the intention of desecrating Christian burial. Instead all these forms attempt to realize a part of the "world turned upside down."[70] Such forms are being transferred from their legitimate place into other spheres; in a wider sense they become "contrafacts." Religious and ecclesiastical matters are easy targets; because of the high aspirations and strict obligations within this realm a small departure from the sacred sphere suffices to achieve a comic effect.[71] It is precisely the candor with which the religious is parodied that often indicates naive piety. At least the religious contents generally remain untouched.

Particularly in the case of Catholic piety these contents essentially cannot be damaged, as here the sacramental validity is grounded objectively and is derived *ex opere operato*. Only where the change to Protestantism understands the sacramental effect *ex opere operantis* does the parody endanger the religious substance. Therefore prohibitions—and our examples, to which many others could be added, prove that a prohibition exists—are at first largely limited to Protestant areas. Only in the course of the last century are parodies pushed into the background everywhere: piety, which by that time tends to be more personally colored, often would no longer allow for parodies. However, in part such parodies, too, became a victim of the general narrowing of the scope for action.

Nevertheless Huizinga's verdict, which attributes nothing but tenacious severity to the nineteenth century, does not entirely apply to the folk culture. Jonas Köpf wrote down the following little song in the small village of Suppingen:

> *Mag au a Lied so hoilig sei(n),*
> *So ghairt a Stückle drei(n):*
> *Ei Bauer, stand auf*
> *Ond füttre dei Schimmel*
> *Ond prügle dei Weib,*
> *Sonst kommst net in Himmel.*
> *Mag au a Lied so hoilig sei,*
> *So ghairt a Stückle drei.*[72]
>
> (Though a song is ever so holy,
> We must add a small piece:
> Hey, farmer, get up

And feed your grey
And beat your wife,
Else you won't go to heaven.
Though a song is ever so holy,
We must add a small piece.)

This text is based on concrete fact, for in this village hardly a song is performed without the addition of an *Anbinder* (attachment), which breaks with the mood of the preceding song.

Such attachments are not entirely new. Friedrich Ranke has shown that in the late Middle Ages the dialectic between the solemn and the grotesque became almost a stylistic principle. For example, in the songbook of the Hätzlerin, praise and abuse of women follow each other in rapid succession; and the writer of the songbook from Lochheim renders sad, emotional songs ironic by adding critical conclusions.[73] It should be investigated if connections from the history of ideas, conceivable particularly for the folk song, lead to the late Middle Ages; however, it is more likely that we have to assume a parallelism: The late Middle Ages followed an era of pronounced intellectual and social order, just as the nineteenth century did; the pathos and ethos of the preceding era melted into sentimentality, which was met with irony as a counterweight. However, the examples cited by Ranke are again "contrafacts" which, as Ranke emphasizes, do not really break the mood established earlier but merely show the other side of a matter. Moreover, as seems to be the case with the Lochheim songbook, perhaps these are nothing but the individual concerns of the writer.

By contrast the *Anbinder* from Suppingen have a more definite position and are more generally diffused. Even if this village in the Alb has a particularly large number of such attachments, as proven by the little Suppingen songbook, *Anbinder* are not a characteristic peculiar to that village. Folk song scholarship has barely paid attention to these little forms, which are easily overlooked and moreover dissolve the "communal mood." However, where the actual process of cyclical singing is accurately described, the same principle appears; even if not every song receives an *Anbinder,* after a whole cycle a few lines may help to find a "way out of the mood."[74]

The "holy" of the line "Though a song is ever so holy" is quite exaggerated. It is the pompously pathetic and sentimental secular song rather than the sacred song to which by all means "We must add a small piece." The Suppingen songbook gives a few typical examples, such as the song of the "handsome red huntsman": his beloved has followed him secretly, and he shoots her in the breast. The song ends with the dialogue:

"Geliebter, was hast du getan?" als sie im Blute rang.
"Die dunkle Nacht ist schuld daran, dass ich geschossen hab."

("Beloved, what have you done?" as she struggled in her blood.
"The dark night is to blame that I did shoot.")

Immediately after this sad ending, the *Anbinder* asks the ironic question:

> *"Was ho dea Jäger so sehr verdrosso,*
> *Dass er hot sei Mädle für an Rehbock gschosso?"*

("What has vexed the huntsman so much
That he would shoot his girl for a roebuck?")

A lovesong begins:

> *Mir ists halt nie so wohl zu Mut,*
> *Als wenn du bei mir bist,*
> *Wenn Deine Brust an meiner ruht,*
> *Mein Mund den deinen küsst*

(I never feel more content
Than when you are with me,
When your breast rests against mine,
My mouth kisses yours)

and in the last verse the song offers the prospect of the yes before the altar, which joins forever: "Then only death will separate me from you." The following text is attached:

> *Mir isch wohl, mir isch wohl,*
> *Mir isch ällaweil so wohl!*
> *Wenn i Geld hau, fahr i Scheesa,*
> *Wenn i koi(n)s hau, mach i Besa!*
> *Mir isch wohl, mir isch wohl,*
> *Mir isch ällaweil so wohl.*

(I am happy, I am happy,
I always feel so happy!
If I have money, I drive a fancy car,
If I don't have any, I make brooms!
I am happy, I am happy,
I always feel so happy.)

Two verses have infiltrated the song *Es kann ja nicht immer so bleiben* (It Cannot Always Stay this Way), which address the younger Napoleon in a self-confident and admonishing manner, reminding him of his defeat at Sedan. However, the attachment shifts to a jocular mood:

> *Napoleon isch nemme stolz*
> *Er handlet jetz mit Schwefelholz,*
> *Er lauft jetz's Gässle auf ond a(b):*
> *Leutla, kaufet mr Schwefelholz a(b).*

(Napoleon is no longer proud,
He now sells matches,
He now runs up and down the street:
People, buy my matches.)

This last *Anbinder* can be dated together with two verses that probably were added later. Others cannot be dated so easily. However, most of these ironic attachments seem to originate in the last century. If not the whole genre, then certainly its tinge, is a response to the sentimentalization of the folk song, even though *Anbinder* are sometimes attached to older, unsentimental songs. The simple people, particularly those belonging to the lower rural level, do not seem to have surrendered to sentimentality as unconditionally as has the bourgeois middle class. This is partly because peasants were not capable of such escalated sensitivity, although they felt and realized the pretentiousness of this sensitivity.

In recent decades, in rural singing this earlier kind of distancing from the sentimental song began to blend with a new-fashioned distancing, which will be indicated in the following examples: The handwritten songbook of a woman from Lothringen contained a parody of Kerner's *Preisend mit viel schönen Reden* (Praising in Many Beautiful Speeches).[75] At a singing event in a village in the Rhön Mountains, parodies of *Freut Euch des Lebens* (Enjoy Life) and *Turner auf zum Streite* (Gymnasts, on to the Fight) as well as a colorful blend of the opening lines of different songs were noted; e.g., *Es braust ein Ruf wie Donnerhall, und wie lieblich sang die Nachtigall am Brunnen vor dem Tor* (A call resounds like thunder, and how lovely did the nightingale sing at the fountain before the gate). A verse was added to the song *An einem Fluss* (By a River): *Und die stürzt sich aus Verzweiflung in die wasserleere Leitung, und die Fulder Zeitung schrieb, sie wär schon tot*[76] (And she throws herself in desperation into the empty water pipe, and the Fulda newspaper reported she was already dead). In a German village in Hungary people sang *Oh Zwetschgenbaum, wie blau sind deine Zwetschgen!*[77] (Oh damson tree, how blue are your damsons!—to the tune of ''Oh Tannenbaum!'').

While the *Anbinder* do not use the melody of the preceding song and thus leave the substance of these songs untouched, the transformations, which on the whole probably occurred later, directly invade the character of the songs. These are parodies in the stricter sense of the word, which retain the form and tune, while the *Anbinder* are more precisely defined as ''travesties,'' which take the content of a song and dress it in a new tune and form. However, compared to the earlier kind of ''contrafacts,'' in both cases the irony has become sharper. That which has been rendered ironic no longer stands far removed and untouched, but is approached directly. While the devotional procession is not actually ''intended'' in the jocular or infamous procession, even though it provides the means and forms, the irony of the song parody aims directly at the spirit and sentiment of the song that it ''intends.'' To this extent the difference between the form of the short *Anbinder* and the entire parody is only one of degree.

This difference is explained by the diversity in origin. While the *Anbinder*, which closely resembles the dance song and the *Schnaderhüpferl* (comical Alpine folk song), seems to derive from the peasant environment, entire parodies essentially originate in large towns and cities. In folk song archives we find many parodies particularly among urban songs; not only ''folk songs'' are parodied but also sentimental songs from operettas and hit songs. Often the parody supplants the original.[78] A few years ago there was a hit song representing a sentimental travesty of Goethe's *Heideröslein* (Heath Rose) that was very popular for some time. However, when a parody of this sentimental *Oh Heideröslein, nimm dich in Acht!* (Oh Heath Rose, Beware!) was written, a live radio audience in Kiel gave it a much higher rating than the original sentimental song.[79] Similarly parodies of emotional broadside ballads became so numerous and so popular that eventually they were mistaken for the "true broadside ballads" which they had helped to drive out.[80]

However, not all of these song parodies were limited to the urban environment. In specific cases a movement from the city to the village has been observed.[81] Mediators were primarily servant girls and laborers. In the villages parodies met with the ironic reaction to sentimentality already expressed in the *Anbinder*. Today such parodies are also quite well known in rural areas at least among the young, and are not confined to industrial workers. Just as the sentimentalization of the folk good traversed all class barriers, so the ironic resistance to it illustrates that the goods of folk culture can hardly be defined in terms of class or social position.

Of course, in towns and cities ironic forms appear more frequently. Here they are not restricted to sobering antidotes to sentimentality but often reach deeply into the structure of traditional customs and social obligations. This is made clear in the typical games of young urban people. Herbert Schöffler describes one "as most characteristic of Berlin": two friends take the bus across Berlin and one deliberately explains the sights to the other in such fallacious terms that eventually the other passengers on the bus intervene.[82] Roda-Roda offers a parallel from Vienna in his story *Wie man das Wienerherz missbraucht* (How to Misuse the Viennese Heart),[83] and similar practices are common in other cities: asking for information about the city one is familiar with; asking the way when one knows it very well; greeting all the people one encounters and evaluating their reaction according to a system of points, e.g., they reciprocate the greeting, they ignore it, or they scold. Such games realize older *Schwank* situations where the moment of the given error is decisive. However, while the *Schwank* is tailored to a specific comic event, in our last example the event continues and very generally plays on the obligatory gesture of greeting: such play is carried by the notion of irony. All of this is only conceivable in the specific context of a large city, where people generally do not know each other and encounters are brief and rare. From this brief and rare quality Georg Simmel has deduced the urbanite's temptation "to act in a way that is pointed, condensed, as characteristic as possible."[84] This, too, is an essential point of departure for the attitude of irony, which is always a consequence of disparate matters; wherever the horizons of experience are uniform, irony is neither necessary nor even possible. By contrast the dissolution of the horizon provokes irony. Nietzsche has shown how historicizing leads "an era into the dangerous mood of self-irony."[85] Similarly the removal of spatial and social horizons relativizes once sacrosanct goods and exposes them to irony. In severe cases irony seizes every given and newly developed cultural good and reshapes and relativizes it accordingly—a productive attitude which forgoes producing any new cultural goods.

These are big words considering the trifling phenomenon of sentimental goods being rendered ironic. It may seem that in this case a minute matter is quite artificially made larger and coarser until it must be measured according to the great standard of the general history of ideas. Certainly no "clear awareness of the eternal agility, the infinitely full chaos," to quote from a definition of irony by Friedrich Schlegel,[86] prevails whenever a parody is sung, a custom is subjected to ironic questioning, or a traditional saying is changed by irony. Another remark by Schlegel, that irony is "no joking matter," applies even to those small incidents. However insignificant the particular incident may seem, the process of irony within folk culture as a whole is important: it complements the process of the freezing of cultural goods in historicized and imitated forms. The irony loosens this solidification without dissolving it completely.

The great influence of irony is most clearly evident in everyday speech. The Dictionary of Colloquial Speech[87] lists numerous examples of ironic escalation and revaluation. Not only the meaning is shifted ironically, e.g., *Pulswärmer* (wristwarmers) stand for boxing gloves,[88] *Staubgefässe* (stamen, lit., dust bins) for garbage cans, *Plattfuss* (flat foot) for a flat tire, *Göttergatte* (gods' spouse) for a husband; even the words themselves and their syntactic concatenation have been changed. One gets betrothed "against" someone;[89] something cuts through *Mark und Pfennig* (German currency terms are substituted for the original *Mark und Bein*, i.e., marrow and bone); a gauze bandage is deliberately called a "compress" or "countess"; one draws "conferences"; goes to see the soccer game in the *Stadium* (instead of *Stadion*, i.e., arena). Even proverbs are changed intentionally. "Das schlägt dem Fass die Krone ins Gesicht"[90] (lit., That throws the head [of the beer] into the face of the barrel) is perhaps primarily used by educated people. However, popular distortions of this kind exist as well, such as "Quäle nie ein Tier zum Scherz, denn es könnt geladen sein"[91] (Never torment an animal for fun because it may be loaded). Such phenomena are too easily ignored as signs of an annoying decline in language, without thinking about their essence.

To begin with we must observe that these linguistic distortions are part of a long literary tradition. Fischart emphasized jocular etymologies: from *Melancholie* (melancholy) he created *Maulhengkolie* (pull-a-long-face-choly), and from *Podagra* (gout) he derived *Pfotenkrampf* (cramp of the paws).[92] In his *Geliebte Dornrose* (Beloved Thorny Rose), Gryphius has tenant Wilhelm talk *mit repetenz* (with repetition) and *gebührenden despect* (due disrespect).[93] He confuses and distorts foreign words as did his contemporary Molière, who turned *hypocrisie* into *hydropiesie* and *grammaire* into *grandmère*.[94] In the nineteenth century Balzac collected witty proverb distortions in his notebook,[95] while Nestroy is the recognized master of such word plays in German. They even invade operas and operettas. In the second half of the nineteenth century Julias Stettenheim, alias *Wippchen*, used this means to augment the comic effect of his reports. Even Theodor Fontane frequently distorted proverbial sayings. The saying *durch Mark und Pfennig* cited above appears in Thomas Mann's *Magic Mountain*,[96] and his Mrs. Stöhr is the unrivaled master of the distorted and misunderstood foreign word. This literary sequence, which could be made more compact and differentiated in a specific study, indicates that such distortions are not necessarily due to a failure in speech or in meaning or to a lack of earnestness. Rather it is frequently an act of alienation that for a few moments allows the metaphorical character of language to shine through, a language which in many ways has become pale and congealed. In some cases this definition applies even to popular alterations and further developments, as "insolent" as they may be. It would take a detailed analysis to determine where such ironic tendencies enter the "Dictionary of the Inhuman."[97]

In ironic linguistic developments the city again takes the lead.[98] Perhaps this is most obvious in the ironic names rapidly applied to new buildings and the like: from the many names given to the monuments of Berlin[99] to the "Tomb of the Unknown Director," as the new theatre in Cologne is known, to *Monte Scherbellino* (Mount of Fragments) for a large heap of debris in Stuttgart.[100] However, ironic language structures and word creations are not limited to the urban environment; when we separate "colloquial language" from "rural dialects" today, we are making a theoretical, historical division. Colloquial and thereby often ironical turns of speech have reached even the most remote villages. To be sure, the limits of popular irony, with their agility, become obvious here more rapidly and clearly than in the cities. For example, the word *furchtbar* (frightful) is often extended in Swabian colloquial speech to the form *furchterbar*. The adverb *fürchterlich* may have contributed to this construction, but it was as unusual in dialects as was *furchtbar;* this is probably an ironic analogy to *wunderbar* (wonderful)—marginally we might also consider *sonderbar* (peculiar). The derivation from irony is supported by the observation that the word is often used in an ironic sense. Thus the exaggerated interpretation of basically harmless events evokes the retort "that would be *furchterbar,* of course." However, the ironic tinge of the word is gradually fading, and if the significant effect of writing did not thwart the development of dialect, the word presumably could simply replace the old form of *furchtbar,* eventually to be used as naively as the latter was used before. Occasionally such naive use can be observed.

This development is characteristic of the life of a language, where innovations rapidly become the norm, where images fade, words become altogether petrified and, as it were, change from appellative denominations to mere names.[101] However, language characteristically indicates the limits of popular irony. Recently Hans Paul Bahrdt showed how the relativization of conventions that were once valid has all but elevated irony to a social convention. However, such irony cannot be codified and cannot enter tradition: "It always remains an individual achievement, meagre though it may be."[102] Forms that are marked by irony can be socialized and traditionalized; but the ironic element must always be achieved individually if it is to retain its ironic quality. To distort a foreign word may be an ironic achievement, even if it is only a repetition; however, it may also be an unconscious copy of a conventional ironic form; it may become the norm and completely loose its ironic character; and finally it may be the result of an unintentional linguistic blunder, not ironic, but of an involuntarily comic nature. This last case is certainly just as frequent as the first and can be comprehended even better from the point of view of social expansion.

THE PYGMALION PROBLEM

The case of the misuse of foreign words mentioned above was first noted when a talkative small-town manufacturer involuntarily used the wrong forms: on Sundays he went to the *Stadium* (instead of the *Stadion*, i.e., arena), he drew his "conferences" (rather than conclusions), in the mornings in his office he assigned *directrices* (instead of directives); thus he was not so much following the path of Gryphius himself as that of his tenant Wilhelm, was not emulating Thomas Mann so much as Mrs. Stöhr. These misuses only spread afterward; perhaps not to the entire population of the town but to more than a small, educated elite. From then on these and similar freely invented permutations were used intentionally and ironically. But even where no involuntary mistake preceded the new usage, such playful distortions are nevertheless directed ironically at an imaginary failure. At an earlier time we could have assumed that they were directed against the kindred of Mr. *Neureich* (nouveau riche) and Mrs. *Raffke* (profiteer), and even now related jokes circulate about such types; however, they have lost some of their poignancy, for we no longer automatically assume a correlation between economic and educational levels, as we have become used to people climbing the economic ladder rapidly. Above all, the dangers to which Nouveau Riche and Profiteer expose themselves nowadays threaten almost everyone, as will be discussed below.

Ulrich Engel has called the linguistic development of the *parvenu* an "inauthentic language movement," as merely exterior forms are altered without affecting the inner form of language and implicitly the whole life-style.[103] He gives as examples of the most frequent kinds of blunders the misuse of words—again primarily foreign words; failure because of regional nuances of speech; use of "hypercorrect" forms as a result of the mistaken generalization of phonological rules. Most of these failures are penetratingly represented in George Bernard Shaw's drama *Pygmalion*, in which two scholars tackle the difficult problem of making a London flower girl of the lowest circumstances presentable to society, even to the court, in the space of a few months. Because these scholars are linguists, and because Shaw himself took an unusual interest in linguistic, especially phonetic, problems, he emphasizes the linguistic side of the educational process. Above all Shaw shows the grotesque incongruity during the first phases between the acquired pronunciation on the one hand and the substance and form of thinking which inevitably derive from the original class on the other; he shows how particularly under emotional stress the original forms repeatedly rise to the surface.

Without doubt the Fabian Shaw is concerned with the possibility of and the obstacles to social advancement. Here he assumes a relatively intact hierarchy and social ranking. We can be certain that the problem itself is not new but merely the point of view, for such upward mobility, with all its stumbling blocks and potential for blunders, has always existed. As early a work as *Meier Helmbrecht* describes how the young Helmbrecht—bearer of the cup that symbolizes immoderation—attempts to move beyond the class structure ordained by God. In that case, too, the poet indicates the disparity between the inherited and the assumed position by linguistic pretensions which turn into the ridiculous.

Speech blunders and misunderstandings were common at all times. The rich field of folk etymology offers many examples which go far beyond the purely linguistic, e.g., appeals to St. Valentine in cases of "falling" fever (to fall = *fallen* in German) and to St. Augustine for help against diseases of the eyes (eyes = *Augen* in German).[104] However, when we contrast these examples with a more recent incident of linguistic misunderstanding, it becomes quite clear that we are dealing with a basically different matter. The host of an inn in Hesse explains his love of singing as follows: "I was born in January. I once read in a calendar that such people are sanguine people [*Sanguisten*]. That is correct, because I have always been a good singer [*Sänger*], just like Mr. O., who formerly directed the choral society and was born on the same day as I."[105] In this case, too, we are dealing with a sort of folk etymology, influenced by the "desire of naive thinking to establish a causality."[106] However, the difference is clear. The etymology attached to the names of saints not only reinterprets the foreign, but the new interpretation becomes binding within the given social horizon. Such folk etymologies are not essentially "wrong"; rather they indicate a sort of transfer from the linguistic sphere of the educated class to that of the simple folk. However, the more recent case of folk etymological reinterpretation is not generally binding, even if it is shared by several people, and the category "wrong" cannot be avoided. Even if at first the interpretation is accepted by everyone, references to the correct form and the correct meaning of the word remain a constant threat (for the real meaning is "sanguine persons"); this fact makes the etymology a mistake.

On closer inspection even these little examples reveal the two major reasons for the shift: for the speakers it is the social expansion, the dissolution of the social horizons, and—partly related to this—for the language it is a huge supply of linguistic resources when compared to earlier times. The destruction of the social horizons generally prevents the assimilation of such a misunderstanding and its becoming the norm for a certain group. Moreover, the destruction of the horizon opens the doors to higher levels of education so that even the little man is confronted over and over again with the content and above all with the language of education. As for linguistic resources, their increase is most clearly evident in today's inflation of words. For a long time it was assumed that "a working man" could get by with 300 words, whereas a man with a university education needed between 3,000 and 4,000 words.[107] Adolf Bach has rightly rejected these numbers as "products of armchair research,"[108] i.e., a very conceited product of someone's desk which entirely fails to recognize the wealth of synonyms in the folk language and its ability to make the most minute distinctions. However, in comparison with today's vocabulary, Jacob Grimm's opinion, which ascribed to the dialects "lexicographic moderation," does not appear wrong. The high numbers resulting from recent studies—approximately 20,000 words for the inhabitants of an industrial village—are probably due in part to recent developments. New areas of expertise and real differentiations demand an enlarged and differentiated vocabulary. Technology participates in this process not only by opening up new areas which call for entirely new groups of words, but also by the rapid and far-reaching diffusion of the entire vocabulary. Primarily newspapers, but also schools, books, movies, and broadcasts provide the simple folk with a huge number of words, word combinations, and sentence constructions which are foreign to the traditional dialects but cannot be excluded from everyday speech.

These many strange forms and words—to some extent words from foreign languages, as many of these have long been popular—cannot be easily assimilated into the given language. Breaks, seams, overlaps, and agglomerations occur which cannot be compared to the changes, which obviously have affected language at all times. Random samples from tape recordings[109] provide many examples of blunders, at least a few of which should be mentioned. A young man talking about his dancing lessons says: "Then a sort of *Mayonnaise* was danced"—a striking mistake of the type we have already discussed. Other blunders are less obvious: A refugee woman reports how they were *zerteilt* (cut up, instead of *verteilt*, divided), in the camp, another contaminates two linguistic images when she says a teacher must "pay much *Eselsgeld*" (donkey money, instead of *Essensgeld*, food money), especially when it is a *frischausgebackener* (freshly baked, instead of *frischgebackener*, i.e., new) teacher. A young man tells of a movie where the hero must leave because he is *schamlos* (shameless), but he really means *ehrlos* (without honor). The more cumbersome structure of the written language, which confronts people in newspapers and bureaucratic writing, leads to distortions which affect even academic circles, such as *meines Erachtens* (according to my opinion), the well-established *ein Herr Sowieso* (a Mr. What's-his-name), and the formula *ein Mann mit namens* (a man of the name of). One of the speakers says that "two days before the *Feindeinwirkung* [enemy influence]" his native place was bombed—here the word enemy influence is limited to the capture of the place. Another person reports "when the *Anbaufläche* [area of cultivation] is begun" in their region, meaning when the cultivation *(Anbau)* is begun. Without doubt some of these cases are influenced by general developmental tendencies in our language.[110] However, none of them fits the scope of the valid, correct rules of language, even if this scope is measured liberally.

Breaks can be identified even in cases that are grammatically correct. When the president of a society says that his club existed "as it were in agony," he is not only applying an incongruously strong expression but a tone that on the whole is foreign to dialect speech. Similar situations arise when a matter is said to have a "long *Werdegang* [growth process]," when a young woman talks of an *Arbeitsvorhaben* (plan for work) for the next day, or when it is said of lowball (a poker game) that everything depends on *"Fassungsvermögen* [self-control] and *Courage* [using the French word *courage*]."* Significantly the sound of such expressions most often clearly sticks out from dialect speech; they are articulated in High German or else in very modified dialect.

All these examples show that the multifarious linguistic data, which nowadays confront even the simple man, are not completely assimilated into his traditional forms of language and concomitantly to his forms of thinking. The linguistic blunders and hybrid forms we have cited seem typical of the parvenu; however, the people who use them hardly fit that term. The concept parvenu does not adequately describe this general social movement, which is also expressed verbally. Faced with this broad movement, it is very difficult to recognize where we may really speak of parvenu-like behavior and how this behavior is expressed in language. However, the process itself is extremely important and cannot be reversed. Today such statements as "unfortunately this era of general education has robbed us of a viable reserve of illiterate people"[111] are as unrealistic as they are rare. On the whole the fundamental democratization of education has been accepted,[112] even though the cultural consequences are frequently still misjudged. Anyone who bemoans the decline of the beautiful old dialects should also join in the lament over the end of illiteracy. It is not without a certain irony that elementary school teachers in particular, whose work necessarily contributes directly to the dissolution of the old dialect, often complain violently and with moralistic undertones about this dissolution.

Any regret that the simple folk is no longer restricted to the "appropriate" educational and cultural goods and any attempt to reduce the folk to goods "appropriate" to it does not recognize that the measure of the simple folk has long changed. Will-Erich Peuckert found in his investigation of "trashy novels" that sophisticated citations play a significant role: Words by Schiller and even sayings of Plato are cited with specific mention of the author's name.[113] These citations feign a level and a value that does not exist, and in that regard they are typical of such inferior serials. However, they also meet a general and quite legitimate need: that no area of our reality, including the realm of higher education, shall remain closed to the simple folk, that at the very least everyone may have contact with the materials of such education. In this sense the simple folk reaches toward linguistic materials outside its immediate sphere of life, at times all too impetuously and clumsily, but nevertheless legitimately.

Here we encounter the essential Pygmalion problem. Shaw's drama explicitly mentions it only once, in the third act, when it becomes forcibly clear to the two linguists that the most important problem is not the linguistic education of the flower girl, but "what is to be done with her afterwards." With Shaw this problem, too, assumes an intact class structure, where for the upper classes a—predominantly linguistic—education, in addition to property and a "name," can be presupposed.[114] This problem can be generalized and applied to our observation: What happens to the folk that, as it seems, has begun to flirt with a partner with whom it cannot enter into a happy relationship; what happens with the simple people who have begun to participate in all of the complexity of contemporary reality? Perhaps this question is decisive for the future of folk culture. So far a comprehensive answer is not possible; however, tendencies are evident which must be considered for such an answer.

Again Shaw's *Pygmalion* may give us a point of departure. After a few studied phrases at her first social appearance, the flower girl Eliza continues to adhere only to the correct phonetic expression, but otherwise relapses completely into her hereditary jargon, which results in a peculiar contrast. However, the guests do not grasp the process at all; instead the strange linguistic behavior is interpreted as a new fashion—an older woman is shocked, her daughter admires "the new small talk," which she decides to adopt herself at the next social event. What is presented in this scene as satirical exaggeration is matched in reality by a nonsatirical general phenomenon: the languages of the upper and the lower classes are moving closer together.[115] Literary naturalism makes the language of the lower social classes acceptable in literary terms and at the same time proves that the claims and pretensions of educated language have shrunk. Likewise the language of newspapers and similar publications is the result of an adjustment between upper and lower linguistic levels: it may be understood as slightly elevated colloquial speech or as standard speech colored by the vernacular.[116] In general the importance and volume of so-called colloquial speech have grown. Even though at all times "middle language levels" have probably intruded between the standard educated language and the folk language, only social expansion could cause these middle levels to become a colloquial language, a language that is not determined by class, that can no longer be defined in sociological terms, and that constantly expands its scope in relation to both the standard educated language and the dialects. Quite naturally the image of the sociolinguistic structure largely corresponds to the image of the social structure itself.[117] Moser's statement that the colloquial level develops "in most regions into a new linguistic base level at the expense of the folk language"[118] is aimed at the linguistic and social upward movement, which includes the encroachments and rejections we have discussed.

Shaw's scene draws our attention not only to this general adjustment between the different linguistic levels and to their mutual approximation but—more specifically—to one of the routes toward such adjustment. The young lady who considers the peculiarly vivid kind of conversation the new social style succumbs to the invigorating effect which unusual forms of language must have in the midst of the monotonous harmony of social manners. This effect is the more pronounced the less active the social horizons; while the latter once provided narrow limits for the exchange of linguistic forms, enticingly multifarious forms are now presented. The general result is indicated by the fact that colloquial speech can no longer be clearly separated from jargon. Even where such a separation is attempted by artificial terminological means, a broad intermediate zone remains— and this precisely is the liveliest zone of everyday colloquial speech. Hans Lipp has said that jargon speaks "as it were beyond the specific matters"; it participates "in taking matters easy."[119] It is this transient quality which nowadays characterizes most social and linguistic encounters. Jargon compensates for this transience by adopting glaring colors and by "alienating" the language. By this process what pertains to everyday life and the most common occurrences in particular is meant to be rescued quickly and for a short time from the rapid flow of the inconspicuous. Typically, sports language has developed many different expressions and phrases for very simple phenomena.[120] It clearly shows the intense rapprochement of colloquial language and jargon. However, the distortion of jargon conceals the involuntary distortion of colloquial forms and phrases as they occur with dialect speakers. When a simple man uses a foreign word incorrectly and when the same foreign word is intentionally distorted in educated conversation, the same result is achieved not just externally and by accident. Rather, the very different processes have a common origin in the destruction of the horizon.

Social expansion generally liberates the notion of language. The fact that efforts at preserving language are directed not only at the standard language but also at dialects is a result of that liberalization. The destruction of the social horizons has broadened the scope of what is considered correct language. Anton Pfalz has shown that frequently in urban speech a number of almost equally valid forms are available rather than a single fixed linguistic form, e.g., "we have" can be expressed in correct linguistic terms with very different phonological forms.[121] The various forms originate from different social classes. After the destruction of the social horizons they have become generally available. They differ only in slight nuances, but are all legitimate. Today this "excess of forms" is neither limited to the cities nor restricted to phonological variations. Because along with the social expansion the former semantic horizons of certain words have dissolved, almost every matter and process can be expressed by a number of words and phrases that are all "correct." Hand in hand with this excess of forms comes a certain excess of meaning, excesses which seem to be in opposition. The latter becomes particularly obvious in the use of words which were once foreign to the folk language. The word *abstrakt* is a good example. Formerly current only in dialects of the Rhine area,[122] the word can now be observed in colloquial language elsewhere. It indicates anything unusual and modern (an "abstract chair"), anything stikingly colorful ("abstract bunch of flowers"), and occasionally a radical, decisive action ("in that case I don't care, I'm abstract about it!"). These meanings are documented; though presumably a number of others exist, these should suffice to indicate that the word can hardly be used "incorrectly." Certainly this is an extreme and quite specific case. However, the tendency is general, and dangerous as it is to the orderly system of meaning in language, it nevertheless contributes to the solution of the *Pygmalion* problem.

Moreover the variation in meaning and the naive use of the word *abstrakt* indicate that the actual complexity of our reality is very definitely influenced, and that things most differentiated are adapted to undifferentiated familiar use. The linguistic blunders we mentioned at the beginning of this section rarely derive from subjective linguistic insecurity; on the contrary, they were uttered with great assurance and often with strong emphasis. Obviously a mistake does not become objectively correct by being made with great confidence. However, in this case such assurance attests to the ability of the simple people to construct a whole, meaningful structure from the confusing array of disparate linguistic and material elements. The reader may have noticed how often the adjective "simple" *(einfach)* has been used in this study to indicate the people of concern to *Volkskunde*. This was done to avoid misunderstandings, to which the concept *Volk* is always exposed. Beyond this, however, the *simple* quality, in fact, is the signature which most validly describes these people. This simplicity has not been abandoned even in the face of our confusing reality; often complicated matters are simply accepted—we may emphasize: *simply* accepted.

At this point linguistic observation joins up with a general account of the world of the folk. We have emphasized linguistic observations because they often open up this world most directly and offer an abundance of examples for our problem. However, the phenomena we expounded are not limited to linguistic matters, but relate to folk culture as a whole: blunders occur also in the popular adaptation of new fashions in clothing. The inflation of words is very obviously matched by the huge supply of material cultural goods; the rapprochement between upper and lower classes is evident, for example, in many manifestations of furnishings, where unusual pieces—"jargon furniture," so to speak—become a habitual necessity. The proliferation of forms and meanings can also be traced in greeting customs; and the security based on *simplicity* in the face of a complicated reality characterizes the folk culture as a whole. We must therefore also recognize the danger to all of folk culture inherent in simplifying the complicated in a short-circuiting, inadequate manner and by putting the stress in the wrong places.

Friedrich Theodor Vischer added another sentence to his definition of "folk" which introduced this chapter:

> We are not talking about those who exist in the indeterminate middle, who are no longer naive without being thoroughly educated, or who have grown dull and wild because of need, or who have acquired the overrefinement of education without its antidote, but we are talking about the mass which is rooted in the old, simple tradition, which has its own education, an education of the kind which is natural when compared to that education which causes the gap. [123]

In the context in which he was working, Vischer did not have to unravel the problems contained in this sentence, for he set up an ideal opposition between folk poetry and literary poetry. [124] In fact even in his time more and more people existed "in the indeterminate middle"; they were no longer part of the naive, "natural" education and did not entirely participate in the other kind.

Today the problem derived from that situation, which we have described as the Pygmalion problem, is more urgent than ever. It confronts any kind of folk education with different and important problems. What can be done in the face of the dissolution of the old bonds? Have all the goods of folk culture lost their educational value because of this, or should those past regulations and bonds now be consciously integrated into the educational process? Can something be done to turn the "indeterminate middle" into a "motherly earth"? Or are all such natural metaphors and the concomitant notions best renounced entirely?

These questions have been raised before in the course of our investigations, and partial answers have been suggested. However, here at the end they once more appear as questions. They are too difficult to be answered wholesale by a pathetic prognosis of decline or by euphemistic praise of the folk; they demand sober reflection and intense sympathy.

CHAPTER
5

RELICS—AND WHAT CAN
BECOME OF THEM

REFUGEE TRADITIONS

Anyone who still talks of refugees nowadays seems to have missed the boat. The official institutions which deal specifically with this section of the population are considered antiquated and superfluous. Even official records were discontinued at the end of 1960, by which time the number of refugees in the Federal Republic of Germany amounted to 10 million: in a sense refugees do not exist any more. This statement does not merely apply to the word *Flüchtling* (refugee), which was commonly used in the years after the war and officially recognized,—e.g., on refugee identity cards—and which at the same time acquired a symbolic charge: the refugee was regarded, to use the subtitle of a study by Elisabeth Pfeil, as the prototypical "Figure of a New Era." The much publicized concept *Neubürger* (new citizen) never caught on. Instead the term *Heimatvertriebener* (expellee) entered the vernacular speech of the Federal Republic, in contrast to the official designation *Umsiedler* (resettler) of the German Democratic Republic, a questionable word which all too easily conceals the fact that the resettlement, flight, and expulsion of millions was a cruel consequence of the National-Socialist conduct of war. Today the concept *Heimatvertriebener* plays a relatively minor role, not because of a distancing from this political bias, but because people are simply convinced that assimilation has been achieved. Refugees—under any name—are no longer an important topic; they have blended into our affluent consumer society: we all read the popular daily *BILD*, we all enjoy the nature programs on television, we are all informed about the latest detergent by television commercials. The sarcastic tone of this—nevertheless correct—statement may serve to indicate that something that has *ceased* to be a problem can certainly be a problem. It is worth talking about the refugees and investigating critically what has become of the traditions they brought with them.

West German *Volkskunde* is not guilty of any neglect regarding the amount of attention it paid to the traditions of refugees. On the contrary, soon after the war the folklore of refugees became an explicit focus. For most folklorists, this seemed to be a direct continuation of their former pursuits. Since the days of the

Romantics, *Volkskunde* has been convinced of its duty to save, at the eleventh hour, what otherwise would be doomed to disappear. The flood of refugees created an almost classic situation for such an impulse. Not only had ethnic groups been uprooted from their former homes, but these groups were widely scattered and their traditions could only be preserved if they were supported vigorously.

These traditions became *relics* not merely in their contemporary context; they had previously been considered as such because of their historical situation. They originated in regions that had largely been regarded as relic areas. At this point the notion of a cultural decline from west to east entered, a notion which, though certainly not wrong, tended to be interpreted too unilaterally. Much of what had been covered up or eliminated by intensive industrialization in the western regions continued to exist in the eastern confines of the German language area, an area which on the whole was of a more agrarian character. Additionally the existence of the many "language islands" (linguistic enclaves) inspired the notion that here one could count on a self-sufficient cultural development, even a freezing of the level of tradition that had been reached centuries ago at the time of emigration. Alfred Karasek-Langer, along with Johannes Künzig the most diligent collector of east German traditions, summarized these notions when he said that in such regions the folklorist encounters much that is part of a "living folk organism" today that can otherwise only be seen in a museum or an archive.

Karasek suffered much less than others from the erroneous assumption that this represents proof of an entirely unbroken tradition. Time and again he pointed out that some of what had passed for medieval, a survival from the time of settlement, really resulted from a wave of Baroque fashion which had reached as far as these eastern areas. Even those groups which did not emigrate until the eighteenth and nineteenth centuries did not simply preserve the level of tradition of their region of origin at that time, but absorbed later elements. For example, in the second half of the nineteenth century Viennese salon culture spread and importantly influenced all Austro-Hungarian regions; it left behind distinct traces, e.g., in the songs of the Danubian Swabians.

The countries of the Danube monarchy provide a good example of a second fact which is ignored by a too narrow view of relics and "islands." The so-called language islands have always been *zones of contact* with other ethnic and linguistic groups, which could well exert a stabilizing influence: The retention of antiquated beliefs in some of the eastern areas depended not merely, or even primarily, on the fact that they had been brought along by settlers from their medieval place of origin but also on the support of related traditions among their Slavonic neighbors. More commonly such contacts must have caused changes. For example, in a number of essays Ingeborg Weber-Kellermann has shown how different ethnic traditions interweave and mutually influence each other. Not even linguistic barriers are decisive in such cases, as is proven by songs from Danubian Swabian villages with macaronic and partly foreign-language texts.

Prevailing notions of relics have paid least attention to the *transitional character of that which does not change*, to put it paradoxically. Relics often were and are assumed to express a continuity of communal culture, which is unchanging and genuine in its substance,[1] while in reality it is precisely the *island situation* which contributed to the stabilizing and in some cases to the freezing of the tradition. Not only did fresh supplies—from upper-class culture—cease or at least slow down, but also in the foreign environment the traditions they had brought with them acquired a considerable *demonstrative value*. At first such demonstrations are primarily related to a rather limited regional consciousness. Nowhere in the language islands had emigration ever occurred under a nationalist banner. A more definite national consciousness, which could build on the awareness of a specific ethnic character, was introduced to the language islands relatively late— e.g., by representatives of the Youth Movement, who had made the preservation of the *Auslandsdeutschtum* (German culture abroad) their goal, as well as by folklorists, who attempted to explain to the population the *urdeutschen* (essentially German) character of their traditions. This, however, changed the function of the relics decisively, even if their appearance remained the same.

Considerable evidence exists to suggest that this was not always the case and that the course of such "preservation" at times resulted in noticeable changes. The magazines and newsletters published in several eastern regions since about the turn of the century contain not only affectionate descriptions of existing traditional goods but also many innovations substantiated by a circular argument: because the east European German language areas were relic areas of old German traditions, they should and could accommodate even more old German traditions. It is certainly not true in every case that *Volkskunde* studies of refugees after the Second World War enthusiastically recorded as relics what had been introduced only years or decades earlier by folk song or folk dance groups, etc., but such changes nevertheless modify the notion of homogeneous relic areas and the continuity of tradition.

A further, related modification is a specific result of the large population movements after the war. When referring to the living folk organism, of which the East German traditions represent a part, Karasek characterized a situation that had already become historical. The enthusiastic collection of traditions beginning after the war took place in refugee camps or any other locality of the new *Heimat*, where the refugees often lived largely in isolation. At the very least the old communicative context was destroyed. The functions which their traditions and goods had had at home were lost, and other functions had replaced them only in part.

Loss of function severely affected precisely those goods which attracted the liveliest interest among folklorists, because these were phenomena which could no longer be observed in our country. This is true of certain objects, e.g., items of clothing, but mainly aspects of oral tradition, such as storytelling. Despite a few exceptions, we can make the generalization that a living *Märchen* tradition has practically ceased to exist in western Germany. An increasingly rational attitude has pushed the stuff of folktales into the world of children, and there they have become subject to pedagogical norms. Fairy tale books, especially the Household Tales of the Brothers Grimm, have allowed the oral tradition to die out. By contrast, in a number of eastern regions the *Märchen* belonged to the context of oral communication. This should not be understood unilaterally: even the East Prussian, Bohemian, and Hungarian-German narrators no longer occupied the central position which was still reported of Finnish and Siberian storytellers at the beginning of this century. Their audience consisted primarily of children, and they did not draw exclusively on oral tradition, but often were avid readers of popular books and pamphlets. Overall, however, the style of communication in many ways resembled that which prevailed in western Germany in the eighteenth and nineteenth centuries. In any case, the *Märchen* was part of a direct and "primary" communicative context.

For precisely this reason traditional narrators grew silent when they were torn from the original context. The new environment no longer provided an audience. Though occasionally grandchildren would listen attentively, even families now evolved very different relationships. Folklore collectors generally report on the isolation of their informants and agree in emphasizing the joy of the narrator at having acquired a small new audience in the form of folklorists armed with tape recorders. Waltraut Werner describes the isolation of a Hungarian-German folktale narrator; the music and singing which had made him popular in his *Heimat* were no longer in demand and now no one would spare the time or had the interest to listen to his "little stories": "Small wonder, that it gladdened his heart when we asked to hear them." Thus bearers and students of relic traditions came together to form a new circle of communication, which expanded through the publications of newspaper articles, essays, books, and records.

As is true of almost all collecting activities within *Volkskunde*, the aim is not only to in a sense deposit those objects into archives but also to return them to the folk and thus to revive them. This aim was inspired by the commonly held desire to provide one's widely dispersed *Landsleute* (fellow countrymen) with a new spiritual center of crystallization in the form of selected, particularly valuable and specific traditions. But a glance at the primary consumer groups of native songs or narratives on records and of corresponding books confirms what Karasek had observed soon after the war: much of what had once belonged to the tradition of broad strata of the population now became the subject of an "upper-class cult of memories." In the new environment the solidarity of *Landsmannschaften* (affiliations of fellow countrymen) was only one means of orientation among many others, and its effectiveness necessarily declined.

A glance at the organized *Landsmannschaften*, which were founded soon after the war in response to the wide dispersion of people, confirms this. Not merely an accidental consequence of the confusion of the war and its aftermath, this dispersion was the result of political decisions. The occupying powers decided on an official policy of complete assimilation, the rapid and absolute integration of the immigrants within the new environment and its population. They proclaimed a universal prohibition of coalitions and aimed for as diverse a mix as possible not only in terms of origin, but also, for example, in terms of religious denomination. Nevertheless certain concentrations in regional distribution emerged, at first for geographic reasons: for Danubian Swabian immigrants southern Germany was simply nearer than northern Germany. But geography was not the only factor, for many more Danubian Swabians settled in southwest Germany than in Bavaria.

Other influences were the notion of "repatriation," the linguistic relationship, and the economics of a region that was mainly rural but nevertheless offered considerable opportunities for industrial employment.

The emergence of such regional and, above all, specific local concentrations often belonged to a second phase: after short intermediate sojourns relatives and acquaintances from the old *Heimat* began to congregate again. It was during this phase that the organizations of *Landsmannschaften* became effective—on the one hand offering semi-official assistance for problems of adjustment and economic security; on the other, acting as centers for the preservation of native cultural goods. Conceivably in a less dynamic situation these *Landsmannschaften* could have provided the organizational structure for firmly centralized subcultures, i.e., consciously restricted, relatively homogeneous groups of a specific type could have evolved. In fact this is true of at best a few smaller groups where the segregation of compatriots is merely accidental, related to the religious separation, which characterizes the group and detaches it from its environment. We could add with some irony that this also applies to the subjective opinion of a small number of functionaries who project their own values on to the groups in their charge.

Often these groups themselves soon lost influence outside their own ranks, and, even where membership has remained constant, their character has changed. This change can be seen in newspaper reports of events organized by *Landsmannschaften* since the last war. During their early years the *Landsmannschaften* acted primarily as relief organizations, and the more colorful side of their work was in the background. When they took up older customs, these were often limited to the narrow confines of their organization or to the *Landsleute* they took care of. For example, a group of younger members of a *Landsmannschaft* visited all the *Landsleute* in the immediate vicinity to perform a New Year's singing and greeting custom. Even here a shift had already taken place: they could no longer walk from house to house as the *Landsleute* lived far apart. However, it remained an internal custom.

Relatively soon, however, it became obvious that at least the younger people no longer relied entirely, if at all, on their *Landsleute*. They established other bonds at their place of employment, during leisure activities in clubs, and through accidental acquaintances at public entertainments. To some extent the *Landsmannschaften* consequently became mediators of sentimental memories for the old, who can do little more than go on directing half-resigned appeals to the younger generation. For example, at a Silesian afternoon gathering in a Westphalian town, a man born in Breslau gave his talk in dialect to please a primarily older audience. He concluded with the statement that the Silesian dialect, "even though powerful and vital," was on the "road to decline," and he demanded that children be taught at least a few Silesian verses at school.

The alternative for the *Landsmannschaften* was to open themselves up to the local population. In the late 1940s the Silesian *Landsmannschaft* organized a *Heiratsmarkt* (marriage fair) in various locations—in Ludwigsburg and Stuttgart, but also in Wedel in Schleswig-Holstein. They referred to the *Gorkauer Heiratsmarkt* (Gorkau marriage fair), which had taken place as early as the nineteenth century

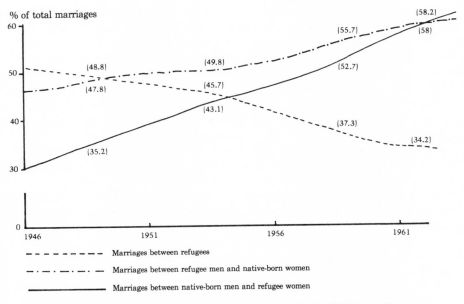

% of total marriages

- - - - - - - - Marriages between refugees

- . — . — . — . — Marriages between refugee men and native-born women

————————— Marriages between native-born men and refugee women

Marriages in the Federal Republic of Germany, 1946–1961 (excluding immigrants from the GDR)

This graph indicates the relatively steady increase in the proportion of mixed marriages, a corresponding decrease in the number of pure refugee marriages, and characteristic differences in the origins of the marriage partners: during the first fifteen years after the war there are many more marriages of immigrant men and native-born women than unions in which both partners are immigrants.

at the foot of the Zobten mountain range, a folk festival at which introductions were arranged which at first were playfully declared "marriages for a day" but frequently led to permanent relationships. Initial attempts to revive the custom after the war were confined chiefly to the Silesians. But by 1957 more than one-fourth of the participants at the great Silesian marriage fair in Stuttgart belonged to the local population. This change parallels the rapid increase in the number of "mixed marriages" revealed in statistics compiled at that time. Attempts at isolation are increasingly thwarted.

Herbert Schwedt observed that in rural communities in Württemberg this compensatory movement was accelerated by the general geographic mobility. The refugees who immigrated to these villages were accepted with fewer reservations—though clearly not without reservations—after two additional waves of immigration had reached villages in the vicinity of cities or villages of somewhat urban character. One group of new immigrants were of a higher economic class and worked in the nearby city. They acquired homes or apartments in the village because they found housing in the city too expensive or because they were seeking cleaner air and a life close to nature. In general they were *not* seeking close contact with the inhabitants of the village and participation in their social life, in contrast to most of the refugees. This led to a higher esteem for the earlier group of immigrants, the refugees, who, compared to the newly arrived occupants of the housing developments and residential estates, belonged to the village.

The same assessment of refugees resulted from the arrival of another group of residents: the foreign *Gastarbeiter* (migrant workers). For the villagers these workers now represented the exotic element from which they could distance themselves; refugees no longer had to play this role. This formulation, however, overstates the case; in critical situations the distance from the refugees that seems to have disappeared may quickly reappear, and there are even cases where *Gastarbeiter* have largely become integrated. In this respect the villages at times offer a more progressive model than do the cities, where the living conditions as well as the larger number of *Gastarbeiter* of the same nationality frequently lead to the development of ghettos. In the urban environment the presence of foreign workers continues to be seen as temporary and is embellished as a "guest" situation. It is more obvious in the villages that we are experiencing a kind of immigration not very different from the post-war immigration as far as acculturation is concerned. However, the difference between the two groups is striking at first and contributes to a further reduction of the obstacles between the native population and the refugees.

The traditions introduced by the refugees are another reason for their opening up to the native population and for a far-reaching adjustment—a rather incidental, but nevertheless very effective motive. In December 1952 a number of newspapers featured the picture of a Silesian baker holding a large cookie sheet covered with *Mohnstriezeln* (poppy seed cakes), a Silesian Christmas confection. Under headlines such as *Striezel aus Rübezahls Heimat* (*Striezel* from the home of Rübezahl, a legendary giant) we are told that the baker need not worry about a lack of customers, for his former *Landsleute* love to buy their native baked goods and that even the local population eagerly partakes of *Striezel*. Precisely because of this no further reports of this confection are published during the following years. This should not be understood in the sense of a direct causal relationship, but in a wider context: Many of the objects and traditions the refugees brought with them could be integrated smoothly into the supply of beautiful and pleasant things available to everyone, things that were advertised and increasingly consumed. Evidence of a specific regional origin may well have served as a particular stimulus for people from this region and to some extent also for other people. However, such objects entered the world of consumer goods in spite of and even because of this fact; here, too, incorporation was achieved.

This statement does not imply that peculiarities and differences which are regionally determined, e.g., in the domain of foodways, have ceased to exist. However, such peculiarities and differences are hardly tangible any more except for statistical comparisons; they are no longer exclusive and, as a rule, the specific regional origin is not noted, except for culinary specialties. During the first years after the war Danubian Swabian immigrants sporadically planted peppers. The local population noticed this by looking across the fence or into their kitchens. At least during the first phase of settlement even the familiar foodways were subjected to observation, and that means at the same time to social control. There is evidence that individual local women adopted the fruit they considered exotic and dared to use it. In "mixed" marriages this seemed natural enough; Danubian Swabians also appeared at markets and sold peppers. When immigrants from the Danubian Swabian area say today that they were the first to introduce peppers to our area, they are certainly correct; however, that is only part of the development. It would be just as correct to say that peppers would now be found in many German kitchens even without the influence of the Danubian Swabians. Today when one buys peppers in a fruit and vegetable store or in a supermarket, one is not buying a Danubian Swabian meal but is simply availing oneself of one of a wide range of products on offer to the consumer. This does not contradict the fact that certain consumer groups have a particular disposition toward peppers because of their Danubian Swabian origin or connection.

Developments similar to those we have demonstrated with foodways can be shown with other objects: something that at first is part of the regional character and at times is all but elevated to a regional symbol by the *Landsmannschaften* enters the channel of general cultural adjustment, via fashionable generalizations or via the leveling abundance of consumer goods which are more or less the same everywhere. According to a number of newspaper reports, at the Christmas celebrations of the East Prussian *Landsmannschaft*, the Christmas tree is decorated with apples and straw stars, as was customary at home. Here we are not concerned with the actual former diffusion of this emphatically plain style of decoration throughout East Prussia, but such simplicity of decoration, which disavows excessive tinsel, has become popular in other areas as well, notably among the better-educated families. And while people from the Erzgebirge particularly value their native woodcarvings at a *Lichtlabend* (evening of lights), we must observe here, too, that these candlesticks in the form of wooden angels and mountain dwellers, various crèche figures, and revolving pyramids are now universally available in craft shops and therefore belong to the general supply of Christmas trimmings in many homes. Folklorists who record this with regret and at times even with indignation forget that they were the pioneers of this development: most often they were the first collectors to decorate their homes, along with the museums, with beautiful folk art from all conceivable areas. It is hardly surprising that since then such "relics" have been manufactured in considerable quantities.

However, we must consider two objections to this thesis of adjustment. The harmless and trifling character of the items discussed hardly needs to be pointed out. This will be discussed again in a more comprehensive context in which this objection cannot be dismissed entirely. In this case, however, we can establish that the innocuous things we have mentioned function as circumstantial evidence. The observations made on these superficial matters also apply to much more important and basic phenomena. It may suffice here to concretize one of these. Various studies have emphasized the importance of Marian piety for the resettlers from the East. On the one hand this bond was viewed as being based on the relatively many places of pilgrimage in the eastern regions which were heavily influenced by the Baroque; on the other hand the perils of the flight must of necessity have reinforced the religious appeal of a protective motherly power. However, the importance of Marian piety was found in the other German regions, as well as in other European countries during the war and the postwar years. Thus the religious orientation of the refugees fuses with the general wave of Marian piety, which even led to new dogmatic commitments by the Church.

The second objection—referring to the problem of relics—is more fundamental. We have been discussing items that are widely available and therefore can easily be generalized, but are there not other traditions which can be understood much more legitimately as specific regional relics? What about costumes, which even in earlier times had the decided function of specifying local or regional identity; and what about customs, which cannot be placed in stores to be bought and thus become generalized?

In general this observation is not limited to pure "objects." One little example: a newspaper reported that at a meeting of Silesian *Landsleute* in a sizable town in northern Germany, the song *Und in dem Schneegebirge, da fliesst ein Brünnlein kalt* (A Cold Stream Flows in the Snow Mountains) was performed as a native song. This is legitimate, for the song originated in Silesia and was included in the 1842 collection of Silesian folk songs by Hoffmann and Richter. Since then it has been printed in the song books of student clubs, youth organizations, and schools, and today it is as popular as any folk song. It is sung during lessons, on excursions, and at public singing events in the cities. In this regard Silesians can point to the particular value of the song, but in the sense of exclusive ownership and, as it were, symbolic representation, it is no longer *their* song.

The decisive argument against the proposed objection, however, lies elsewhere: It can be demonstrated that even the seemingly unique, no matter how specific in detail and outward appearance, has become interchangeable in its essential substance. This must be explained in more detail.

I will choose costume and its function as an example. In many places some of the refugees were immediately recognizable by their dress, a simple costume that largely eschewed changes of fashion, or by specific attributes of such costume, e.g., a dark kerchief. Understandably this was most striking in the larger cities. This at first very foreign element to a slight extent persists even today, though it no longer attracts much attention. Here, too, adjustment has progressed. The catchword *Tracht* (costume) no longer evokes this common dress of old people, but beautiful festive costumes for special occasions: To put it bluntly, it evokes costume groups, clubs, and large displays and events where mainly girls in costumes fulfil a sort of ornamental function.

Almost all *Landsmannschaften* include such groups, and in some cases they are even differentiated by age and additional functions. They proudly display their costumes, and in the solemn speeches costumes are almost always considered as embodying the old *Heimat*. By wearing the costume one desmonstrates one's love of and loyalty to the old *Heimat*. We cannot ignore the fact that even these costume groups could not remain completely isolated; i.e., that local people often participate, and that often the costumes no longer conform to the originals but have been newly styled on the basis of certain elements of the old costume. The crucial element, however, is the demonstrative function assigned to the costume.

We can only very conditionally compare such demonstrative functions to those that formerly accompanied the wearing of costumes, i.e., primarily internal demonstrations of class, position, importance, and perhaps beauty. Now, by contrast, we are dealing with an external display function. This process is not limited to costume, it is merely particularly and immediately obvious there. Even the customs of the refugees were increasingly pervaded by this demonstrative element. It was an inevitable process because many of these customs had basically become "obsolete," for on the whole they lacked a more direct function. If we follow the internal history of the *Landsmannschaften* for the last two decades, keeping this aspect in mind, we realize that the "theatrical" element of customs was increasingly emphasized. It then took only a small step to turn theatrical custom into custom as theatre. By the mid-fifties there were many reports of festive occasions of *Landsmannschaften* which preserve "the pre-Christmas customs of the Sudeten Germans," "the old customs of the Silesian *Heimat*," or "Danubian Swabian wedding customs"; and only a closer look reveals that this "preservation of customs" had been transposed to small theatrical pieces ("An Advent Evening," "Rübezahl Pays Us a Visit," "Evchen's Wedding").

With this demonstrative function it does not matter which costume group and which specific costume we are dealing with at a particular moment. The above observations apply equally to the costume groups of the local population, with at most a difference in degree. Because the *Heimat* creed of organized *Landsmannschaften* is largely de-specified and de-concretized—hardly any of their members still retain the illusion of a return—it fuses into an "abstract sense of *Heimat*," as formulated by one of the historians of the *Landsmannschaft* movement. It is hardly a misrepresentation to say that what is expressed here is a universal, freely available conservatism which can be activated in different directions.

Thus it is only consistent that an approximation to the local population takes place not only when refugees settle down inconspicuously but also and particularly when they demonstrate a consciousness of their origin. External signs of this process are mutual *Heimat* Evenings, *Heimat* Days, and the like, where the specific traditions of individual regions at most contribute a colorful garnish, while the true focus is the sentimental creed of the *Heimat*, as expressed, for example, in many nineteenth-century songs. This creed, rather vague in itself and generally attuned to the notion of blissful memories, is almost always of a national, or at least political-conservative nature. In such events the role of the refugees is no longer fundamentally different from that of the local population; they merely engage in such activities more frequently, as far as we can determine from somewhat intensive, if not systematic, observation over a lengthy period of time.

A qualification is necessary at this point regarding the lump assessment of "the refugees." The concept has been used in a somewhat statistical sense, so that in individual cases and individual groups differentiations and deviations have to be expected. In 1956, after exactly one decade of acculturation, I attempted to establish a rough chart for the individual typology of the process of settling down. Using numerous observations and individual examples I differentiated between the characteristics *perseverance/adaptation* and *naive/sentimental*. The continued wearing of the old costumes without regard to the new environment would fall into the category of naive perseverance, while the demonstrative efficacy of the costume groups would be an example of sentimental perseverance. The various types of adaptation are neglected in the present deliberations, e.g., the relatively rare type of sentimental and therefore emphatically zealous adaptation, occasionally described as "costume converts"—those individuals who eagerly adopt the costume of their new home. The category of naive adaptation is neglected as well, even though it is certainly not unusual and thus supports to some extent the thesis of completed assimilation.

Obviously these types do not describe autonomous psychic conditions, but indicate how characteristic attitudes are socially transmitted in complex ways. The positive correlation between age and the tendency to insist on what is old should make this clear. Regional origin as well predetermines position on the typological chart. Members of *Landsmannschaften* and immigrants who have had to defend their traditions are naturally disposed toward a sentimental relationship to tradition and *Heimat*. The same is true of regions that were relatively heavily industrialized, where people therefore experienced a disruption in their relation to their traditions. By contrast, the population of the countries along the Danube, with their predominantly rural life style and their long experience of ethnic interchange, tend to have a more naive reaction to these problems, even in an urban environment. Herbert Schwedt has emphasized that the place of resettlement and its structure may also be partly responsible for the actual attitude. He uses the example of village communities: while smaller, primarily rural villages made an "assimilation" impossible from the outset, the opportunity for assimilation was much greater in villages of mixed functions, particularly in regional centers.

The types sketched above can thus occur in combinations (as is true of all typologies) and this should be assumed for most of the actual cases. Moreover, these types can change. An impetus present at first can be bent or receive a new definition. With reference to the examples quoted here, we must acknowledge that the four-part division corresponds to an early phase of assimilation rather than to current conditions. The efficacy of the costume groups shows that sentimental persistence and sentimental adaptation somehow coincide here, so that this network of coordinates no longer seems to play an important role. Nor does the concept of sentimentality continue to apply to the situation. Someone basing an investigation on the emblems, scrolls, and festive speeches of such events may want to retain that category. However, for the participants these often just represent a kind of drapery which permits their naive performance of certain leisure activities and provides a framework for the possibility of communication.

On the other hand it is not appropriate to reduce the description of such processes to the recording of this naive performance. Just as the grand words of the festive orators lend this performance a certain solemn mood, so it invests the intentions of the orator with their power. In order to indicate this shift in function of "old" traditions in a catchword, the formula *political folklorism* seems appropriate. The concept of folklorism was introduced to folkloristic discussion primarily by Hans Moser. Never strictly defined, the concept indicates not so much clearly circumscribed attributes as a certain process: the process of a folk culture experienced at second hand. The concept addresses the widespread fact that folklore—in the widest sense, not limited to oral tradition—appears in contexts to which it originally did not belong. This will be discussed later in more detail. However, the fundamental definition is immediately clarified by the image of a *Trachtentreffen* (meeting of costume wearers). Here the costume has an entirely different function from the one in earlier eras of rural, and to some extent, urban life.

The powerful economic reasons for and political implications of folklorism are easily ignored in favor of its picturesque aspects. However, when we are faced with folkloristically embellished refugee traditions, this political aspect becomes quite clear. Some striking examples are letters to the editor in the form of dialect poems with vengeful content, printed in newspapers specializing in reminiscences and *Heimat*. But the realm of political folklorism involves more than just such extreme cases; it includes that complicated relationship of performances which at first seem apolitical to concomitant political agitation. Frequently demonstrative adherence to old traditions is used to serve a general and often quite stubborn political conservatism. Here the motives for adhering to traditions can be very diverse: at one extreme, religiously based loyalty to that which is old; at the other, the simple enjoyment of colorful tradition. However, the powerful "pilgrimages of the expellees," which often feature speeches by conservative politicians as well as by ecclesiastics, and the costume festivals, with their flags and coats of arms, place the relics into aa political context. When the present is furnished with the ornaments of the old and the "original," the future often seems merely the projection of a lost past.

TOURISM AND FOLKLORISM

Traditions of refugees at first seem to be a special case. These traditions are radically torn from their original contexts and are transplanted into a new environment. What was once a more or less self-evident expression acquires a demonstrative character in the new environment, even where this is not intended. Thus we can explain the mutation which the concept folklorism alludes to. However, our description has shown that the forms and functions which consequently develop do not differ from those that can be observed among the local population. To be sure, the traditions transplanted from the East are more easily influenced by the spell of minority folklorism; but this is not an intrinsic characteristic. In any case, even local people develop a consciousness of *Heimat* which is expressed in forms of folklorism. While they have not ventured abroad, the world has come to them.

If one seeks an image that contrasts with the powerful population movement after the last war and has a high degree of perseverance, one might well turn to rural mountain villages or to remote valleys high in the mountains where the flood of refugees has not reached. To put it more generally: one would seek out relic areas, relatively sparsely populated regions that are not affected by industrialization. But by this visit the folklorist proves that mobility has advanced to these regions. Even travel for scholarly reasons in a sense is part of the mighty stream which has long been washing over these regions, too—the stream of tourism.

This situation affects the relics of the relic areas, as an anecdotal example may illustrate. In the Montafon, one of the beautiful valleys of Vorarlberg, a master carpenter showed me a piece of furniture he was about to attack with his knife. It was a new chest made in the style of old Baroque peasant furniture. A closer look at the ornamentation he was carving revealed a date. Somewhat surprised I read "1793." The answer the man gave to my question was not at all elusive, but rather an explanation given with naive self-evidence: he had made an exact copy of the chest, including the date, which had always stood in his livingroom, and tourists much preferred such furniture to modern pieces. This isolated, harmless incident hints at the peculiar interplay between tourists and local population in resort areas, at the process which has led partly to the freezing of the cultural style of whole regions and partly to rapid changes. It alludes to the relationship between tourism and folklorism.

The folklorist who is thus confronted with a "relic" in an area of tourism has a choice of interpretations: He is taken in, really believes it to be a relic, and if the fake is revealed to him, he still has the chance to refer to the antiquated type of the construction. Or, he is not taken in, but distinguishes rigorously between the genuine evidence of old folk culture and the crude imitation merely produced with the tourist in mind. He then might talk of "folklorism" and use the concept derogatorily for anything that diverges from what is truly genuine and original. However, the question remains whether he, too, after all, has not been taken in, for the function of the "genuine" chest is the same as that of the "fake" chest. Perhaps the real old chest would not have been preserved if tourists—including folklorists—had not admired such pieces of furniture on earlier visits to the village. At least the appreciation such furniture enjoys today was to a certain extent introduced to the villages from outside. It is precisely this appreciation which leads to the production of fakes which, however, are not fakes; for in this case the old is not taken to be historically correct but assumes the much more general claim of "original" and beautiful. This statement is not meant to favor any cheap sham culture or to render everything equal. But the difference between "genuine" and "fake" should be relativized. Functions adapt, from both the perspective of the foreign visitor and the perspective on him. Thus folklorism does not present a limited arrangement, a particular performance for tourists; instead folklorism belongs to the comprehensive horizon of tourism as a whole.

In addition to practical demonstrations, the relationship between tourism and folklorism can be deduced from a few steps of theoretical reflection. Tourism has a long prehistory, ranging from the knightly voyages of adventure in the Middle Ages to the obligatory gentlemanly tours of the nobility. However, its development is most closely related to industrialization. The nation that was first and most thoroughly industrialized also led in the development of tourism: not only were Englishmen the discoverers of the subsequent centers of tourism, but the first agency for organized group travel was established about a hundred years ago in England by Thomas Cook. The close relationship between the industrial world of work and leisure travel can be deduced from statistics even today. Statistics show that income level is not the only and perhaps not even the primary factor determining the frequency of vacation travel; the specific environment of theeler is extremely important. People living in cities or in predominantly industrial environments travel most frequently. However, the barriers of tradition certainly have some influence—small farmers admittedly have little time and money to spare, but it would somehow contradict the stereotype of the farmer if he were simply to leave his land for a while. In addition to such obstacles it is certainly a decisive point that a yearning for the other, the very different, tends to grow particularly within the industrial working world. In a contest, a French magazine once asked its readers what they expected of a voyage. The (female) winner wrote briefly and to the point: "le différent." The quality of difference inherent in vacation and travel is more definite (to put it more cautiously: it appears more definite to those concerned) the more one's own work is organized and determined by others.

This compensatory relationship defined even the potential vacation destinations: they had to be far removed from civilization and have a certain original quality, particulary in the beginning of tourism. High mountains and, to a somewhat lesser degree, the sea became preferred destinations only secondarily for medical reasons; primarily these areas were considered oases of untouched nature within the vast desert of industrial work and mechanized life styles.

However, even these areas were not entirely uncultivated and devoid of people. On the contrary, visitors had to rely heavily on the local population and their services. But the visitors expected that these people, too, should personify a piece of nature. They did not tolerate any break in style. Thus they determined for the natives—to use an expression that slightly caricatures, but nevertheless fits the situation—the role of the earthy, robust, vital, plain, *naturally* living human being who was as far removed from the "veneer of civility" of the cities as from the hectic rhythm of their working lives. A volume of the satirical pamphlets *Fliegende Blätter*, published more than a century ago, contains a description of a *Gasthausscene in Tirol* (A Scene at a Tyrolean Inn). The guest, unmistakably a Prussian tourist, is sitting at the table; the host, in costume, is standing near him. "Good evening, Sir!" says the host (politely), "would you like to stay here for the night?" The tourist replies colloquially: "Yes. But why don't you use *Du* [the familiar form of the second person pronoun] when you talk to me?" The host consents and continues more informally, "Want something to eat?" The tourist answers in the affirmative, and the host subsequently addresses the waitress (politely): "Stanzi, please fetch a bottle of wine for this gentleman!" The tourist, surprised: "Why do you address the girl so politely?" (i.e., using *Sie*, the polite form of the second person pronoun). The host answers, "Well, here at home we no longer call each other *Du*. We only behave as coarsely as that with gentlemen from England or northern Germany, or by special request."

No doubt this scene at the inn is constructed somewhat artificially and is therefore not entirely representative: even today many innkeepers address their Stanzis

"A Scene at a Tyrolean Inn." From *Fliegende Blätter.*

with the familiar *Du*. This artificial scene in all its plainness nevertheless indicates a few lines of development of folklorism influenced by tourism:

1. Tourists confront the local population with a standardized role expectation; they do not look for their equals, but for the powerful charm of the earthy and original.

2. Local people accept this expectation and seek to do it justice; they adopt the role demanded of them.

3. To the extent that this leads to conflict with their own norms they are playing a double role: among themselves and in the private sphere they are participating in economic and cultural progress; when dealing with tourists they are pretending to be living relics of a past era.

As far as the development of folklorism is concerned, this double role became increasingly inevitable for the simple reason that even touristic areas could not avoid the twentieth century and had to satisfy the growing external demands of the visitors. Today the double role has become so obvious that it is no longer concealed but is consciously acted out. However, it is worthwhile to consider not merely this final phase, but also the earlier development.

In 1802, Dr. Deneken from Bremen made a contribution to the *Neue Teutsche Merkur* published by Christopher Martin Wieland, entitled "Über die Sitte der Städter, den Sommer über sich in Bauerhäusser einzumiethen (On the Custom of City Dwellers of Renting Summer Accommodations in Farmhouses). This habit was then relatively new, for reports of such summer resorts increased only in the course of the eighteenth century. Moreover, only a few people could afford such vacations in the country. This applies even though accommodation was not expected to be luxurious. The article printed in the *Merkur* makes this very clear. It describes rural life in warm colors but does not exaggerate. Instead the author has a keen eye for the toil and meagerness of the farmer's existence, and points out that even the vacationer escaping from urban life must share some of this burden. He gives a few warnings, which directly contrast with the language of later tourist brochures: a country sojourn would "involve many deprivations," and all tender souls should be advised against it.

Apparently the picture of the vital and earthy peasant was painted the more glaringly the less directly the visitors came in contact with him. Only when tourism had been developed enough to ensure tourists a high degree of "individual existence" and a certain amount of comfort was there an urge to enjoy at least the spectacle of such earthy and original local people. This enjoyment combines two contrasting motivations: the first is an essentially sentimental relationship, i.e., the search for and the apparent rediscovery of lost nature; in the second this distance from nature is savored as well as deplored. The tourist deigns to lower himself from a higher level of evolution and completes his personality by submerging himself temporarily in that earlier level. Certainly these are grand and somewhat complicated words considering the rather uncomplicated and fleeting matter which a vacation in the mountains represents. But we are concerned here not so much with the tourists as with the local population; for them the attitude of the visitors became an important permanent influence.

On the occasion of his Italian voyage of 1828/1829, Heinrich Heine drew a character sketch of the Tyrolean which begins with the malicious sentence "The Tyroleans are beautiful, cheerful, honest, well-behaved, and of unfathomable obtuseness." In his behavior toward visitors

> The Tyrolean has a sort of smiling, humorous servility which has an almost ironic tinge, but which nevertheless is meant to be profoundly honest. The women of the Tyrol greet you in such an obligingly friendly manner, the men press your hand so roughly while acting in such a droll and affectionate manner that you could almost believe they were treating you like a close relative, at the very least like one of them. But far from it, they never fail to remember that they are merely simple people and that you are a distinguished gentleman who certainly enjoys it if common people "raise themselves toward him"[2] without bashfulness. And in this they show a correct natural instinct; the most rigid of aristocrats are glad to find an occasion for condescension, for it is just by such acts that they experience how highly they are placed.

The splendidly ironic coinage "to raise themselves" precisely characterizes the role which the visitors press upon the local people. Because in reality they are situated on a lower level and lead a simpler life (which meant a fuller and more self-contained life, according to views already current at that time), they are expected to encounter the visitor with a hearty *Du*. And where strangers become a permanent institution, the attitude of hearty servility becomes entrenched.

Heine's travel images take a particularly critical turn in describing the traveling Tyrolean singers, who earn money in this role and carry folklorism to other countries. At a concert in London, he

> heard those songs which are yodeled so naively and piously in the Tyrolean Alps and sound so lovely even to the northern German heart. . . . Then my entire soul was distorted in bitter indignation, the pleasant smile of genteel lips stung me like snakes and I felt as if I saw the purity of the German words most rudely abused and the sweetest mysteries of German spiritual life profaned before a foreign mob. I could not join in the applause for this shameless exploitation of what is most bashful, and a Swiss gentleman, who feeling the same left the hall with me, remarked quite correctly: 'We Swiss, too, provide much for money, our best cheese and our best blood, but we can hardly listen to the Alphorn being blown abroad, much less blow it ourselves for money.'

Heine's observation is remarkable for the information it contains on an early form of folkloristic export which had reached its first heyday in the 1820s: at that time the Rainers from the Zillertal traveled all over Europe and parts of America. This escalated rapidly until even fake Alpine singers appeared; in Leipzig, four "Tyrolean children" were discovered to be enterprising Saxons. But above all Heine's remark is important because it documents the prejudice of the otherwise so clear-sighted and acrimonious critic. We could even speak of "touristic" prejudice. Together with the like-minded Swiss he assumes the permanent bond of cultural forms to a land or a region, to the motherly native soil, and he notes without irony that human lives are more easily detached from this soil than are such cultural goods. As a romantic tourist, he believes in the authenticity of the offering when he encounters it in a living context, just as tourists today talk enthusiastically about authenticity wherever local culture is presented to them on the spot, though the question was probably justified then as well as now whether all of this really happens quite as naively and bashfully as it appears to the enraptured visitor.

Friedrich Theodor Vischer later described from a distance how he too once fell victim to a similar temptation:

> From Linz I began a walking tour to Salzburg and the Tyrol. For the first time in my life I saw high mountains, wild passes, giant battles between water and rocks, the life of the Alps and the herdsmen, peasant folk of a yet unbroken, vigorous type, free and fresh of mind, proud in posture and step, picturesque costume. I was as if electrified, elevated in each nerve, delighted by this unknown, new world of poetry.

Vischer then describes his return, how the more modern localities suddenly appeared to him artful and frivolous, and adds: "I did not consider that I myself had traveled across these green valleys between the glacier-clad mountains in the garb of the city-dweller and with the observing eye of education which has outgrown the poetry of the direct experience." After recognizing this situation, Vischer later directed many a critical statement at what was served up to the tourists. In any case, an ironic echo of the criticism of the Swiss gentleman cited by Heine occurred several decades later, when Vischer has the hero of his novel *Auch Einer* (Another One) describe his ascent of Rigi Mountain: He departed while it was still night so as not to have to "witness the fellow who in old Swiss costume blows the *Kuhreigen* [cow tune] at sunrise and then collects tips at the inn," and consequently he asks for an *Abschreckungs-Baedeker* (Baedeker to deter tourists).

A small, humorous contribution to this imaginary *Deterrent Baedeker* was provided a year later by Mark Twain. The narrator details his protracted attempt to experience the sunrise from the top of the Rigi. Twice he wakes up around noon, a third time he accidentally experiences the setting of the sun, and even though morning after morning an *Alphorn* blower blasts his way through the corridors of the hotel and subsequently collects his tips, only on the fourth day does a freezing Mark Twain manage to reach the peak in time. In the same context he describes another folkloristic experience: the "Tyrolese Warbling." During the ascent he hears yodeling. Finally a sixteen-year-old shepherd boy appears, and the hikers, full of joy and gratitude, give him a franc to keep on yodeling.

> So he jodeled and we listened. We moved on presently and he generously jodeled us out of sight. After about fifteen minutes we came across another shepherd boy who was jodeling, and gave him half a franc to keep it up. He also jodeled us out of sight. After that we found a jodeler every ten minutes. We gave the first one eight cents, the second one six cents, the third one four, the fourth one a penny, contributed nothing to Nos. 5, 6, and 7, and during the remainder of the day hired the rest of the jodelers, at a franc a piece, not to jodel any more. There is somewhat too much of this jodeling in the Alps.[3]

This caricature anticipates a future phase of development when an *Abschreckungs-Baedeker* is no longer necessary: it has been replaced by hundreds of advertising pamphlets. Although they seem varied and of different quality, they always announce the same blend of concocted original state of nature and equally concocted natural quality of the local population, of landscape and folklore.

This standardization across wide distances today appears to be an expression of commercial serial production, which also characterizes the tourist industry. Its formation involved many factors, a complicated interplay of demand and supply. Within tourism a whole list of regional and racial stereotypes has at least been fixed, if not formed. The earthy *Renommierbayer* (Bavarian Braggart) evolved not so much from Bavarian self-identity as out of a role expectation on the part of tourists visiting an undeveloped area. For the local population such self-stylization often served to cover up their economic needs and difficulties. As an example, Richard Weiss has pointed out that the urban-determined longing for nature spread to the Alpine population via their cow and herding songs as early as the first half of the nineteenth century. Through these songs "even the mountain dweller gradually became familiar with the poetic view of herding bells, Alpine glow, *Edelweiss* and *Alpenrosen* [alpine flowers], joyful shouts and the sounds of the *Alphorn* as an unrealistic, but beneficial self-glorification of his difficult existence."

For the tourist, however, the confirmation of his expectations is essential. Local people and their activities too must conform to the norm and must more or less explicitly become a "sight" to make the impression a stronger one, a clichéd experience. For the tourist, folklore mediates between the need for peace and relaxation and the need for constant activity and distraction, which is carried over from the world of work to the vacation. Advertising both *Ruhe und Brauchtum* (Tranquility and Folklore), as has been done for years in some resorts in Upper Bavaria, does not really present contradictions. Rather, folklore is here considered the legitimate, traditional amusement that basically does not interfere with the need for relaxation.

This is a rough sketch of the entire development, and it deals only with the high roads of tourism. If we include all of the territory, we encounter significant shifts of phases. Many of today's tourist areas were opened up relatively late, so that they experienced the entire development in an abbreviated and therefore modified form. In other areas the beginning phase of tourism—characterized by the semi-distant and semi-respectful relationship between tourist and local population—lasted far into the present century. For example, in some Alpine tourist localities the vacationers of this beginning phase are still remembered. They were called a different name from the one used now; i.e., people talked and still talk about the "tourists," which only later became "vacationers" (*Urlauber*). A single concrete example may show how the developmental tendencies described above are repeated on a small scale.

I have chosen a small mountain village in a side valley of the Montafon Mountains of Vorarlberg, a village which originally did not even deserve that name. It was a "seasonal settlement," a term that in this case indicates cattle farming, not tourism. In the spring the cattle were driven from the farms in the valley to the mountains, and some members of the farmers' families stayed there until winter in the high *Maisässen* (May abodes). For centuries foreigners had been passing through the village, for near the *Maisässe* a mule path led into Switzerland. From time to time people stopped there, for instance, itinerant wine merchants from Lombardy with their small pack horses. A small inn catered to those who traversed the pass, and by the end of the nineteenth century the first alpinists and summer vacationers from Germany and Switzerland arrived in this high-altitude location. A little later manufacturers began to buy farm properties. The locality was built up, and tourism began to flourish when the amusements of the new winter sports were added to those of the summer season. Gradually the loose assemblage of *Maisässe* became a real village—no longer a peasant village. however, but a tourist center full of inns and places of accommodation for visitors, with ski cabins and ski lifts, a swimming pool, and marked hiking trails.

Here, too, distinct phases of touristic development correspond to distinct phases in the evolution of folklorism. The first tourists adhered to the style of the summer visitors described as early as 1802 in the *Neuen Deutschen Merkur*. They were easily satisfied and did not expect the local population to change their rural life-style. However, they raisesd the esteem of this life-style and thus contributed to the glorification of the peasantry, which gradually turned into forms of self-glorification, modest and restrained though they were at first. To begin with the local people did not see any reason to deviate from their usual activities. At that early stage very few of them realized the opportunity which the new trade of tourism offered and expanded their *Maisässe* into permanent farmsteads with several spare rooms for rent.

This introduced the second phase of touristic and therefore also folkloristic development, characterized by the hectic buildup of all touristic establishments and—related to this—the equally hectic demolition of all traditional forms. The old log buildings were replaced by quickly built stone houses. Where once kilometers of trestle fence stood, soon only scanty remnants provided a pathetic photographic motif while barbed wire now surrounded the pastures. The cattle were no longer festively decorated when driven into the valley, but were rapidly loaded into trucks and transported away.

This development lasted until about fifteen years ago and obviously did not merely affect the external image, which displayed the symptoms of change, but also the internal conditions—the social interactions, attitudes, and opinions. According to several critical observers among the villagers, an increasing insecurity began to spread. For example, a Capuchin priest who takes care of church services reports that people no longer knew how to position themselves and how to behave at funerals, not to mention that the once customary lying in state in the home had long been abandoned in deference to the guests. This, too, is merely a symptom, but a symptom which reaches beyond the rather ornamental sphere of the examples cited above. There are hints of the insecurity of behavior which arises when not enough is available to satisfy all valid norms. The village had developed into a flourishing tourism center, but it had definitely ceased to be a village. The consequent dissatisfaction of the population was one reason for certain efforts at "renovation" that can be called "folklorism."

Obviously the tourists themselves were not entirely happy with the modernization which neutralized all distinctive features. The hectic buildup provoked a boomerang effect. Despite their need for comfort, the visitors wanted to be able to admire some of the style of the old herding and farming village. At least the summer visitors then and now want to relax in a real village, not in a touristic no-man's-land. Conservative attitudes prevailed, but there was not much left to be preserved. If the old was to be presented to visitors, it had to be created anew. The guest rooms were furnished with new peasant furniture like that made by the carpenter in the valley. Houses were built as elsewhere in a sort of generalized *Heimat* style, popularly described as "Swiss houses"—even, and in particular, outside Switzerland. These are commonly understood as gabled, white-washed stone houses, with large, broad windows, low roofs, and balconies decorated with flower boxes.

This shows that the answer to the given provocation did not have to be newly invented. It presented itself, regularized and in part prefabricated, by the fully developed tourist industry. To quote from an Austrian tourist magazine: "Whoever comes to visit us wants to see folk costumes and listen to folk songs, he envisions brass bands and *Schuhplattler* [a kind of folk dance] and his vacation would not be a real vacation if he could not see and experience some of this." It is obvious that such a premise is conducive to all conceivable forms as well as deformities of folklorism. The former cattle barn at an inn in the village of Vorarlberg was expanded into a dance hall and bar, and it is here that we regularly find the largest number of visitors. We hardly need to mention that the supply of souvenirs is as questionable as anywhere else. In souvenirs, too, the aspect of the old, the native, and the primitive is put to lucrative use, even though the observation of a market researcher applies in many cases: "Souvenirs are things made in Japan, sold in Italy, admired in Germany." Here, too, it is obvious that the return to what is regionally specific, to local production, basically does not change much. Today in East Allgäu only 20% of the cowbells are made for cows, while 80% are made for visitors, who take home these factory-fresh relics of a world that has been lost to them. Certainly if the item is marked "made in Germany" the souvenir is directly related to the location of one's vacation, but the question remains whether it can be passed off as "authentic" when contrasted with "inauthentic" imported items.

This statement is not meant to encourage indifference toward the process observed here. However, we may ask whether the categories of authentic and inauthentic are sufficient to provide a clean division. For the local conservator—and that often means: the amateur folklorists of the region—the case is obvious: old customs that have been revived are authentic even if they are transferred from one neighborhood to another. In the village on which we have been focusing our attention, at the *Funkenfeuer* (sparkling fire) custom on the Sunday after Shrove Tuesday, for a while the fire was lit by the local schoolchildren. By contrast whatever cannot be legitimated as traditional custom is considered inauthentic, particularly any kind of "display" which involves "artists" from outside the community. Thus the local mask traditions would be authentic, while the *Fasching* race on skis, with visitors often joining in, would be inauthentic. However, even the local participants do not make this kind of distinction, or they do so only after having accepted this historically oriented category of the authentic. They can hardly make such a distinction, as their active interest often includes specifically new elements. It is said that native folk dances were performed in the Samoan Islands in 1963, on the occasion of a visit by Stewart Udall, then United States Secretary of the Interior. However, immediately after he and his entourage left, the natives began to dance the Twist and the Madison. We can generalize from this example without reservation. Even if young people did not assign to all things modern a certain positive value from the outset, the modern is at least held in equal esteem with ostensibly old matters, and many organizers present it in this manner. For example, a demonstration of dog training, mountain rescue techniques, old brass music, the First of August festival, the new *Heimat* song *Du kleines Haus am Gletscherrand, leb wohl!* (Oh Little House at the Rim of the Glacier, Farewell!) from the jukebox, the costume parade, and the fashion show—all are listed by the Swiss tourism center Saas Fee, in no particular order and with equal emphasis, as available to visitors, who on their own would hardly have the potential or the inclination to distinguish between authentic and inauthentic in the sense that the conservators would.

There are signs that distinctions are dropped not only because of a lack of appropriate criteria for differentiation, but that in many ways such an attitude hits the mark. "Tyrolean evenings" regularly take place in a village of the northern Tyrol, where tourism has developed rapidly since the end of the last war. They include performances of the *Schuhplattler* by dance groups, the singing of sentimental alpine songs, and earthy *Schwänke* on stage. As the highlight a goat is pulled by its tail into the hall, and the visitors, most often from northern Germany and Holland, are offered goat's milk to drink. A teacher from this village expressed his disgust at these Tyrolean Evenings: what was being offered here was neither authentic nor native folk good; he was just in the process of getting rid of these events and introducing "village evenings" instead. I inquired if the village still had special traditions, such as old songs and dances which had been handed down and which he might present at these village evenings. The answer was no, but at a certain place in Innsbruck one could get songbooks and dance books, and with the help of such documents a real evening of customs could be put together. Certainly we do not want to attack the teacher's intention to reform the all too commercial "original" quality of the Tyrolean evenings. But does the concept "authentic" apply any more accurately to what the teacher now intends to introduce? In fact, we could ask the malicious question whether in a few years or decades the next teacher might not have to reinstitute "Tyrolean Evenings" because he realizes that the village evenings are not authentic either.

The spiral movement which emerges indicates something of the inevitability of the inauthentic; it shows that in the context of tourism, which is largely an economic phenomenon, the same system of reference remains valid for both the authentic and the inauthentic. Among an abundance of pictures in the souvenir book *Schweiz*, published by the Swiss tourist board, about 40 percent are scenic photographs, mainly of the high mountains, devoid of people and of just about anything man-made. Twenty-five percent depict old cities. About 20 percent are pictures of colorful Swiss folklore, 7 percent show images of crafts and agriculture, and 5 percent are pictures of industry and transportation. This is a rather distinctive publication and all are "authentic" presentations. For example, there is an impressive picture of the Marché Concours with captions in four languages: "Marché Concours in Saignelégier: Volksfest von urwüchsiger Kraft—Fête populaire débordant de naturel—Festa popolare die antiche origini—A full-blooded country fête." Here we get an indication of the point of transfer. The "urwüchsig, débordant de naturel, di antichi origini, full-blooded" refers only in part to the matter depicted; more importantly these words and the subject matter itself refer to providing a profile for a specific travel destination within the tourist industry. To quote a tourism advertising specialist: "Publicity becomes marketing communication for the tourist market, too. Publicity's mandate is to raise the demand for certain products and to make them better known in marketing-strategic and tactical terms. Publicity has the further mandate of establishing a profile according to given functional goals." Folklore is one of the essential means of creating such a profile.

If we acknowledge this context we come to the paradoxical conclusion that the so-called inauthentic, insincere events and forms are, in fact, more appropriate while the so-called authentic and serious ones, by contrast, are sometimes more dangerous because they are associated with an evaluation that conceals strong economic interests. It is by no means rare that the architects of the Austrian *Heimat* style, the vigilant preservers of regional folk dances and folk songs, and the revivers of old customs succumb to the self-deception that they have become detached from the bonds of commercial entanglements and social constraints, that they are voluntarily returning to the "essential," while their aims are serving a folklorism that belongs to a very specific phase of socioeconomic development. Thus we could make the provocative overstatement that the artificially antique bar in the former cattle barn is, in fact, a more honest and appropriate product: no sane person would claim that it preserves native values or symbolizes a happy rustic past, or that it is part of the timeless style of folk tradition.

There are arguments that might be used to provide a more "playful" interpretation of the folklorism of tourism, an interpretation burdened with neither too much *Heimat* soil nor too intensive a cultural anguish. This corresponds first of all to the attitude of the tourists themselves. The tourist today experiences the place and environment of his vacation less fully than was the case in former times. Even if he intends, for once, to "tune out" completely, he generally remains connected to the rest of the world via the mass media and by communication with other tourists. Therefore his experience of the vacation site and what it has to offer is less absolute and unconditional than it once was. Moreover, today's tourist is much more used to living his own life in various roles than was true of his predecessor some decades ago. He, too, is not only employee and father, but a member of various clubs, a soccer fan, a television viewer, and much more; and to that extent he no longer tends to consider folkloristic roles as absolute. Even though now as then he bundles what is offered into clichéd notions, for him these clichés have lost their unconditional and ideological character. Finally he no longer needs to have his own freedom affirmed by the local population, as the tourist's urge for freedom is essentially confirmed by and operates within his own group. The pioneer of tourism who wanted to be addressed familiarly by his host thereby tricked himself into experiencing a feeling of freedom which he had lost in the industrialized, bureaucratic, conventionalized everyday world. Today, by contrast, conventions among tourists themselves have loosened. Psychologists who observed groups of tourists coined the memorable catchword *Brennerspritze* (Brenner Injection). It is not only young people who lapse into a strange euphoria when they cross into a foreign country, and begin to address their fellow travelers familiarly and demonstrate their newly won freedom within their own group by adopting casual clothes and casual manners.

However, to stay within the framework of our anecdotal example, local people now may again address their guests politely, and their folkloristic presentations are no longer understood as existential forms but as a friendly background. For the local population, too, this freedom to engage in mere play may be an important gain. After all, folklorism as a mythically exaggerated form of life, as an ideologized attitude, not only determined the external forms of costume and custom but also constituted an internal barrier which hampered progress toward modern conditions and relationships. By contrast folklorism as mere play allows for the possibility of perceiving the occasional presentation of ancient things as a matter of costuming and of going down the road of technical progress and urbanization in spite of such demonstrations—the only way to save some of the historical substance, which would otherwise be subject to freezing and decline.

In some places the population began to identify with its locality only when the economy stabilized through tourism and led to a playful self-representation. Because vagrants settled there in the eighteenth century, a hamlet of the eastern Black Forest grew from a manorial estate into a small village. Most of the inhabitants became peddlers. During the nineteenth century they specialized in locally made brushes and brooms. In the 1930s a brush factory was established, and even before the Second World War the village had 40 brush makers. This specific vocational structure as well as the dubious origin of these people contributed to a depreciative attitude toward them in the vicinity. Stories of their eating roast dog meat were circulated, and they were given extremely ugly nicknames, as is usual in such cases. However, after the Second World War this particular village was exceedingly successful in attracting tourism, probably not least because the population engaged in a sort of "flight forward" regarding this type of business. They put up with numerous personal restrictions and identified more or less in unison with this new trend. Because peddling encountered economic difficulties, most of the inhabitants went to work in the factory. Thus tourism was introduced during a phase of general change, and just about all of the population profits from it. Noteworthy local souvenirs, which have been available for some time, are particularly beautiful handmade brushes. Though this certainly is no momentous matter, as a symptom it could indicate that the population, because of the economic consolidation and the specific constellation of the tourism development, has gained sufficient distance from its past to begin to deal with it and to overcome it in folkloristic terms. We have reason to believe that this is not the only case of its kind.

However, such a friendly background should not mislead us into overlooking the fact that even such a change is accomplished within the closed horizon. In his theory of tourism, Hans Magnus Enzensberger has pointed out that today's tourist practically cannot escape the "sight" as the "standardized basic element of the tour." Even where attempts are made to replace "sight-seeing" with "life-seeing," i.e., to open up as much as possible of the living everyday reality of the locality to the touristic encounter—even there the element "sight" is not overcome at all, rather the "life" of such an encounter is destroyed. According to the result of a comprehensive inquiry, people who flee the working world and consider their vacation a phase of "extreme leisure" and probably extreme freedom, do not escape the laws of that working world any more than those who seem to live free from it within their "natural reserves": in many respects the elements of the tour are just as much preprogrammed and prefabricated as what the resorts have to offer. This is the specifically touristic form of a universal phenomenon which will be discussed later: that programs of flight—including folkloristic programs of flight—do not contribute to an escape from the industrial society and its conditions.

FOLKLORE AS A COUNTERWORLD

One of the many tourist attractions of the Allgäu is the *Wilde-Männle-Tanz* (dance of the wild men) in Oberstdorf: Fourteen sturdy young men don tight linen costumes to which lichen from the mountain forests have been sewn. With wooden clubs and drinking goblets made of birch they appear on a stage decorated with fir boughs. They perform more than a dozen different leaping dances, some of which demand artistic abilities. For a long time the dance was held only once every five years. Such intervals are primarily due to economic reasons and make sense particularly for strenuous presentations that involve time-consuming preparations. This also explains why the more or less monumental Passion Plays— for example, in Oberammergau, in Erl in the Tyrol, or in Waal in Swabia—have not become annual events. However, regardless of the practical considerations the rhythm itself becomes part of the tradition, so that a deviation is not easily accomplished. Nevertheless—and this hardly needs explanation—a schedule of much more frequent performances has evolved in Oberstdorf under the influence of tourism.

It is the more remarkable that such shifts have colored the explanation of the origin and meaning of the dance insofar as to make them appear even more mythological than before. In 1957 one of the largest regional newspapers in southern Germany reported that this summer the *Wilden Männle* once again,

> as in all previous decades and centuries, [performed their dance,] which has been preserved as the oldest cult dance from time immemorial until today. . . . Young sons of mountain farming families from Altoberstdorf perform it generally at lengthy intervals as a privilege that has been handed down through the ages from generation to generation. It is no dance in the ordinary sense, but a dance play with a pantomime of Germanic origin, probably a last remnant of ancient liturgical choral dances performed before the Germanic heathen god Thor. The belief in the wild men was once spread over all of Germania as well as across France, England, and parts of the Slavonic countries. They formerly played an important role in Oberstdorf folk legend as little dwarflike, gnome-like beings of a rather harmless, often mischievous nature who, moving quickly, appeared suddenly and disappeared just as fast.

Similar reports could be read twenty years earlier. In 1938 *Schwabenland* (Swabian Country), a "magazine of cultural politics" printed an article on the dance which also mentioned "ancient tradition." The wild men are described "as symbols of the eternally creative forces of spring, which bestow new life after the long hibernation of frost and solidification," as "symbols of the eternal fertility of the earth as well as of men." The article emphasizes that "men of the old established families of Oberstdorf" perform the dance, men who are "tied to the land and soil where they have lived for many generations." However, the fact that the dance did not really grow so immediately from this soil and that it was cultivated for strangers even then can be deduced from a note at the end of the long article: "Performances of the *Wilde-Männle-Tanz* by the Mountain Costume and the *Heimat* Preservation societies in Oberstdorf, with the support of the National Office for Propaganda, are scheduled on the following days: June 20, July 10, July 24, August 14, and August 28." One would like to add that these are Sundays during the vacation season, when special trains and similar arrangements promised to make it most profitable.

The interpretation in this essay was substantiated by, and probably derived from, contemporary folkloristic literature. Even Adolf Spamer, who is otherwise quite skeptical when confronted with quick mythologizing, regarded the performances as belonging to the category of "cult dances as magical practice." Though he realized that the Oberstdorf dance was traditionally performed toward fall and exhibited "a number of recent showy features," he viewed it as an ancient custom: "Such club dances probably were the precursors of the old Germanic sword dances which are described in Tacitus' Germania."

Hans Moser established the questionable quality of such interpretations and in this context has referred to older scholarly literature on the custom. Interestingly enough these writings do not insist nearly as much on the antiquity and the mythical origin of the custom as do more-recent reports. Even here the notion is discussed, e.g., by Karl Weinhold, that the performance "is rooted in ancient spring customs" and that the wild men "personify the trees of the forest, which are imagined to be alive." More sober references are also made. At least the folklorist closest to the custom, Karl Reiser, the collector of the Allgäu, definitely rejected any notions that the dance was a "continuation of ancient liturgical choral dances in honor of the god Thor" or that the wild men were "a copy of the earliest inhabitants of the country, who were increasingly pushed into the mountain valleys by the immigrating Germanic tribes." He adhered to the actual picture and spoke of a "dance play consisting of gymnastics and pantomime," which he thought derived most likely from a "*Fastnacht* [carnival] entertainment." He relied exclusively on archives dating no earlier than the year 1811.

At that time, Clemens Wenzeslaus, the Elector of Trier, and his sister visited Oberstdorf. Wenzeslaus had been the sovereign of the Augsburg diocese, to which Oberstdorf belonged until 1803, when the latter became part of Bavaria. We may assume that for the people the ecclesiastical dignitary personified a gilded past and that he was honored with a special reception. At that occasion the people of Oberstdorf performed their dances as wild men and presented the sovereign with a "joyful song," which reads in part:

Sey's uns erlaubt! Erlauchteste
Vor Euch aufzuspielen!

O Möchtet doch Ihr Edelste
Ein Vergnügen fühlen!

(Grant us permission! Most illustrious,
To play before you!
O that you, most noble one,
Might take pleasure in this!)

Evidently the most noble audience took pleasure in it, for later the Elector called
the dancers to his nearby summer residence for another performance, presumably
for a more substantial noble audience. In subsequent years the people of Oberstdorf undertook regular "artistic excursions" to perform in Lindau, in Constance,
and in Switzerland.

To be sure, the performance of the dance underwent manifold changes then and
in the following years and decades. Karl Reiser attributed this to the specific
form of transmission: because no records were known, one had to rely on the
memory of older dancers. However, another reason should be considered. Quite
obviously people were not shy about adjusting the performance to changing circumstances, the prevailing taste, and the audience. The fixing of such a tradition
at a previously attained allegedly ancient stage is generally a very late phenomenon. As long as traditions are truly alive, they keep on changing. This is most
obvious in the texts of the songs performed, some of which are rendered topical
in all but grotesque fashion. For example, around the time of the founding of the
nation the performance of a lengthy song included the following text:

Dem tapferen deutschen Heere singt
Der wilde Mann sein Lied,
Und für den deutschen Kaiser springt
Der Faun sich gerne müd.
Hoch über Klüften und Gestein
Singt er mit frohem Mut,
Und für den freien deutschen Rhein
Gibt Leben er und Blut.

(To the brave German army
The wild man sings his song,
And for the German Emperor
The faun gladly springs until tired.
High above chasms and rocks
He sings with joyful spirit
And for the free German Rhine
He gives his life and blood.)

The evidence of such shifts could almost support the thesis of continuity, and
arguments frequently followed those lines. Accordingly even the earliest record of
1811 would document a degenerated late phase of the custom which originally
belonged to a much more serious context. The notion that wild men had been

invented in Oberstdorf in 1811 would be quite absurd. Not only are they part of older legend traditions but also the appearance of wild men had been noted long before the nineteenth century. In festive parades of the Baroque era masks of wild men—and at times wild women—were favorites. These parades are related to the tradition of the Trionfi and the tournament processions of the Renaissance, which at festive occasions included representations of the gods of antiquity, allegorical figures, significant occupational groups, and even animals. During this time wild men participated in the parades in the large cities which were mainly influenced by patricians, such as the *Schembartlauf* of Nuremberg. The tradition goes back even farther: the woven tapestries of the High Middle Ages frequently use the motif of the wild man, and special circumstances led to the recording of a late medieval courtly celebration where a wild men's dance was the central feature: Early in 1392 the wedding of a young knight to a maid of honor was celebrated at the French court. King Charles VI and five noble guests danced the wild men's dance, "la danse des sauvages," in linen costumes to which hair had been glued. One of the costumes was ignited by a torch; only the king and one other dancer could save themselves. The other four became victims of the "Bal des ardents," as the celebration was later called. According to Froissart's chronicle, the king later made a pilgrimage to Notre Dame and donated a mass to the victims, not least to placate the agitation which had grown among the population.

Documents of representations of wild people are so numerous that they could fill a substantial volume, but the meaning attributed to such figures is not uniform at all. With some justification Hans Ulrich Roller calls the wild man the "chameleon of the Middle Ages" in his investigation of the Nuremberg *Schembartlaufen*. However, at least in a negative respect the meaning can be considered consistent: "wild" is what exists outside prevailing norms, outside convention, no matter if this represents the idyll of the simple life, alluded to in Hans Sachs' verses of the "wood people," or the uncanny, as personified in the wild men of some Middle High German poetry. In any case, the wild man is the opposite of convention, an "escapist" figure, and this applies to the entire long sequence of evidence.

This seems to provide a powerful example of the continuity that was so vigorously disputed. On the other hand, important qualifications must be made: The chain of transmission does not lead to the realm of cult, but to a more or less theatrical role play. Wild people do not originate in cultural expressions of the "folk" but in predominantly playful customs of the upper social class. And, particularly with reference to the actors, a characteristic shift occurs over time to which the concept continuity does not do justice.

Although it is dangerous to base such observations on a single example, in this case we can deduce a typological sequence which is verifiable by additional examples. In the first phase, the "folk" and its tradition do not yet offer the upper classes a pretext for the playful escape from convention. Certainly the figure of the wild man does not resist the label "folk belief," and it can hardly be doubted that notions of forest spirits and the like were widespread. The courtly counter-dances do not essentially conjure up folklore, but a plausible counterworld of a different kind—figures of their own mythology, if we interpret this word some-

Wild Man as Shield Bearer

what loosely. No folk actors are mentioned; the courtly society remains largely separate. This increasingly changes in the processions of the Renaissance and Baroque eras, which are much more open to the public and require the folk at least as an audience. According to Friedrich Sieber, "The art of performance, not the art of disguise, is the aim of this type of theatricality." He further shows that larger groups of the population were included in the representative plays. Troupes of cheerful peasants in colorful costume and diligent craftsmen in simple working dress now appear in the processions. They mediate between the courtly demonstration and the audience, which itself is an integral component of the festive essence. Richard Alewyn has even gone so far as to state that basically only the folk, which was amazed by the display of magnificence, profited from the festivities; for the upper classes such demonstrations merely meant a rigorous and exacting role play. This is a coquettish reversal of the usual formulas of exploitation—correct insofar as it focuses on the collaboration of all strata and all classes, but also one-sided, as there can be no doubt about either the additional burden to which the working population is subjected here, or the fact of a role play simply imposed from above, which relates entirely to the center of courtly society. Even more so than in the processions, this is obvious in the courtly "inns" and "peasant weddings," where the nobility celebrated in the style, and sometimes even in the costume, of the rural population, which again called for the participation of numerous extras from the surrounding peasant communities.

Role expectation was gradually accepted with fewer and fewer reservations in the third phase, which can be observed (though not in pure form) in Oberstdorf in the beginning of the nineteenth century. Peasants and workers (often miners) took part in the Baroque processions along with the wild people and the "folk"; on the one hand the "folk" and the mythical group functioned as a component of a great world theatre, which also included biblical figures and antique gods; and on the other, they provided this world theatre with a distinct counterpart to the court. Later on the "folk" so to speak adopted the entire role play; it celebrated its own earthy originality, and playful mythicizing is one of the means to achieve this: the wild men were now represented by young fellows. At first the orientation toward the nobility persisted; the dance was not simply performed but was performed for the former sovereign. This changed eventually; however, the next documented performances were characteristically arranged in cities, where some interested parties among the bourgeois public could be expected. The final phase set in only gradually; it is a phase where the social distance, at least at first glance, no longer seems to influence the intentions underlying the performance and seems to be replaced by a spatial distance: the dance is no longer performed for noblemen but for visitors from other regions.

Folklore as a counterworld: this formula summarizes a whole series of motivations. First of all it implies a search for nature from the distance of conventionalized etiquette. The counterimage, to cite a book title by Giuseppe Cocchiara, is called *L'eterno selvaggio*, The Eternal Savage and The Eternal Wild. Insofar as this contrasting image is embodied in a lower social class, the justification of sovereign power also plays a role; the thought that those below in their natural existence really lead a much better life serves as an excuse for the often far-reaching power over the other social classes. But this association is realized in only the rarest of cases. The experience of social distance is not only used to focus self-confidently on comical aspects of the simple folk—the peasant as a *Schwank* figure—but also to register sentimental melancholy—the cheerful peasant as an enviable being. This sentimental attitude, however, does not remain limited to the upper class; it enters the consciousness of the other classes as well. The notion of "folk culture as a counter world" becomes popularized.

This development can be traced without difficulty in very diverse areas. We first encounter many of today's *Fasnacht* masks in the context of masked processions at the courts. The large cities in turn developed colorful activities, which are still typical of the *Karneval* (carnival) along the Rhine in the nineteenth century. By contrast some of the masks were adopted only very recently in the villages, often to replace much simpler forms, e.g., blackening and masks made from soot. Such mask traditions are "cultivated" by organizations, guilds, and clubs, in an active mutual program of visits and celebrations, which at first glance are no longer influenced by other social strata.

Even beautiful folk costumes—this term typically refers to colorful festive costumes rather than to traditional working dress—often developed and thrived best in the vicinity of great courts and important urban centers; for a long time they, too, functioned as a counterworld. While the early books on costumes of the

Schweizer-Trachten

aller Kantone für Damen und Herren halten wir in reichhaltiger und grosser Auswahl am Lager. Diese Trachten eignen sich für jeden Anlass, wie Umzügen, Ball- und Festanlässe, Bazars, Tombolas, Aufführungen etc.
Wir liefern diese Costumes immer in kompletter Ausstattung und sind dieselben nach Originalen ausgeführt. Jede Kantonstracht, gleichviel ob Dame oder Herr, ist in verschiedenen Qualitäten und Ausführungen am Lager, sodass also Miet-Costumes zu jedem Preise und sich jedem Zwecke anpassend prompt geliefert werden können.
Die einzelnen Trachtenbilder ersehen Sie auf dem Umschlage. Detaillierte Offerten und Kostenvoranschläge gerne zu Diensten.

Costume Rentals for Festive Processions

Renaissance era pictured mainly foreign, exotic garments, from the end of the eighteenth century on the exotic aspect of native costumes was increasingly discovered. Costumes were presented to the rich and educated public in colored engravings, and later photographers, too, paid attention to costumes. Sunday after Sunday a Betzingen farmer dragged young people in costume to Tübingen, where Paul Sinner had arranged folksy scenes in his studio, using peasant furniture and spinning wheels. His hand-colored photos were sold not only in the vicinity, but as far away as America. The daughter of this pioneer photographer relates that at first the farmers reacted "with suspicion" and swore when they recognized themselves in the showcase. However, this "lack of understanding" would gradually be overcome, she thought. In fact, the consciousness of social distance, to some extent expressed in clothing, was replaced by a sense of representation. The role expectation of the upper classes was accepted, and the role was adopted. Increasingly costume was viewed as an external sign of love of *Heimat*, of a patriotic and even religious disposition; and where the old costumes had disappeared, new costumes were created. This paved the way for costume societies.

In another example, in 1806 Adam Müller mocked the increasingly popular notion that certain "nature poets" achieved artistic perfection out of pure naivité:

From time to time such creatures, considered rare phenomena in these regions, appear and let themselves be seen and gazed at like wild animals or people with fish scales. It really amazes me that the human sense of economic speculation has not yet thought of substituting the many remaining traveling shows of dancing bears with the more popular nature poets, for it seems much easier to make a peasant boy produce a sort of rhyme and song via the frequent blathering of Wieland's poetry than to make a bear dance.

What Müller suggested ironically soon became reality. By the second quarter of the nineteenth century "nature singers" were travelling throughout the country, and the educated public, which longed for things unaffected by education, applauded. Where the audience was accustomed to judging by artistic standards and did not ask for a natural counterworld, the traveling singers failed. Moritz Willkomm notes in his travel memoirs that "two nature singers from Steiermark," who enjoyed much applause in Paris and at the royal court in Madrid, earned nothing but sneers and ridicule from the audience in Granada. However, this was a kind of exception no longer found in Germany, where meanwhile the realm of song, too, was affected by a mass movement of relic preservation. From their beginnings choral societies felt close ties to folk song. The fact that folklorists ignored this movement and looked for "real" relics in ever more distant regions is another story.

The formula "Folklore as a counterworld" also characterizes many of the encounters of the arts with popular traditions. At least the formula achieves this more easily than the long-held assumption of a direct and unbreakable bond between *Dichtung und Volkstum* (poetry and folk tradition, the title of a former literary journal), of folk song as the seedbed of all great music and of the revival of the plastic arts out of the spirit of folk art. The formula "Folklore as a counterworld" is more pregnant than precise; the relationship does not shift merely in nuances, but repeatedly undergoes fundamental changes. Anyone who attempts to sketch the development in a simple scheme runs the risk of failing to recognize essential conditions; above all a more detailed investigation of art and folklore should never lose sight of the fact that aesthetic prior judgments on the relationship of art to reality also influence their relationship to popular traditions.

Despite uncertainties and provisional qualifications, we can establish a sequence comparable to the developments described above. A first phase represents a conscious playful identification from a relatively large distance; here we might mention pastoral plays, which capture in formulaic-idealistic fashion an alleged rural reality, including folklore and alleged folklore. In a second phase people believe that they have really discovered folk poetry, folk tradition, etc., and aspire to a more existential form of encounter, frequently all but a fusion of the arts and folk traditions. However, this impulse rapidly reaches limits and weakens; what remains is a distanced presentation of a decorative sham reality. In painting this is expressed in the many embellished rural genre scenes, in poetry most vividly in stories of village life. Even more typical are operettas, where colorfully folkloristic elements assume a position similar to that of exotic scenes.

If we attempt to pursue the sequence of particularly poignant phenomena into modern times we could add: pastoral play—operetta—*Heimatfilm* (a film glori-

Genre Painting of a Christmas Scene

fying one's native area). In the last the sham reality has turned into a real sham. At least in the beginning the great spectacular operettas were tailored mainly to a bourgeois public, which enjoyed the picturesque folk world; but obviously such fixed limits can no longer be easily drawn for the *Heimatfilm*: here the "folk" seems to find delectation in its own image, and if this does not correspond entirely to the clichés of the screen, it more or less directly emulates those clichés. Films of life in the mountains, such as those produced by Luis Trenker, with their overwrought, mendacious ideals, not so much *de*scribed alpine customs as *pre*-scribed them. There are examples showing that such films have added to the mendaciously authentic behavior of the mountain dweller acquired by the population.

But this line of development hardly touches on the more important artistic achievements at the meeting place of art and folklore. Signs of a much more fundamental concern are evident particularly in our century—specifically in reaction to the superficial folklore of operettas. Béla Bartók collects Hungarian folk tunes; as with Smetana, Janáček, Kodály, and others, his artistic activities serve a social and national duty and his compositional sketches are inspired by elements of folk music. Around the time of the First World War, the artists of the *Blauer Reiter* were inspired by Upper Bavarian *Hinterglasmalerei* (*verre églo-misé*, a type of painting on glass); in 1922, Max Picard published *Expressionis-*

tisches Bauernmalerei (Expressionist Peasant Painting), in which he interprets religious *Hinterglasmalerei* as evidence of Expressionism, and this alleged peasant art provides the Expressionists with impulses for the technique, composition, and even the contents of their work. In this connection, among a wealth of other instances, there is Bertolt Brecht's concern with folk drama, which should not be understood as mere concern with existing folklore but which is also influenced by elements of folk theatre.

The quality that unites these very diverse approaches, and at the same time distinguishes them from the shallower forms of artistic folklorism, is the radicalism of their concern. These artists did not stick to the "cultivated" forms of folklore, which by the nineteenth century had become the harmless object of bourgeois entertainment. Instead they sought elementary forms of presentation, which still existed aside from established cultural activities. They did not use such elements as pleasant pieces of decoration, but integrated them into their own creative concept. They did not refer to these elements because they saw in them the comfortable quality of the antiquated that had ceased to be problematic, but on the contrary because they recognized in them provocation and potential for "alienation."

In Brechtian style we could say that Brecht's concern with folklore is to a large extent part of his efforts to fight against the "culinary" theatre, against an art which allows the audience to be carried and propelled contentedly by the fable of the moment. Again, the anticulinary fight can never be reduced merely to this aspect, as it was too difficult and too protracted, and in some respects hopeless. However, this does not change the fact that folklore became integrated into works of art not only as the counterworld of a harmless and pleasant past but also as an expression of provocation. The developmental sequence of the function of folklore as a counterworld, which we have indicated and verified by several examples, is questioned because of this fact, which points beyond the realm of art; at the very least it should be supplemented.

The development outlined above could be understood as a sequence of Romantic movements, where each case begins with a specific social stratum seeking an orientation toward certain other, lower ranks. Though done playfully, it assumes the clearly biased attitude that the lower ranks personify a more "natural" state. The concept "Romantic" is here divorced from its purely epochal meaning with good reason. Norbert Elias investigated the *Soziogenese der aristokratischen Romantik im Zuge der Verhofung* (The Sociogenesis of Aristocratic Romanticism in the Process of the Spreading of the Courts) and showed how "a sentiment of longing for the countryside" evolved from the "gap between the comparatively high degree of complication and differentiation of life at the court and the relatively uncomplicated life in rural groups." This sentiment of longing was expressed in all sorts of playful, cultural forms. In fact, even here or at the latest at the Baroque courts we encounter the same attitude which later was turned into more of a principle by Rousseau. However, the bourgeois Romantic movement, too, searched for a social image to counter its feelings of alienation and focused on the "folk," i.e., the rural folk, the focus of almost all such retrospective attitudes. When applied exclusively to the peasantry, this last step seems fairly well characterized: the glorification by others becomes *self*-glorification, the role play first imposed from outside is adopted.

However, this limitation to the peasantry distorts the genetic lineage. It ignores the fact that the structure of the population has changed decisively, and not only very recently. Agricultural historians date a phase of equilibrium between agricultural and industrial production at about the mid-nineteenth century. But this was a short phase, and the notion of equilibrium conceals the dynamics of the social processes which resulted in the industrial society. Had the folklorists' concept of "folk" indicated a demographically established condition, it would have had to consider the worker too for at least a century. Instead "folk culture" remained a system of rural relics which was stylized as the permanent and essential foundation of all culture. This is true not only of *Volkskunde*, but also represents the prevailing bourgeois view of culture.

The concept folklore, if loaded with current associations, fails when we refer to "proletarian" culture, which is still relatively unknown. Workingmen's culture has certainly become "domesticated" for the most part too; in many respects it has been adapted to the values and norms of older cultures to such an extent as to excuse the equation of the two to a certain degree. In this cultural sphere, too, we find many motifs of escape: the "small piece of happiness," e.g., *Schrebergärten* (small garden plots) and *Gartenzwerge* (garden gnomes), pious verses on wall plaques, and *Vereinsmeierei* (club fanaticism). However, a concept such as "workers' romanticism" is typically unconvincing; workers' romanticism is peasant romanticism adopted from the bourgeoisie. The essential domain of workers' folklore—if this term is used in a somewhat neutralizing manner—represents a counterworld in a different, more aggressive sense. Folk song scholarship has meanwhile established not only that the entire sphere of the workers' song has been ignored for decades, but that all critical deviations from the more or less idyllic folk song were consciously eliminated by collectors and publishers. However, such deviations did exist—verses were reshaped to express need and distress aggressively rather than to soothe feelings about troubles, and songs expressed a bellicose spirit of both a national and a social character.

But the tradition of "Folksongs of a Democratic Character" reaches beyond the emergence of the industrial working class; it certainly includes "peasant" songs. Here it becomes clear that the current notion of "folk culture" was not merely attached to a historically outdated level of development but largely included the earlier levels as well. The culinary quality, to refer to the key concept of Brecht's dramatic technique, did not stem from the reality of an intact folk world but was a distortion of perspective—the result of a tacit prior decision which considered the "folk" and its cultural expressions as a pleasant backdrop rather than as an active force and as a social problem.

The function of folklore in our time is characterized by the fact that this backdrop can no longer be located exactly within the social structure. The statement that workers enjoy "rural" folklore as much as does the rural population is to some extent correct. The distinction between the two groups is not fundamental—a distant role play in one case and a consistent self-representation in the other. Rather, folklore represents a counterworld in the sense of a relation of avoidance and escape for these two population groups, as indeed for all population groups. To put it differently: as forcefully as one may insist on the original and authentic quality of some parts of folklore, they do not escape the destiny of folklorism. The concept of folklorism does not indicate a closed area, with its own laws dating back to the preindustrial era; instead folklorism is a component of the culture industry.

FOLKLORISM AND THE CULTURE INDUSTRY

Jeremias Gotthelf set many of his peasant narratives in the Emmental Valley, not only because he knew the area well but also because he recognized in its affluent and independent farmsteads a safe prerequisite for the continuity of peasant customs, which he considered basically timeless. Bernhard Luginbühl, a Swiss sculptor, has recently made the same valley the subject of an aggressive color film, full of provocative happenings, which mercilessly describes the contemporary life of the Emmental farmers. He told journalists:

> The Emmental farmers are not as great liars as we are. They no longer give their animals names. They talk about product. They produce meat. On Sundays they listen to *Ländler* [slow country waltzes] because they need to recuperate from what they do. They view the land as a building site for apartment complexes that pay rent. Only those who later take the product from the freezer in the form of a veal cutlet still believe in the idyll.

These remarks, like the film itself, generated some indignation in Switzerland. They make it clear that agricultural work has become entirely subject to the laws of the market. Quite rightly the remarks insist that the farmers have consequently divested themselves of false ideological inferences and have identified with their actual economic situation. However, these remarks possibly announce a kind of contrasting rural myth, according to which the farmer is the one who most clearly perceives economic pressures and confronts them most soberly. Only the allusion to the *Ländler* on Sundays contains a note of reservation. This allusion fits the lineage of what we have described as folklorism, and it could be extended to the overall diagnosis without any difficulty. For example, the farmers give their animals sentimental names, but in practice these animals are products. The farmers talk of green zones, of nature, and of rural vacation areas; that raises real estate values. They listen to *Ländler* and appeal to ancient tradition; but this tradition now is nothing but movable scenery.

Though such an extension has not been tested empirically in the Emmental Valley, it is verifiable as a more general statement. In any case, such a correction prevents the misunderstanding that folklorism is restricted to those who have lost the authentic folk culture because of external circumstances, i.e., by reason of living in the city, while elsewhere folk culture cheerfully continues to exist. Certainly there is a connection between the degree of "alienation from nature" and the degree of "sentimentality about nature" and all its cultural forms: a person who wants to listen to folk songs is more likely to find them at a public event in the city than in a village inn. But a certain "cultivation of song" exists even in the village inn with singing circles and clubs. Generally neither the urban-rural model nor the rather difficult definition of social classes suffices to assign folklorism its place. The ubiquity and the general diffusion of folklorism correspond to the totality of society.

The statement that folklorism is part of the culture industry demands further explanation. Adorno and Horkheimer introduced the concept "culture industry" in 1947. It replaced the term "mass culture," which they had used originally, to make it clear that we are not dealing with "something like culture rising spontaneously from the masses themselves, the contemporary form of folk art." According to Adorno, the planned production of merchandise tailored for mass consumption exists in extreme contrast to folk art. The culture industry makes use of technological means to keep the masses down, and therefore to "integrate" them socially in a monumental process of stupefaction. This technical aspect only applies to some of the phenomena usually characterized as folklorism. Writing about the *Heimatfilm*, Adorno says, "No *Heimat* survives its treatment in the films which celebrate them and all the unique features on which they depend to the point of mistaking one for another." If we understand folklorism in a wider sense and begin with the thesis advocated here that folklore today cannot appear except in the mutative form of folklorism, then this fact cannot refer to the external form of production and sales. Folklorism exemplifies the fact that not only are economic structures tied immediately to the area of production and marketing but also that their social and thereby implicitly cultural consequences reach beyond them. Folklorism is a contrary phenomenon. On the one hand, it is a "secondary, administered folk world," as Wolfgang Brückner characterized it; on the other hand and simultaneously it is effective precisely because it has the semblance of the nonadministered, the original, the spontaneous, the naturally evolved. Adorno explained this using the example of the musical element in the Youth Movement. It was a rather elitist movement in folklorism to begin with, but its views and goals became quite popular: "The more the administered world spreads, the more it prefers events which offer the consolation that things are really not quite so bad. The yearning for that which has remained undamaged by the process of socialization is mistaken for the very existence of the same and even for some supra-aesthetic essence."

Generally this observation is not disputed. However, for *Volkskunde* it often acquires a different nuance. Should we replace "the more it prefers" with "the more it needs"? This question has several dimensions. It aims at a kind of statistical "necessity," but at the same time it suggests that there is also something positive in the fact that people withdraw into a world which is determined by others and which runs counter to their entirely organized, technological existence.

The statistical argument does not refer exclusively to folklorism, but to the culture industry as a whole. The apparently progressive social technologists and managers of the culture industry insist that it must be attuned to given needs, that the supply is determined by the demand, and that what is wanted on such a massive scale must obviously be important, if not vital. Clearly a purely elitist notion of culture, which fails to consider these needs in its discussion, reveals a relatively cynical attitude. However, blind submission to the needs which are constantly reproduced by the apparatus of the culture industry is no less cynical. Adorno has always defended the attention paid to the position of the culture produced against such a superficial "functional" view: "The importance of the culture industry for the spiritual household of the masses does not exempt us from reflection on the objective legitimation, the *An sich* [per se] of the culture industry. Least of all does it exempt therefrom a science which considers itself pragmatic."

This *An sich* does not mean the fictitious realm of timeless cultural values. It refers to an orientation toward social potential rather than banal reality, towards objective human opportunities which result from the position of the forces of production. In a certain sense the other question, regarding the necessity of folklorism, belongs in this context: Are there not attempts at humanizing, at a new self-determination and spontaneity, contained in the retreat to forms of former folk culture, which are often preindustrial in origin and structure? This question should not simply be ignored. It definitely renders an essential motif of folklorism tangible—the need to escape from a world that has become extremely unintelligible and unwieldy into a realm that is intelligible, manageable, and familiar. But here, too, appearances are deceptive when it comes to the fulfilment of such needs. What appears as an enclave of the authentic (relative to objects this again means as a relic) is in reality most often contrived, organized, prepared, and at the very least "cultivated."

Moreover such enclaves are generally extremely harmless areas; they do not exert any further beneficial influence on society. It is no accident that much of folklore (in the widest sense—from the collecting of old furniture to the techniques of women's crafts, such as patchwork) is integrated into the realm of the hobby. Folklore itself has become a hobby; it belongs to the realm of leisure activities, which seem to provide a contrast to work but remain related to it, as leisure merely provides an inconsequential framework for the intervals between work periods.

But where folklore surpasses the mere hobby, where it is concerned with values, it almost always assumes the character of regression. Only those who believe in an unchanging substance and in unchanging social structures can possibly hope for salvation from that result. In fact, the values thus retained (often those we discussed earlier in our critique of fundamental concepts) do not offer any answer to today's truly pressing problems; they are mere images of escape, which are continually reproduced. In this matter the realm of folklorism differs only in degree from events in which the culture industry is directly revealed: patriarchal community structures determine not only the dramas about *Heimkehrer* (returned soldiers or prisoners of war) and of poachers and village *Schwänke* in amateur theatrical performances, but also the majority of German soap operas and family series shown on television.

The relationship between folklore as a neutral hobby and folklore as a mediating agent of antiquated values can be defined more closely. When compared to the whole of the current culture, folklore is reduced to a peripheral role area. However, peripheral roles achieve higher esteem precisely because they are interpreted as substantial *Sein* (existence) or at least as existentially important roles. The "professional folk types" mentioned by Hans Moser—folklore pros who hardly ever take off their costumes or abandon their calculated folksy behavior—do not unconditionally confirm this connection: in part this is nothing but a lucrative professional role for them, as is obvious in tourist areas. But some of these permanent representatives of folklorism are also part of the group of officials and ideologists whose goal is raising the esteem of folklorism.

In 1965 the Fachgruppe Brauchtumspflege (Expert Group on the Conservation of Customs) of the German Heimatbund (*Heimat* League) passed a resolution which reads in part: "Customs express what animates and moves man and human communities in their innermost spheres." Obviously in this case something that has become peripheral and relatively meaningless is attached to a postulated central meaning; the loss of function—loss of immediate, precise functions—of a custom is compensated by a vague postulate of inner meaning. Clearly this attitude, which is held by important conservators—and we should not merely think of "groups of experts" but of an army of well-meaning teachers, ecclesiasts, and other dignitaries—has had repercussions on the reality of customs. *Brauch* (customs) became *Brauchtum* (tradition); the outward appearance of customs was increasingly detached from the playful element often present at first. What no longer possessed an immediately obvious social function at least had to be endowed with a deep meaning.

This development, anticipated in certain procedures of the "historicizing" of customs, began intensively in the nineteenth century. Typical of this development is the *Trachtenbewegung* (costume movement). The significance of costumes had decreased because the flat country was made accessible to industrial products, the waves of fashion accelerated, and attitudes toward hygiene and working conditions changed. However, Heinrich Hansjakob, a cleric and writer from the Black Forest, was representative of many others when he observed that the costume became the guarantor of religion, the sign of love for one's *Heimat*, of loyalty to the family, and of patriotism. It was this process of ideologizing, and not a natural, rural conservatism, that made sure that costumes were preserved and at the same time stylized to become festively solemn, even though they were more colorful than the old forms of peasant dress. The increasing colorfulness is related to the new, indirect commercial function of costume, for which the way was paved by the process of ideologizing. The catalogue of a provincial exhibition on travel and tourism in Stuttgart in 1912 includes an essay on Swabian folk costumes, "one of the last and most peculiar phenomena of the class consciousness of the peasants of the past." According to the author, probably the Swabian costume was "little known only because these regions have not yet become the hiking destination of travelers to the same extent as other German regions." The contradiction between these assertions is only an apparent one. In fact this historically influenced upward revaluation supported today's economic function of publicity.

The influence of such an "endowment with meaning" becomes obvious in the paradoxical development of the carnival. Once and again critics of carnival customs record the grim, serious way of celebrating customs, and they often interpret it as a sign of degeneration related to the overwhelming entertainment offered by television and other mass media. In fact this phenomenon is much older and is, to a certain extent, the result of a *Rücklauf* (process of flowing back): of the adoption of scholarly and semi-scholarly interpretations by the actors themselves. Friedrich Hebbel noticed in 1859 that "our New Year's Eve, with its obligatory lead smelting and assorted hocus-pocus, which no one believes in any more, is nothing but an exercise in memory, a short recapitulation of German mythology; and our carnival walks on stilts and should not feel insulted if it is called an Ash Wednesday in disguise." Representatives of particularly active *Fastnacht* regions may object to this statement and criticize the unduly serious author from northern Germany. But in this instance the tribal arguments do not hold water, for a fair number of newspaper articles from those very regions voice the same opinion, if more moderately. Nowadays the jesters' all but sacred, serious view of customs has become altogether excessive. The slogan of the "clean carnival" evokes a condescending smile only among outsiders; concerned organized participants revere it like the motto of a banner. More or less revealing forms of dress, popular because of today's liberated fashion, are still strictly taboo in carnival clubs. Carnival events often degenerate into all but military ritual, characteristically labelled "letting off steam." It is precisely this refinement which encourages commercial use, e.g., by radio and television programs.

The dialectic of authentic and inauthentic already taken up in the section on tourism fits this context as well. Not merely characteristic of a small shabby, sham part of folk culture, the dialectic renders the whole area problematic, and therefore also the concept of folk culture itself. In an 1872 lecture on "A Historian's Alpine Excursion," Wilhelm Heinrich Riehl mentions the contact between mountain farmers and their urban neighbors. He attempts to comprehend "the artistic image of these entangled opposites" within the *Passion Play of Oberammergau*:

> Only a very few notice that this passion play fascinates them most irresistibly precisely because of its contradictions. It is performed by farmers, a proportion of whom are *not yet* farmers and a larger proportion of whom are *no longer* farmers, by artists, who are particularly attractive because we cannot really call them artists . . . half nature, half art; half rural, half capital city; born in solitude, preserved in solitude, and placed on the large stage of an Alpine valley in front of a Sunday audience made up of all nations: in short, all one could possibly desire, but no longer anything original, harmonious, and whole. And exactly this murky blend—let us be honest!—provides the greatest charm for a satiated worldwide public. . . .

Once again Riehl proved to be a keen observer. He noticed that the cooperation between the "folk" and the educated elite has its stylistic consequences. To broaden the meaning, one could say that the forms of folklorism gravitate toward a middle position between actual originality and distant sentimental yearning. Riehl further recognized that from that distance the illusion of an authentic quality cannot easily be grasped. The greater the distance, the more deceptive the appearance. In Joseph Roth's "Story of the 1002nd Night," the Shah of Persia, on a state visit to Vienna, sees "riders in Persian costume" for the first time with his own eyes (previously he has seen them only "on the portraits of my ancestors"). He mistakes a brothel for an occidental castle and the prostitute Mizzi for a rich countess. This narrative only intensifies and renders exotic what characterizes folklorism, too, and what Riehl described in the Oberammergau example.

What Riehl did not recognize in his presentation is even more important: The development he observed in Oberammergau was no isolated case, but points to that process of folklorism where all other traditions had to end up too. Riehl believed that what was really original could be localized and preserved, that the truly genuine would not fall victim to changing social and economic conditions. But it was precisely the conservative characterization of "genuine" that pushed traditions into the field of view of the ever-increasing sentimental public; it provided for a longer life-span of the old only where the authentic was presented as authentic and therefore lost its original function and original authenticity. What is shown here in Riehl's case applies to a whole squad of scholars, conservers of *Heimat*, preservers of customs, and the like. *Volkskunde* referred so loudly and vehemently to the authentic, the old, and the original that it had to become conscious, and this changed its character.

Riehl and others believed in the preservation of the authentic, old, and original because of their reliance on a fundamentally static conception of society. Such a conception assumes that folk traditions do not belong to a historically defined level but to a basically timeless substance. Folklorism changes folklore in its essence, but is based on this assumption: because the antiquated is thought to be "authentic" and therefore timeless, it is rescued in a time alien to it, necessarily changed, but for all that admired and regarded with amazement.

This de-historicizing impulse at the same time blurs the social boundaries and indicates one function of folklorism, which lends it support from many sides, at least from above and below. From above folklore can become a demonstrative means to a partial downward adaptation. Objects like peasant furniture or costume fashions do not exist apart from the scale of prestige, but are part of it. Beyond that they are also valid as signs of a certain distinguished simplicity; anyone attracted to such objects avoids being considered a snob. His wealth and social status are, as it were, inevitable factors to be endured by fate; in reality his heart belongs to other, simpler things and there he joins the other social classes.

This reduces to one common denominator what, in fact, is subject to very different conditions. Even peasant fashions publicized in magazines of interior decorating exist in a different context from, for example, costume fashions, which have a relatively long tradition in some regions. The latter became accepted in the salons early in the nineteenth century in parts of Bavaria and Austria, because of the hunting fashions worn by the house of Wittelsbach. Since the beginning of our century it has also become the dress of "the official class in

"A Strange View of Relationships." Social distance: caricature of peasants
From *Fliegende Blätter,* 1861.

mountain localities, the business people of the Steiermark, or the resident owners of country estates." According to Rudolf Kriss this dress looks the same "from about Lindau via Munich to Vienna, consisting of long *Loden* [woolen] pants with green piping, and a jacket of fashionable cut that constantly undergoes small modifications but reveals a conscious renunciation of any strictly regional characteristics and corresponding adornment." The social status value is described by Kriss: "While wanting to adapt, one nevertheless keeps a certain social difference." In fact, the standardized fashion costume achieves both. It demonstrates membership in a tradition which, according to the notion of the followers of the costume fashion, is a generally "native," common one that includes various levels of society. However, what is emphasized is a so-to-speak elevated Sunday tradition which has nothing or very little in common with the difficult everyday world of the farmer. The extent of the radical consciousness of class distance, particularly from the peasantry, which is evident well into our century, could be documented by hundreds of caricatures, some of them malicious. Even if we invoke the individuality of the laws of comedy and point to the peculiar longevity of comic types, we must admit that the choice of that which has a comic effect is a consequence of real attitudes.

The symptom of folklorism in costume fashion can be substantiated from below as well as from above. The professional ascriptions given by Rudolf Kriss— officials and small business people alongside owners of country estates—permit the conclusion that we are dealing with a phenomenon that is not primarily, or even exclusively, typical of the upper ranks of society. Instead forms of folklorism distinctly seem to be components of the "ritualism" with which members of the "upper lower class" emphatically and stubbornly adopt the dominant norm of the upper middle class; Friedhelm Neidhardt calls this "the flight into adaptation." Where such an adaptation obviously takes on class-specific forms, the danger exists of being considered a *parvenu*. This applies even to the attempt to deviate from the traditional dialect by using a more-sophisticated form of speech, and should apply similarly to certain more-sophisticated forms of dress. By contrast costume fashions are not considered genteel in this sense. Rather they are considered distinguished and thereby rank relatively high without being tied to obtrusive social pretensions.

In this connection a more serious and politically portentous case of ritualism comes to mind: the conduct of many members of the middle class—more precisely the upper lower class— in the years before 1933. The economic crises reduced many employees practically to the level of the proletariat, and this led them to emphasize the middle-class positions, the bourgeois pretensions and ideologies, i.e., to strengthen the National Socialists. We do not intend to establish a connection to the theme of folklorism on the narrow track of concrete examples, though it is certainly striking that the cult of *Janker* (mountain jackets) and *Dirndl* dresses spread vigorously in the years after 1933. Hermann Göring and other leading figures of the party at times enjoyed being seen in costume, and the Alpine foothills became an important base and decision-making center of National Socialism. However, other, contrasting references can be made: the painter Franz Marc and his wife consistently wore Bavarian costume, or—more directly related to National Socialism—some of the Bavarian costume societies showed signs of vehement resistance to the party and its tendencies toward "political coordination." Therefore it would be absurd simply to describe the fashion and cult of costume as peculiar to the Nazis.

Instead the connection can be made on a somewhat more abstract level: Folklorism paves the way for other trans-social identifications by blurring and hiding distinct social identities. Folklore, which Maxim Gorki, in a 1934 lecture on folk poetry, proclaimed an instrument of class struggle, has long assumed the opposite function and now bridges social antagonisms. This is true not only of folk poetry but of folklore in the widest sense. Furthermore it does not merely apply to Western social systems, where folklorism is a sign of and simultaneously a means to the spread of the bourgeois culture. It feigns a strong and healthy middle in a more or less noncommittal cultural realm, creates the illusion of a connection with tradition which is passed over by all truly essential decisions. Within Eastern social systems folklorism demonstrates the smoothing out of all social oppositions using non-bourgeois pretexts—but here, too, in the picturesque realm of relatively noncommittal phenomena.

In either case it is important that the sense of social adjustment and social conformity mediated or at least reinforced by folklorism facilitates identification not with social units but with others of a geographical or political nature. Even the consciousness and sense of *Heimat* which evolved in the course of the nineteenth century should be viewed in close connection with the rise of folklorism. A socially defined folklorism is also conceivable where certain classes or professional groups demonstrate their specific traditions. We could cite examples from crafts or peasant customs where this kind of demonstration is obvious. Here the tendency to represent the social whole by a specific custom has been pressing to the forefront at least since the nineteenth century, i.e., representing the community, the region, the country, or even the entire nation as in the "rural" thanksgiving celebrations on the Bückeberg. As a whole folklorism is thus an expression of a diluted social consciousness and—contrary to all ceremonious proclamations in official speeches—it generates little social and political engagement. Heiner Treinen has concluded on the basis of empirical research that the "sense of *Heimat*" based largely on the relationship to intimate groups rather hinders participation in the communal social system and orientation to a larger social context, but it promotes an "emotional relationship with the locality" which encourages politically relevant interactions. If we proceed from this distinction, folklorism is frequently seen as providing the relationship with the locality with an abstract "sense of *Heimat*." This function is appealed to only where it finds an echo in ideologies, e.g. in the National Socialist forms of politics.

The compensatory and in many ways camouflaging character of folkloristic events is obvious where minorities, often politically disadvantaged, arrange particularly colorful demonstrations of their folklore. The folklorism of minorities becomes evident especially where smaller folk groups differ from the rest of the nation not only in cultural details but also in such fundamental respects as language. These include the Welsh in Great Britain, the Flemish, the French-speaking population of the Aosta Valley, the southern Tyroleans, the Sorbs in Lusatia, the many diverse ethnic groups in the Balkan nations, especially Yugoslavia. Even this tentative list indicates that for some political constellations the sudden change from a merely folkloristic consciousness of the self ("we") to a militant national consciousness can occur readily. In such a case folkloristic phenomena easily become signals of revolt and resistance. This does not call for a negative evaluation a priori. But it is precisely the folkloristic emphasis which most often shows that the consciousness of self ("we") and therefore the resistance are tied to false, i.e., historically antiquated, forms and ideas. For example, it is no accident that in the southern Tyrol folk costumes symbolize the claim for independence. For the politically important German representatives of the southern Tyrol, too, costumes often embody the "essential" folk culture, which is contrasted with the negative image of an international "culture of luxury." Progressive forces have ironically renamed this "essential folk culture" a *Lederhosenkultur* (culture of leather pants). They realized that such a twofold division is slanted and that an opposition which recognizes socially antiquated forms as the essential, must lead to false judgments and consequences in the sphere of economic and general political concerns as well.

Here, as always, folklorism is granted a scope for action, but really important switches and processes take place outside of it. This statement is not limited to cultural activities, but it can be verified in that realm: folklorism offers something old-fashioned and the more important developments occur elsewhere, entirely independently and not influenced by it. But folklorism is not mainly a component of primary communication, while the other part of culture has been taken over by the media of the culture industry; instead folklorism is fully integrated into the latter: The *Heimat* show on the radio immediately follows the broadcast of a jazz session; in several popular television series affluent business-men, hotel directors, or doctors wear the distinguished, simple costume, to mention this trifling piece of evidence once more. Such examples give folklorism its positional value; they show its impotence with respect to progressive cultural processes, but they also show its power in the conservation of antiquated attitudes.

Karl Kraus once said "much confusion" would "arise between the *Kyffhäuser* [legends] and *Kaufhäuser* [department stores]" in the realm of German legend. In light of the present situation, this ironic prognosis would probably be questioned: Folklorism is the means used to protect the allegedly essential folk culture from actual development, and it is done with the help of all of the technology of the culture industry. Folklorism makes it possible to pretend that the issue is the *Kyffhäuser*, while the real movement of culture is carried by the principle of the *Kaufhäuser*, i.e., consumerism. Folklorism seems to preserve culture in a realm of the original and authentic; it denies the connection between culture and industry, which in reality has given folklorism its weight.

Notes

Translator's Preface

1. For a detailed discussion of this development see the introduction to *German Volk-skunde—A Decade of Theoretical Confrontation, Debate, and Reorientation (1967–1977)*, edited and translated by James R. Dow and Hannjost Lixfeld (Bloomington: Indiana University Press, 1986).
2. Ibid.
3. See the congress papers *Heimat und Identität—Probleme regionaler Kultur*, edited by Konrad Köstlin and Hermann Bausinger (Neumünster: Karl Wachholtz Verlag, 1980), 9–24.
4. For example, "Traditional branches of folklore are oriented toward cultural objectivations, toward 'goods.' These have been to a great extent the real and exclusive items of folklore. . . . German polarization of culture and civilization, which developed very early in the technological world, continues to affect our conceptions of preindustrial life. If we ignore this one-sidedness, we can justify the limitation of research interests to 'goods' when considering relatively closed and uniform cultures. In these cultures every objectivation has its relatively precise and elevated place of value. Among Alpine herdsmen, for example, who are virtually illiterate and who have only meager contacts with the valley, a custom is observed, songs are noted, carvings are collected, and work processes and implements are recorded. . . . we can certainly draw the conclusion that in such *relatively* closed cultures every individual objectivation has a *relatively* high expressive force" (Dow and Lixfeld, 28–29).
5. See also Grimms' *Deutsches Wörterbuch*, vol. 12 (Berlin: Deutsche Akademie der Wissenschaften, Abteilung II, 1852; reprint Leipzig: S. Hirsch, 1951), 453–511.

Introduction

1. *Versuche* 20–21 (Berlin, 1950): 85–101; cf. 94.
2. Hanns Koren, *Volkskunde in der Gegenwart* (Graz-Vienna-Altötting, 1952), 81.
3. See Hugo Moser, "Volk, Volksgeist, Volkskultur. Die Auffassungen J. G. Herders in heutiger Sicht," *Zeitschrift für Volkskunde* 53 (1956/57):127–140.
4. Wilhelm Heinrich Riehl, *Die Volkskunde als Wissenschaft in Culturstudien aus drei Jahrhunderten* (Stuttgart, 1859), 205–229; esp. 215; also Gerhard Lutz, *Volkskunde* (Berlin, 1958), 23–36; esp. 29.
5. *Die Volkskunde als Wissenschaft*, 216 (see also Lutz 1958:29).
6. Cf. Eduard Hoffmann-Krayer, *Die Volkskunde als Wissenschaft* (Zürich, 1902) (see also Lutz 1958:43–60).
7. Adolf Spamer, *Vom Problem des Volksgeistes zur Volkskunde als Wissenschaft. Wesen, Wege und Ziele der Volkskunde* (Leipzig, 1928), 20–29; esp. 29 (see also Lutz 1958: 15–22; esp. 22)
8. Cf. Willy Hellpach, *Deutsche Physiognomik* (Berlin, 1942), 8–9, where Johannes Scherr's comment that *Volk* is "the great play on words of world history" is cited.
9. Friedrich Georg Jünger, *Die Perfektion der Technik* (Frankfurt, 1949), 4.
10. Translator's note: The translation of *das einfache Volk* as "the simple folk" is, of course, not idiomatic English. However, Bausinger explains at the end of the study that the literal meaning of the word "simple" is essential to his understanding of *Volk*. I have therefore decided against the more idiomatic "the common folk."
11. Translator's note: Lacking an adequate idiomatic English term, cultural *Gut* and *Güter* have been translated as cultural "good" and "goods" throughout the study. This follows the precedent set in the translation of Bausinger's essay "A Critique of Tradition" in *German Volkskunde—A Decade of Theoretical Confrontation, Debate, and Reorienta-*

tion (1967–1977), edited and translated by James R. Dow and Hannjost Lixfeld (Bloomington: Indiana University Press, 1986), 26–40; see esp. 28–31. "Good" here indicates a cultural objectivation, i.e., a cultural expression or product.

12. See Hermann Bausinger, Markus Braun, and Herbert Schwedt, *Neue Siedlungen* (Stuttgart, 1959), 13–15.

13. Fedor Stepun, *Die Objektivitätsstruktur des soziologischen Erkenntnisaktes* in *Soziologie und Leben* (Tübingen: Carl Brinkmann, 1952), 63–78; esp. 67.

14. Hans Arnold, "Das Magische des Films," diss., Munich, 1949, 9.

15. Leopold Schmidt writes in this sense: "In the final instance for *Volkskunde* the essential is not the saint's statue, but the relationship of the human being to it" (*Formprobleme der deutschen Weihnachtsspiele* [Emsdetten, 1937], 2). The term coined by Schmidt, *Gestaltheiligkeit* (*Gestaltheiligkeit im bäuerlichen Arbeitsmythos* [Vienna, 1952]), i.e., sacredness of figures, is such a term specific to *Volkskunde*, even though in its characteristics it retreats from the functional view in favor of the mere motif-historical search for ideal figures. For functional approaches in *Volkskunde*, see in addition to works of the Frankfurt school under Schwietering and Richard Weiss's *Volkskunde in der Schweiz*, the dissertation by Helmut Möller, "Untersuchungen zum Funktionalismus in der Volkskunde," Göttingen, 1954.

16. See Carl Gustav Jung and Karl Kerenyi, *Einführung in das Wesen der Mythologie* (Zürich, 1951), 38n5.

17. Ernst Tröltsch, *Der Historismus und seine Probleme*, Gesammelte Schriften, vol. 3 (Tübingen, 1922), 763. See also Otto Friedrich Bollnow, *Zufall und Missverständnis in der Geistesgeschichte* in *Minotaurus. Dichtung unter den Hufen von Staat und Industrie* (Wiesbaden, 1957), 203–220, esp. 216. Within the field of *Volkskunde*, Josef Dünninger, Hans Moser, Dieter Narr, and Leopold Schmidt are the main scholars concerned with a new approach to the Enlightenment.

18. Otto Friedrich Bollnow, *Das Verstehen* (Mainz, 1949), 82.

19. I owe sincere thanks to the Faculty of Philosophy at Tübingen and particularly to the examiners who have accepted this work as an inaugural dissertation, even though it does not shy away from engaging in the seemingly transient to and fro of our present time.

1. The Technical World as "Natural" Environment

1. *Unter Krahnenbäumen—Bilder aus einer Strasse*, by Chargesheimer, text by Heinrich Böll (Cologne: Greven Verlag, 1958).

2. Julius Schwietering, "Wesen und Aufgaben der deutschen Volkskunde," *Deutsche Vierteljahrsschrift für Literatur wissenschaft und Geistesgeschichte* 5 (1927):748–765 (see also Lutz 1958:143–157).

3. Leopold Schmidt, "Wiener Volkskunde," *Wiener Zeitschrift für Volkskunde*, supplementary vol. XVI (Vienna and Leipzig, 1940).

4. Hans Commenda, *Volkskunde der Stadt Linz an der Donau*, 2 vols. (Linz, 1958, 1959).

5. Here we should mention the *Bayrisches Jahrbuch für Volkskunde* of 1958, all the essays of which are dedicated to the folklore of Munich.

6. This is clearly shown by Wilhelm Brepohl's studies of the *Ruhrgebiet* (see esp. *Industrievolk im Wandel von der agraren zur industriellen Daseinsform, dargestellt am Ruhrgebiet* [Tübingen, 1957]). Recently Josef Dünninger and Alfred Karasek have repeatedly pointed to these transitions.

7. Joseph Klapper, "Volkskunde der Grosstadt," in *Handbuch der Deutschen Volkskunde*, vol. 1 (Potsdam: Wilhelm Pessler, n.d. [1934]), 103–119; esp. 103 and 119.

8. Translator's note: The term was coined by F. L. Jahn in *Deutsches Volksthum* (1810); it connotes national characteristics, inherent essence, activity, and life of the folk.

9. Josef Dünninger, *Volkswelt und geschichtliche Welt* (Berlin, Leipzig, Essen, 1937); esp. 21–31.

10. See Josef Dünninger, "St. Erhard und die Dollingersage," *Bayrisches Jahrbuch*

für Volkskunde 1953:9–15; Hermann Bausinger, "Volkssage und Geschichte," *Württembergisch Franken* 41 (1957):107–130; esp. 124–125.

11. This is particularly obvious in the research done in Bavaria by Hans Moser and K. S. Kramer; see also p. 33 below.

12. Alfred Weber has emphasized this and thus separated civilization from culture with its processes of unique creations. See his essay "Prinzipielles zur Kultursoziologie," *Archiv für Sozialwissenschaft und Sozialpolitik* 47 (Tübingen 1920/21):1–49; he also contrasts "evolutive" and "morphological" cultural observation. This contrast touches on the oppositions mentioned above.

13. See Wolf Häfele, "Geschichtlichkeit und Metaphysik," manuscript of the Institut für Neutronenphysik, Karlsruhe, 1958:12; and Werner Heisenberg, *Das Naturbild in der heutigen Physik, Rowohlts Deutsche Enzyklopädie* 8 (Hamburg, 1955), 21.

14. See Bolte-Polívka, *Anmerkungen zu den Kinder- und Hausmärchen der Brüder Grimm*, vol. 5 (Leipzig, 1932), 240. Translator's note: the author mistakenly gave the date of vol. 5 as 1912.

15. XII, 11. Cited by Gerhard Rosenkranz, "Die Völker Asiens und die Technik," *Evangelische Missionszeitschrift für Missionswissenschaft und evangelische Religionskunde* 13 (1956):97–100 and 129–143; see esp. 129.

16. Friedrich Georg Jünger, *Die Perfektion der Technik* (Frankfurt, 1949), 225.

17. See René König, ed., *Soziologie* (Frankfurt a.M.: Fischer Lexikon, 1958), 214–219. See the pronounced blending of the concepts in *Trübners Deutsches Wörterbuch*, vol. 5 (Berlin, 1954), 33–34.

18. See esp. the essays on this subject in *Kölner Zeitschrift für Soziologie* 7 (1955).

19. René König 1958:87.

20. See Hermann Bausinger, "Vereine als Gegenstand volkskundlicher Forschung," *Zeitschrift für Volkskunde* 55 (1959):13–15.

21. This characteristic has been emphasized by Wolfgang Schadewaldt, *Natur—Technik—Kunst* (Göttingen, Berlin, Frankfurt, 1960), 16–23.

22. Friedrich Bollnow, *Einfache Sittlichkeit. Kleine philosophische Aufsätze*, 2d ed. (Göttingen, 1957), 24.

23. Ibid., esp. 122.

24. *Die Perfektion der Technik*, 178.

25. Max Mikorey, *Phantome und Doppelgänger* (Munich, 1952), 44.

26. See Bausinger, "Schwank und Witz," *Studium Generale* 11 (1959):699–710.

27. "Vergangenheits- und Gegenwartsvolkskunde—Volkskunde und Soziologie," *Kölner Vierteljahrshefte für Soziologie* 9 (1930/31):407–429; see esp. 417.

28. See Otto Weiss, "Josef Anton Harz und das oberschwäbische Singspiel," diss., Tübingen, 1927, 6.

29. For example, the description of the Gral by the Younger Titurel affectionately details the "mechanism of the doves"; see Albrecht von Scharfenberg, *Jüngerer Titurel*, edited by Werner Wolf, vol. 1 (Berlin, 1955), 88–89, verses 352 and 353. I owe this reference, as well as many other helpful hints, to Professor Wolfgang Mohr, Tübingen.

30. Franz Oberthür, *Philipp Adam Ulrichs, ehemaliger öffentlichen Lehrers der Bürgerlichen Rechte an der Hohen Schule zu Würzburg, Lebensgeschichte*, 2d ed., (Sulzbach, 1824), 110–112. I owe this reference to Dr. Dieter Narr, Eschenau. As to Ulrich, see also Josef Dünninger, "Beharrung und Wandel im fränkischen Dorf," *Soziale Welt* 9 (1958): 275–281.

31. See Will-Erich Peuckert, *Pansophie. Ein Versuch zur Geschichte der weissen und schwarzen Magie*, 2d ed. (Berlin, 1956), esp. 83 and 474–478. See also H. Bächtold-Stäubli, ed., *Handwörterbuch des deutschen Aberglaubens*, vol. 1 (Berlin and Leipzig, 1927), 241–243.

32. For example, see J. Huizinga, *Homo ludens. Vom Ursprung der Kultur im Spiel, Rowohlts Deutsche Enzyclopädie* 21 (Hamburg, 1956), 165.

33. Jeremias Höslin, *Meteorologische und Witterungsbeobachtungen, auf neunzehn Jahre, sammt einer Anweisung hierzu, und den erforderlichen Tabellen* (Tübingen: Auf-

gestellt und bekannt gemacht von Jeremias Höslin, Pfarrern zu Böringen auf der Wirtembergischen Alb, 1784).

34. *Ludwigsburger Kreiszeitung,* October 14, 1950.

35. Manuscript, 236.

36. Personal communication from Professor Helmut Dölker.

37. Gustav Sauter, *Philipp Matthäus Hahn, der "Mechanikerpfarrer"* (Ebingen, 1939), 28.

38. Chr. Ulr. Hahn, ed., *Philipp Matthäus Hahns hinterlassene Schriften* (Heilbronn and Rothenburg, 1828), 25.

39. Max Engelmann, *Leben und Wirken des württembergischen Pfarrers und Feinmechanikers Philipp Matthäus Hahn* (Berlin, 1923), 60–61.

40. The fact that the development of technology was often advanced by priests points to a connection which has briefly been mentioned before: technology was regarded as an expression of ahistorical, divine laws of existence; therefore it did not have to stand in opposition to religion. Nevertheless Hahn was plagued by doubts, particularly, it seems, insofar as his strong preoccupation with technical reflections threatened to prevent him from fulfilling his official duties as a priest. In the *Echterdinger Neujahrsbetrachtung* of 1784 he blames himself for being "too preoccupied with mechanical matters" when he should be trying more "to please his Lord in heaven."

41. This ambivalent concept is appropriate here, as manifold and ambivalent ideas are described.

42. This concept coined by Belshaw is explained by Andreas Lommel, "Der 'Cargo-Kult' in Melanesien. Ein Beitrag zum Problem der 'Europäisierung' der Primitiven." *Zeitschrift für Ethnologie* 78 (1953):17–63; esp. 46.

43. See Jürgen Pechel, "Ein Kult beunruhigt Neuguinea," *Stuttgarter Zeitung,* January 11, 1958. See also Gerd Koch, *Südsee—gestern und heute. Der Kulturwandel bei den Tonganern und der Versuch einer Deutung dieser Entwicklung* (Braunschweig, 1955).

44. See Andreas Lommel, "Traum und Bild bei den Primitiven in Nordwest-Australien," *Psyche* 5 (1951):187–209; esp. 204–206.

45. Ortega, *Betrachtungen über die Technik* (Stuttgart, 1949), 96.

46. See Gerhard Rosenkranz, "Die Völker Asiens und die Technik," *Evangelische Missionszeitschrift für Misssionswissenschaft und evangelische Religionskunde* 13 (1956):97–100 and 129–143; esp. 134–137.

47. Ibid., 134.

48. Prince Pückler, "Briefe eines Verstorbenen," *Stuttgarter Zeitung,* February 4, 1956.

49. Karl Meyer, *Gedichte,* 2d ed. (Stuttgart and Tübingen, 1839), 127.

50. It is worthwhile investigating from this point of view the special position of Max Eyth, who has provided theoretical comments on these questions.

51. Arthur Weber, "Franz Graf Thun, der Geisterseher," *Chronik des Wiener Goethe-Vereins* XLI (Vienna, 1936):19–31; cf. 27.

52. The confidence, energy, and enthusiasm typical of the remarks made by theoreticians, engineers, and technicians concerned with space travel may partly be explained in similar fashion.

53. Siegfried Gerathewohl, *Die Psychologie des Menschen im Flugzeug* (Munich, 1954), 194–195.

54. Peter Purzelbaum, *Mit Maske und Anker* (Oldenburg and Berlin, 1937), 146–147.

55. *Die Perfektion der Technik,* 139–140. The fact that F G. Jünger uses images from nature to remove technology from the realm of the customary (*secunda natura*) and to emphasize its demonic aspects is a revealing indication of the relative quality of "naturalness."

56. The following is quoted from Robert Musil, *Mann ohne Eigenschaften* (Hamburg, 1952), 39–40: "If it is the realization of archetypal dreams to be able to fly and to travel with fish, to tunnel through under the bodies of giant mountains, to send messages with god-like speed, to see and listen to the invisible and the far, to hear the dead speaking, to

let oneself sink into a wonderful sleep of regeneration, to see while alive how one will look twenty years after one's death, to know in glistening nights a thousand things above and below our world which formerly no one knew, if light, warmth, power, enjoyment, comfort are archetypal dreams of mankind—then today's research is not just science, but a kind of magic, a ceremony of the highest power of heart and brain, before which God opens one fold of his coat after another, a religion whose dogma is permeated and carried by the hard, courageous, flexible, knifelike cold and sharp ideology of mathematics.''

57. The common name for these cavities, *Wetzrillen,* is often erroneous. They do not always derive from this Easter custom, but were also created during times of epidemics when stone dust was shaved off for medicinal purposes.

58. Personal communication from Heinz Schmitt (Ph.D. candidate), Weinheim.

59. See p. 77 of this study.

60. Karl Reuschel, *Volkskundliche Streifzüge* (Dresden and Leipzig, 1903), 122.

61. Johannes Bolte, ''Die Altweibermühle. Ein Tiroler Volksschauspiel,'' *Archiv für das Studium der neueren Sprache und Literatur* 102 (1899):241–266; see 247–248. See also Joseph Gregor, *Das Theater des Volkes* (Vienna, 1943), 93.

62. Collection of posters in the *Heimatstube* of Neresheim.

63. Heinrich Lützeler, *Philosophie des Kölner Humors,* 10th ed. (Honnef: Rheinbücher N.F.V., 1955), 56–57.

64. See Paul Gerhart, ''Motor mit Gefühlsantrieb,'' *Christ und Welt,* May 3, 1956. The temporary ''old car craze'' reigning in England and partly in America does not contradict this general state of affairs: it represents a somewhat ironic regression to an earlier level.

65. Martin Heidegger, broadcast lecture, *Südwestfunk,* February 17, 1956.

66. See Walther Rathenau, ''Die Mechanisierung der Welt,'' *Sozialwissenschaftliche Schriftenreihe* 7 (Schwenningen, 1948):16.

67. See Hermann Unger, ''Die Krisis des deutschen Volkslieds,'' *Deutsches Volkstum* (Hamburg, 1938), 843–847, esp. 845; and Fritz Spieser, ''Das Leben des Volksliedes im Rahmen eines Lothringer-Dorfes,'' *Bausteine zur Volkskunde und Religionswissenschaft* 8 (Bühl-Baden, 1934):n71.

68. See Raimund Zoder's review of Walter Wiora, *Das echte Volkslied* (Heidelberg, 1950), *Jahrbuch des österreichischen Volksliedwerkes* 2 (Vienna, 1953):148; also Zoder-Klier, eds., *Lieder aus Niederösterreich,* vol. 1 (Vienna, 1932), 11; vol. 2 (Vienna, 1934), 23.

69. See *Das deutsche Volkslied* 45 (1943):72.

70. Leopold Schmidt, ''Die österreichische Maskenforschung 1930–1955,'' *Masken in Mitteleuropa* (Vienna, 1955), 4–71; esp. 47.

71. Ruth Lorbe, ''Das Kinderlied in Nürnberg,'' *Nürnberger Forschungen* 3 (Nuremberg, 1956):80; see Reinhard Peesch, *Das Berliner Kinderspiel der Gegenwart* (Berlin, 1957), esp. 51–52.

72. Wilhelm Brepohl, *Industrievolk im Wandel von der agraren zur industriellen Daseinsform, dargestellt am Ruhrgebiet* (Tübingen, 1957), 240–241.

73. See, for example, Max Peinkofer, ''Das mechanische Ölbergspiel zu Hohenegglkofen,'' *Schönere Heimat* 46 (1957):298–299.

74. See Heinz Küper, *Wörterbuch der deutschen Umgangssprache* (Hamburg, 1955).

75. Johannes Köpp, ''Das Volkslied in der Volksgemeinschaft,'' in *Die deutsche Volkskunde,* edited by Adolf Spamer (Berlin, 1934), 299–308; esp. 306.

76. Communication from Dr. Willi Müller, Schwieberdingen.

77. Peter R. Hofstätter, *Gruppendynamik, Rowohlts Deutsche Enzyklopädie* 38 (Hamburg, 1957), 18.

78. See Kurt Stavenhagen, *Kritische Gänge in die Volkstheorie* (Riga, 1936), 29, 58, 95; and Herbert Freudenthal, *Die Wissenschaftstheorie der deutschen Volkskunde* (Hanover, 1955), 103–104.

79. See Hermann Bausinger, ''Strukturen des alltäglichen Erzählens,'' *Fabula* 1 (1958):239–254; esp. 244–245.

80. See Hermann Bausinger, Markus Braun, and Herbert Schwedt, *Neue Siedlungen* (Stuttgart, 1959), esp. 121–123.

81. *Schwäbische Zeitung* (Leutkirch), December 7, 1956. The term "club," which is characteristic of such associations, combines ideas from high society with those from the sports world. Sports associations also often have the word "club" in their names, following the original English model. The sports element in such associations should not be underestimated, as sport in general has replaced and dissolved almost all competitive elements in former folk customs.

82. See Bausinger, Braun, and Schwedt, 113; and Josef Dünninger, "Beharrung und Wandel im fränkischen Dorf," *Soziale Welt* 9 (1958):275–281, esp. 277. Similar reports exist from many other localities.

83. Folkloristic investigations of the Ludwig-Uhland-Institute at Tübingen; Markus Braun, "Tscherwenka II," manuscript, 1954, 13.

84. Herlinde Knorr, "Das Volkslied im Leben eines hessischen Dorfes," diss., Marburg, 1945, 32.

85. Ernst Jünger, *Der Arbeiter* (Hamburg, 1932), 73.

86. Lothar Rudolph has collected important material on this subject. See his "Stufen des Symbolverstehens auf Grund einer volkskundlichen Untersuchung in Berlin über drei Symbolformen (Christophorus, Hahn, Johanniterkreuz)," *Kirchengeschichtliche Studien* 1 (Berlin, 1959).

87. For the development and dissemination of these festivals, see, among others, John Meier, "Muttertag," *Zeitschrift für Volkskunde*, new series 8 (1936):100–112; Eduard Strübin, "Der Muttertag in der Schweiz," *Schweizerisches Archiv für Volkskunde* 52 (1956):95–121; J. Ällig, "Wie ein neuer Brauch entstehen kann: Der Valentinstag in Norwegen," *Schweizer Volkskunde* 40 (1950):7–9; Anton M. Keim, "Geschäft schafft Brauchtum—zu den St. Valentins-Grüssen," broadcast of the Südwestfunk, Studio Rheinland-Pfalz, February 14, 1959.

88. *Stuttgarter Zeitung*, December 24, 1955.

89. Translator's note: Euphemism for the famous remark by Götz von Berlichingen, "Kiss my ass."

90. Heinrich Lützeler, *Philosophie des Kölner Humors*, 10th ed., (Honnef, 1955), 71–72.

91. Individual references in Hermann Bausinger, "Lebendiges Erzählen," diss., Tübingen, 1952; see also Lutz Röhrich, *Märchen und Wirklichkeit* (Wiesbaden, 1956), 150.

92. Thomas Mann, *Zauberberg*, special ed. (Stuttgart: Fischer Verlag, 1954), 843.

93. Jean Paul, *Sämtliche Werke*, vol. 16, 1st sec., (Weimar, 1938), 46.

94. Helmut Plessner, "Soziologie des Sports. Stellung und Bedeutung des Sports in der modernen Gesellschaft (Persönliche Welt—Arbeitswelt)," *Jahrbuch 1953/54 der Studiengesellschaft für praktische Psychologie*, edited by H. Petri (Lüneburg, 1954), 70–81, esp. 72.

95. For example, see "Märchen um die Todeskilometer," *Stuttgarter Zeitung*, March 17, 1956.

96. See C. G. Jung, *Ein moderner Mythus. Von Dingen, die am Himmel gesehen werden* (Zürich-Stuttgart, 1958).

97. Hans Arnold, "Das Magische des Films. Ein Beitrag zum Problem der Wirksamkeit magischer Einflüsse in der Gegenwart unter besonderer Berücksichtigung des Films," diss., Munich, 1949.

98. Cited from Leopold Schmidt's study *Das deutsche Volksschauspiel in zeitgenössischen Zeugnissen vom Humanismus bis zur Gegenwart* (Berlin, 1954), 49–50.

99. See Anton Dörrer, "Hochreligion und Volksglaube. Der Tiroler Herz-Jesu-Bund (1796 bis 1946) volkskundlich gesehen," in *Volkskundliches aus Österreich und Südtirol; Hermann Wopfner zum 70. Geburtstag*, edited by A. Dörrer and L. Schmidt (Vienna, 1947), 70–100.

100. Folklore studies of the Ludwig-Uhland-Institute, Tübingen; Hans Rüss, "Csobánka," manuscript, 1954, 43.

101. Paper given by Hans Dreger at a conference attended by folklorists and Protestant ministers, Frauenkopf (near Stuttgart), May 30, 1954.

102. *Anton von Buchers sämmtliche früher gedruckte Schriften* (Munich: Joseph von Klessing, 1822), vol. 6, 440.

103. Johann Mokre, *Grundriss der Arbeiterkunde* (Vienna, 1950), 52.

104. Personal communication from Dr. Hannelore Roth; see her dissertation, "Tageszeitungen als Quelle der volkskundlichen Forschung," Tübingen, 1956, 95–96.

105. Hofstätter, *Gruppendynamik,* 17.

106. See Leopold Kretzenbacher,"Freveltanz und 'Überzähliger,' " *Carinthia* I 144 (Klagenfurt, 1954):843–866; Hermann Bausinger, "Volkssage und Geschichte," *Württembergisch Franken* 41 (1957):107–130; esp. 119–120; as well as the literature mentioned in both essays.

107. Georg Simmel, "Die Grossstädte und das Geistesleben," in *Brücke und Tür* (Stuttgart, 1957), 227–242, esp. 238–239. An older source for the *quatorzième* of mythological importance is possibly evident in the custom reported from Karlsbad of adding a fourteenth table setting for the "stone guest" at a dinner for thirteen (Leander Petzoldt, typed questionnaire on the subject of *Der Tote als Gast,* i.e., the Dead Person as Visitor, Mainz, 1960). Perhaps a late form of the superstition has fused here with a notion that did not originally pertain to it.

108. See "Glückszahl am Auspuff," *Stuttgarter Zeitung,* July 18, 1956.

109. See Carl Jantke, "Bergmann und Zeche," in *Soziale Forschung und Praxis,* vol. II (Tübingen, 1953), 180.

110. *Stuttgarter Zeitung,* June 23, 1958 (sports section). Similarly the "charging" of a small piece of fabric is more important than its origin in Wolfgang Borchert's tale "Vielleicht trug sie ein rosa Hemd" (Perhaps she wore a pink shirt).

111. See H. Husmann, "Lebensformen und ihr Wandel beim Arbeiter in Hamborn," *Rheinisch-westfälische Zeitschrift für Volkskunde* 4 (1957):1–39 and 133–214; esp. 193.

2. Spatial Expansion

1. In this connection the research at the Bayrische Landesstelle für Volkskunde must be mentioned explicitly; see the fundamental statements relating to investigations of archival sources in Hans Moser, "Gedanken zur heutigen Volkskunde," *Bayerische Jahrbuch für Volkskunde* 1954:208–234, esp. 221–228; and the studies of Karl-Sigismund Kramer, *Die Nachbarschaft als bäuerliche Gemeinschaft* (Munich-Pasing, 1954), and "Bauern und Bürger im nachmittelalterlichen Unterfranken," *Veröffentlichungen der Gesellschaft für fränkische Geschichte,* series IX, vol. 12 (Würzburg, 1957). Similar research was done in southwest Germany by Friedrich Heinz Schmidt-Ebhausen ("Kirchenkonventsprotokolle als volkskundliche Quelle," *Württembergisches Jahrbuch für* Volkskunde 1955:49–65) and Willi Müller (in all issues of *Hie gut Württemberg*).

2. Various chronicles, particularly from the sixteenth century, give a lively impression of this influence. See, for example, *Zimmerische Chronik,* edited by K. A. Barack (Freiburg and Tübingen, 1881–1882).

3. Josef Dünninger, "Beharrung und Wandel im fränkischen Dorf," *Soziale Welt* 9 (1958):275–281; esp. 279.

4. See Leopold Schmidt, *Die Volkskunde als Geisteswissenschaft. Gesammelte Abhandlungen zur geistigen Volkskunde* (Vienna, 1948), 13.

5. See above all the paper by Dieter Narr presented at the *Dorftagung des Schwäb. Heimatbundes 1954* (printed in *Hie gut Württemberg,* 6/9, 10; 7/2, 3, 7) and the work of Gerhard Lutz, "Die Sitte—zu den philosophischen Grundlagen der Volkskunde," *Zeitschrift für deutsche Philologie* 77 (1958):337–361, and "Sitte, Recht und Brauch" (paper given at the Staatliche Akademie Comburg on February 4, 1959), *Zeitschrift für Volkskunde* 56 (1960):74–88.

6. Mathilde Hain explains the contradiction and tension between strife at the individual level and the relative unity at the community level by the fact that everyone is obli-

gated to *Sitte*, "but not so much in terms of personal encounters, as to an authoritative higher order," which is generated by the group itself "as an irrational-spiritual entity." See *Das Lebensbild eines oberhessischen Trachtendorfes* (Jena, 1936), 83.

7. See esp. Dieter Narr, "Zum Euphemismus in der Volkssprache," *Württembergisches Jahrbuch für Volkskunde* 1956:112–119, which also contains the following examples. Specific references are not given.

8. Karl Pfaff, *Geschichte der Stadt Stuttgart*, vol. 1 (Stuttgart, 1845), 26–27.

9. Anton Birlinger, *Aus Schwaben*, vol. 2: *Sitten und Rechtsbräuche* (Wiesbaden, 1874), 309–310.

10. Ibid., 310.

11. *Schwäbische Zeitung*, February 20, 1958.

12. Folkloristic studies of the Ludwig-Uhland-Institute in Tübingen; A. Hermann, "Sarata Kr. Akkermann," manuscript, Tübingen, 1954, 35–38.

13. See Hermann Bausinger, "Schwank und Witz," *Studium Generale* 11 (1958):699–710; esp. 101–102.

14. See Gerhard Lutz, "Sitte und Infamie. Untersuchungen zur rechtlichen Volkskunde am Phänomen des Verrufs," diss., Würzburg, 1954, 99–105; and Ilka Peter, *Gasslbrauch und Gasslspruch in Österreich* (Salzburg, 1953), 81.

15. See Ruodi's words in the first scene of Schiller's *Wilhelm Tell*.

16. Hermann Bausinger, "Von der Mundart im südlichen Oberschwaben," *Schwäbische Heimat* 6 (1955):69–72; esp. 71.

17. Conventional directions can be adapted to this evident spatial awareness within a limited horizon; however, they are essentially abstractions. Recently notions derived from maps have become increasingly influential, i.e., "up in northern Germany."

18. See Gottfried Henssen, *Ungarndeutsche Volksüberlieferungen* (Marburg, 1959), 19–20.

19. Leopold Schmidt, "Karl Ehrenbert Freiherr von Moll und seine Freunde," in *Volkskunde als Geisteswissenschaft* (Vienna, 1948), 31–58; see esp. 45. See Paul Zinsli, *Grund und Grat* (Bern, n.d.), 202–203.

20. P. Beck, "Redensarten und Ausdrücke aus dem mittleren Oberschwaben," *Schwäbisches Diözesanarchiv* 6 (1889):88.

21. Immanuel Kammerer, "Handschriftliche Aufzeichnungen zur Volkskunde Neubronns," at the Württembargische Landesstelle für Volkskunde Stuttgart, 71.

22. See *Elsassland, Lothringer Heimat* 15 (Gebweiler, 1935):44.

23. The—often improvised—four-liners are definitely "songs to be sung" and as such they tend to have a local entry connection. Professor Wolfgang Mohr has called my attention to the Norwegian "Gamle Stev."

24. Jonas Köpf, ed., *Suppinger Liederbuch* (Stuggart, 1953), 58. See Karl Reuschel, *Volkskundliche Streifzüge* (Dresden and Leipzig, 1903), 121.

25. Hugo Moser, *Schwäbischer Volkshumor* (Stuttgart, 1950).

26. Hugo Moser, "Sprachgrenzen und ihre Ursachen," *Zeitschrift für Mundartforschung* 22 (1954):87–111; esp. 100.

27. See Hermann Bausinger, Markus Braun, and Herbert Schwedt, *Neue Siedlungen* (Stuttgart, 1959), 183–193. Markus Braun, who planned this chapter, referred to Otto Friedrich Bollnow's presentation of "space experienced" in its "system of different levels" (see *Zeitschrift für die gesamte innere Medizin* 11 [1956]:97–105).

28. Taken from Leopold Schmidt, *Das deutsche Volksschauspiel in zeitgenössischen Zeugnissen vom Humanismus bis zur Gegenwart* (Berlin, 1954), 74.

29. Emilie Altenloh, *Zur Soziologie des Kino. Die Kinounternehmung und die sozialen Schichten ihrer Besucher* (Jena, 1914), 20.

30. Martin Heidegger, *Sein und Zeit*, first half, 5th ed. (Halle, 1941), 105.

31. Theodor Litt, *Das Bildungsideal der deutschen Klassik und die moderne Arbeitswelt*, 5th ed. (Bonn, 1958), esp. 18–26.

32. The more the familiar, the unity of theory and practice, recedes in reality, the more decisive becomes the philosophical attempt to reinstate this unity. Ernst Bloch em-

phasizes—as an essential foundation and an essential result of the philosophy of Marx—"that truth is not just a theory-relationship, but a theory-practice-relationship throughout" (*Das Prinzip Hoffnung* [Frankfurt, 1959], 311). The phenomenological trend in philosophy, as exemplified by Heidegger, is also based on concrete *Umgang*, on what is familiarly "available."

33. A monograph on the stranger and the strange place could yield important information on the essence and the thinking of the simple folk. It would be necessary to investigate relevant archives, remarks from travel reports, and semantic fields in specific dialects. The sociological dissertation by Willi Schwarz, "Der Fremde und das Volk," Cologne, 1938, which culminates in a "review and preview of the Jew as a stranger to the folk," is at most of interest for the history of the discipline.

34. See pp. 14–16 above.

35. See Hermann Bausinger, "Eine Albwanderung im Jahre 1790," *Blätter des Schwäbischen Albvereins* 61 (1955):21–25; esp. 24.

36. Erk-Böhme, *Deutscher Liederhort*, 2 vols. (Leipzig, 1925), 332; also Hermann Bausinger, "Volkslied und Schlager," *Jahrbuch des österreichischen Volksliedwerks* 5 (1956):59–76; esp. 72.

37. See Otto Elben, *Der volkstümliche deutsche Männergesang, seine Geschichte, seine gesellschaftliche und nationale Bedeutung* (Tübingen, 1855), 116.

38. *Schwäbisches Tagblatt*, Tübingen, June 16, 1958.

39. *Stuttgarter Zeitung*, May 16, 1955.

40. See Hans Magnus Enzensberger, "Vergebliche Brandung der Ferne—Eine Theorie des Tourismus," *Merkur* 12 (1958):701–720; and Hans-Joachim Knebel, *Soziologische Strukturwandlungen im modernen Tourismus* (Stuttgart, 1960).

41. See *Stuttgarter Zeitung*, August 7, 1956.

42. See Alfred Karasek-Langer, "Volkskundliche Erkenntnisse aus der Vertreibung und Eingliederung der Ostdeutschen," *Jahrbuch für Volkskunde der Heimatvertriebenen* 1 (Salzburg, 1955):11–65; esp. 62; and Bausinger et al., *Neue Siedlungen*, 125–126, 130, 143.

43. Otto Elben, *Der volkstümliche deutsche Männergesang*, 265.

44. Hugo Moser, "Vollschwäbisch, Stadtschwäbisch und Niederalemannisch im seither württembergischen Oberschwaben," *Alemannisches Jahrbuch* 1954:421–437; esp. 434; see also *Mittlere Sprachschichten als Quelle der deutschen Hochsprache. Eine historisch-soziologische Betrachtung. Antrittsvorlesung* (Nijmegen, 1955), 18.

45. See the references in Bausinger et al., *Neue Siedlungen*.

46. Richard Weiss, "Alpiner Mensch und alpines Leben in der Krise der Gegenwart," *Die Alpen* 1957:209–224, see 219.

47. With the following headlines: "There was a Brouhaha and then a crashing sound: many dishes were broken." "If the bride does not hail from the same village as the bridegroom, she enters ceremonially with the bridal cow." "Tear a small piece from the veil—it is conducive to affluence and brings you luck!" "A piece of singed material." "One has to step on the money." "Since ancient times salt and bread have protected against need and poverty."

48. Leopold Schmidt, *Die Volkskunde als Geisteswissenschaft* (Vienna, 1948), 19–20, emphasizes that this does not mean that a certain action is taken unconsciously, but "that the relevant tradition, of which this action is a part, is not made conscious as such." By comparison such presentations indicate the traditional connections of certain actions at least in part, even though they are not always primarily concerned with education but are often rather cunningly aimed at evoking deeper levels covered by rational attitudes.

49. Even the concept *Volkskunde* often indicates not only the study of the folk and its traditions but at the same time the knowledge of the folk itself in the sense of the English concept "folklore," coined in 1846 by Thoms. See Leopold Schmidt, 1948, 10–11.

50. See Hugo Moser, *Uhlands Schwäbische Sagenkunde und die germanistisch volkskundliche Forschung der Romantik* (Tübingen, 1950), 19–23.

51. Elben, 289–303.

52. Elben, 110 and 141–146.

53. See Schmidt, 9–10.

54. Alfred Weber, *Kulturgeschichte als Kultursoziologie* (Munich, 1951), 418.

55. Wilhelm Heinrich Riehl, *Die Familie. Die Naturgeschichte des Volkes*, 9th ed., part 3 (Stuttgart, 1882), 153.

56. Willi Müller, "250 Jahre Ludwigsburger Strassennamen," *Schwäbische Heimat* 5 (1954):77–80; see 80.

57. A special study could specify the details of this model; however, it would also have to consider the "exceptions" to the model, e.g., the fact that streets named after places, by which we understand big exit routes, infiltrate suburban areas individually (Flensburger Street in Kiel) or in clusters (Neusiedlung in Karlsruhe-Rintheim). Specific references are found in the presentation of the individual new settlements in Bausinger et al., *Neue Siedlungen*.

58. Ibid., 128–143, which also contains several examples of "pillars" supporting available goods.

59. C G. Jung, *Ein moderner Mythus. Von Dingen, die am Himmel gesehen werden* (Zürich and Stuttgart, 1958), 17.

60. See Hermann Bausinger, "Strukturen des alltäglichen Erzählens," *Fabula* 1 (1958):239–254; esp. 251.

61. Willy Hellpach, *Deutsche Physiognomik* (Berlin, 1942), 17.

62. A clear example is a novel by the best-selling author Hans-Ulrich Horster, which was first printed in the radio magazine *Hör zu* and later turned into a film. Entitled *Ein Student ging vorbei* (A Student Passed By), this novel provides insights into the alleged everyday bourgeois world of Tübingen, but it is also much concerned with the "allure of high society," which is specifically mentioned several times. The scene occasionally switches to Paris, where several strange, fascinating Mexicans play a major role.

Publishing efforts of many magazines and the popular press are partly distinguished by the attempt to refer the faraway world to the familiar world; the perspective of the butler is characteristic of the "historical" reports and expositions. These are attempts to make the faraway familiar; however, no amount of violence can remove the real distance.

63. *Schwäbische Zeitung*, January 18, 1956.

64. *Das Narrenbüchlein. Närrische Gesänge für den Narrenverein Riedlingen* (Riedlingen, 1926), iv.

65. Translator's note: While the standard German terms for carnival or Mardi Gras are *Fastnacht* or *Karneval*, optional spellings in local dialects are *Fasnet* or *Fasnacht*.

66. Albert Fischer, *Villinger Fastnacht einst und heute* (Villingen, 1922), 58.

67. Theatrical questionnaire of the Ludwig-Uhland-Institute in Tübingen, 1955; communication from the head of the village theatre at Diepoldshofen.

68. Oskar Eberle, " Die Japanesenspiele in Schwyz," *Jahrbuch der Gesellschaft für Schweizerische Theaterkultur* (Lucerne, 1935), 5–33; see esp. 11–13.

69. *Hundert Jahre Narrenzunft Frohsinn Donaueschingen* (Donaueschingen, 1953), 20–21.

70. Anton Dörrer, "Hochreligion und Volksglaube. Der Tiroler Herz-Jesu-Bund (1796 bis 1946) volkskundlich gesehen," in *Österreichische Volkskultur*, vol. 1, Wopfner Festschrift (Vienna, 1947), 70–100; see 95.

71. Leopold Schmidt suggests this concept; see his "Die österreichische Maskenforschung 1930–1955," *Masken* 1 (Vienna, 1955):4–71; esp. 39.

72. See Moritz Fürstenau, *Zur Geschichte der Musik und des Theaters am Hofe des Kurfürsten von Sachsen*, 2 vols. (Dresden, 1861), vol. 1, 88–89; Werner Fleischhauer, "Fasnacht und Maskerade an Stuttgarts Herzogshof," *Schwäbische Heimat* 6 (1955):3–6; Hermann Bausinger and Maria Kundegraber, "Ein Maskenzug im Jahre 1591," *Masken* 2 (n.d.).

73. See Rudolf Brotanek, "Die englischen Maskenspiele," *Wiener Beiträge zur englischen Philologie*, XV (Vienna and Leipzig, 1902):283–302.

74. Heinrich Düntzer, *Goethes Maskenzüge* (Leipzig, 1886), 87–88.

75. See Brotanek, "Die englischen Maskenspiele," 68 and 220.

76. See Hermann Bausinger and Maria Kundegraber; also Otto Richter, "Das Johannisspiel zu Dresden im 15. und 16. Jahrhundert," in *Neues Archiv für sächsische Geschichte und Alterthumskunde,* 4 vols. (Dresden, 1883), 101–114; esp. 109.

77. Hans Moser, "Zur Geschichte der Maske in Bayern," *Masken* 1 (Vienna, 1955):93–141; see 112.

78. See Fritz Brüggemann, *Vom Schembartlaufen* (Leipzig, 1936), 52.

79. An explanation of the connections between the image of the noble, elegant, courtly heathen of the High Middle Ages and the affectionate portrayal of the Black King in late medieval pictures of the three Magi could be attempted in a monograph on the figure of the Moor in German poetry, plastic arts, etc.

80. Franz Kirnbauer, "Der Vogel Strauss als Sinnbild des Eisenhandels," *Österreichische Zeitschrift für Volkskunde* 61 (1958):254–257.

81. See Hermann Bausinger, "Wallfahrten im Kreis Ludwigsburg," *Hie gut Württemberg,* Supplement, *Ludwigsburger Kreiszeitung* 8 (1957):86–87, 89; (1958):3–4, 10–12.

82. Ernst Jünger, *Der Arbeiter. Herrschaft und Gestalt* (Hamburg, 1932), 51.

83. See Alfred Götze, *Das deutsche Volkslied* (Leipzig, 1929), 6–7.

84. Immanuel Kant, *Bestimmung des Begriffs einer Menschenrasse* (1785), 125. Cited after Erich Vögelin, *Die Rassenidee in der Geistesgeschichte von Ray bis Carus* (Berlin, 1933), 47.

85. See Ludwig Andreas Veit, *Das Aufklärungsschrifttum des 18. Jahrhunderts und die deutsche Kirche* (Cologne, 1937), 12–15.

86. Friedrich Heer, "Die Russen, die Chinesen, die Atombombe, und wir," *Magnum* 21 (December 1958):32–34 and 54; esp. 32.

87. See Hans Plischke, *Von Cooper bis Karl May. Eine Geschichte des völkerkundlichen Reise- und Abenteuerromans* (Düsseldorf, 1951). Plischke defines the exotic more narrowly: in it he recognizes the result of the tiredness with European culture around 1900, as expressed in the works of Rimbaud and Gauguin. In fact, exotic impulses are much older, and measuring novels and narratives according to their anthropological content is problematic. Often these are exotic, not "anthropological," novels.

88. Walter Benjamin, *Einbahnstrasse* (Berlin and Frankfurt, 1955), 14.

89. Today a further related transfer symbolically indicates faraway areas: "Nights in Hawaii."

90. See Otto Weiss, "Josef Anton Harz und das oberschwäbische Singspiel," diss., Tübingen, 1927, 11.

91. Friedrich Karl Baron, *Die Volkslieder der Deutschen* (Mannheim, 1834–37), vol. 5, 547–548; see also 531.

92. Salonia, *Ludwigsburg* 5 (February 4, 1855):9.

93. Heinrich Weber, "Die Storndorfer Lieder. Der Liederschatz eines Vogelsberger Dorfes, gesammelt in den Jahren 1907–09," *Hessische Blätter für Volkskunde* 9 (1910): 1–125, see 3 and 120–121. The fact that similar songs were sung not just by the lowest classes is proven by a *Reservistenlied* printed in *Kneipzeitungen aus dem Tübinger Lichtenstein* (Tübingen, 1890), 177–178. This song also sings of love in Africa.

94. See Hermann Bausinger, "Volkslied und Schlager," *Jahrbuch des österreichischen Volksliedwerkes* 5 (1956):71.

95. *Constanze* (Hamburg), January 1953.

96. See *Schwäbische Zeitung,* January 10, 1958.

97. This also explains why, within these firmer horizons, *Sitte* and fashion are hardly differentiated; most dialects do not indicate any difference. See p. 64 above.

98. Walter Wiora, *Das echte Volkslied in Musikalische Gegenwartsfragen* 2 (Heidelberg, 1950), 49.

99. Hans Ruess, "Csobánka," manuscript at the Ludwig-Uhland Institute in Tübingen, 61.

100. See Friedrich Kluge, "Heimweh," *Zeitschrift für Deutsche Wortforschung* 2 (Strassburg, 1902):234–251. Actually, the word *Heimweh* does appear in the Articles of

the Guilds of Craftsmen of the Honorable Council of the City of Rottweil (1785); but here those who "only crawl around the boundaries" during their journeyman's years, the *Heimjammerer* (lit. "those who moan and wail for their homes"), are attacked (Art. VII). It is significant that the clearly pejorative word *Heimjammerer* has now been retained in the vocabulary, while the word *Heimweh* has spread.

101. What is demonstrated here in the goods of folk culture has its parallels and to a small extent its basis in philosophical developments. While the philosophy of the Romantic era still dealt with man's reconciliation with the hereafter from the viewpoint of the *Heimat*, the problem of *Heimat* in the course of the nineteenth century increasingly proves to be in a more secular sense the problem of the identity of man and the world. This is demonstrated in such contrasting endeavors as Marx's philosophy and Riehl's cultural sociology. Marx wants to retrieve man from his alienation by means of humanizing nature and naturalizing man; Riehl defends the unity and comfort of the home in the face of the threatening dissolution of traditional orders. It is tempting, but would lead too far in this case, to draw from these approaches a "left" and a "bourgeois" line of development to the present.

102. See Wilhelm Brepohl, "Die Heimat als Beziehungsfeld. Entwurf einer soziologischen Theorie der Heimat," *Soziale Welt* 4 (1952):12–22.

103. The chapter on *Heimat* in Bausinger et al., *Neue Siedlungen* (156–193) attempts to capture specifically the barely conscious connections to the *Heimat*. Any study of this kind has to investigate the native character of cultural goods, which is to be found in the subjective familiarity and therefore in the objective ties to tradition—this is obvious in the alteration of the song repertoires of choral societies and in the churches. Beyond this such a study must also demonstrate the spatial and social relationships which produce a feeling of familiarity and being at home; here the fleeting but regular contact with certain professions (merchants, postmen, gas station attendants, etc.) plays an important role, as do the regular use of the same train, frequent visits to the same cinema, etc.

104. Alfred Karasek, "Die sudetendeutsche Volkserzählung im industriellen Zeitalter," paper presented at the Staatliche Akademie Comburg, February 5, 1959.

105. Many references are contained in Bausinger et al., *Neue Siedlungen*.

106. Helmut Schelsky, "Die Flüchtlingsfamilie," *Kölner Zeitschrift für Soziologie* 3 (1950/51):159–177; see 163. See also Helmut Schelsky, *Wandlungen der deutschen Familie in der Gegenwart* (Dortmund, 1953).

107. See the works of Eduard Sprangers, esp. *Der Bildungswert der Heimatkunde*, 3d ed. (Stuttgart, 1952); also Johann Friedrich Dietz, *Das Dorf als Erziehungsgemeinde*, 2d ed. (Weimar, 1931); and Diedrich Rodiek, "Der bäuerliche Lebenskreis und seine Schule," diss., Berlin, 1932.

108. The strong and basic need for a sense of *Heimat* is sometimes particularly obvious among "new" students, again to a great extent among refugees. They often pay particular attention to lectures explaining details of the new environment and thus develop more intentionally what other children build up in less-conscious manner during the constant process of getting used to the *Heimat*. The topic "Refugee children and instruction classes on the native region" deserves intensive treatment. Such treatment, however, would also have to consider soberly where the potential for acquiring a sense of home exists within a heavily industrialized environment.

109. See Hermann Bausinger, "Oberschwäbisches Theaterleben jetzt und einst," *Württembergisches Jahrbuch für Volkskunde* 1957/58:49–70.

110. Vogt Kr. Wangen, *Schwäbische Zeitung*, December 15, 1955.

111. See "Härtsfeld-Heimatlied tönt in aller Mund," *Aalener Volkszeitung*, February 8, 1956; and " 'Härtsfeld-Heimatlied' geht um," *Schwäbische Post*, March 23, 1956.

112. See Hans Commenda, "Der Liederschatz einer Mühlviertler Bauernfamilie," *Jahrbuch des österreichischen Volksliedwerkes* 2 (Vienna, 1953):39–47; esp. 45.

113. *Stuttgarter Zeitung*, July 15, 1957.

114. *Schwäbische Zeitung*, October 10, 1958.

115. Hans O. E. Gronau, "Heimatfeste—einmal kritisch beleuchtret," DHD, 1955.

116. See, for example, *Schwäbische Zeitung,* April 19, 1956.
117. *Aalener Volkszeitung,* May 14, 1956.
118. Written communication from the *Landesgewerbeamt Baden-Württemberg,* June 11, 1954.
119. This constitutes an important subject for contemporary *Volkskunde.* The *Atlas der deutschen Volkskunde* lists innovations of folk life, such as choral and sports societies and the regional distribution of soccer playing (map 36a–36d, part 3 of new edition). But technological innovations as well, which tend to be quickly declared "everyday phenomena," should be investigated with respect to their regional and social relationships. Walter Hävernick has studied schoolboys' sailor's suits in Hamburg from 1900 to 1920 from these points of view and has obtained very remarkable results ("Kinderkleidung und Gruppengeistigkeit in volkskundlicher Sicht," in *Beiträge zur deutschen Volks- und Altertumskunde,* 4th vol. [Hamburg, 1959], 37–61). Other modern sartorial habits should be similarly investigated. Futhermore we could inquire into the use of certain types of cars and motorcycles, the diffusion of central heating, the sale of oil furnaces, the frequency of certain types of roof, the spread of television, the number of cinemas per capita, etc. All these phenomena are no doubt also influenced by economic manipulation; however, demand, which at least in part reflects characteristic needs, largely determines the supply here, too.
120. See p. 97 below.
121. Letter of November 9, 1954.
122. See Gerhard Zaddach, "Der literarische Film," diss., Breslau, 1930, 58–59.
123. *Stuttgarter Zeitung,* July 6, 1956.
124. *Schwäbische Zeitung,* October 1, 1957.
125. *Schwäbische Zeitung,* July 29, 1958.
126. *Stuttgarter Zeitung,* May 22, 1956.
127. Hans Moser emphasizes in "Gedanken zur heutigen Volkskunde," *Bayerisches Jahrbuch für Volkskunde* 1954:208–234, that "pure" scholarly theoreticians have probably never existed, and neither have "phenomena that can be explained by *one* cause and interpreted according to *one* idea," 225.

3. Temporal Expansion

1. Helmut Plessner, "Die Technik und die Gesellschaft der Zukunft," *Stuttgarter Zeitung,* February 4, 1956, 17.
2. See Hermann Wein, "The Department of Social Relations in Harvard," *Psyche* 1954:191–205; esp. 196–197.
3. Walter Hävernick, "Ursachen der Akzeleration. Ein Erklärungsversuch aus volkskundlicher Sicht," in *Beiträge zur deutschen Volks- und Altertumskunde,* 4 vols. (Hamburg, 1959), 63–66.
4. See Willy Hellpach, "Die Beschleunigung der Erlebniszeitmasse," in *Biologie der Grossstadt,* edited by B. d. Rudder and F. Linke (Dresden and Leipzig, 1940), 60–74; also Hellpach, *Mensch und Volk der Grossstadt,* 2d ed., (Stuttgart, 1952), esp. 67–77; and Hellpach, *Deutsche Physiognomik* (Berlin, 1942), 70.
5. *Mensch und Volk der Grossstadt,* 75.
6. See Hermann Bausinger, Markus Braun, and Herbert Schwedt, *Neue Siedlungen* (Stuttgart, 1959), 142–143.
7. See for the following as well, Alfred Lowack, *Die Mundarten im hochdeutschen Drama bis gegen Ende des achtzehnten Jahrhunderts* (Leipzig, 1905).
8. Hellpach, *Mensch und Volk der Grossstadt,* 71.
9. See Elisabeth Pfeil, "Fremdheit und Nachbarschaft in der Grossstadt," *Studium Generale* 8 (1955):121–126; esp. 122.
10. A cultural "consumer attitude" is spreading, parts of which could almost be interpreted in terms of economic categories. However, the fact that this, too, merely indicates an escalation and that the need for rapid changes is very old is proven by the late

medieval topos "a new song"; nevertheless it is necessary to investigate the extent to which this formula really belongs to new songs and for how long it remains tied to individual songs over extended periods of time.

11. Lucius Burckhardt, "Die Wohnkultur als Gegenstand der Soziologie," *Der Monat* 12, No. 139 (1960):31–36.

12. See Alfred Weber, *Kulturgeschichte als Kultursoziologie* (Munich, 1951), 418 and 426.

13. Gottfried Benn, broadcast lecture, Süddeutscher Rundfunk, March 7, 1954.

14. Gottfried Benn, *Reden* (Munich, 1955), 61.

15. See Ernst Troeltsch, "Der Historismus und seine Probleme," in *Gesammelte Schriften*, vol. 3 (Tübingen, 1922), 757.

16. Since Tinbergen "horizon of expectation" is defined by political economics as a time limit in the future beyond which no reliable expectations are possible.

17. Martin Heidegger, *Sein und Zeit*, first half, 5th ed. (Halle, 1941), 114.

18. See Hermann Bausinger, "Man—Bemerkungen zu einem volkskundlichen Grundbegriff," manuscript Festschrift for Helmut Dölker, 1954.

19. *Deutscher Liederhort*, 3 vols. (Leipzig, 1925), 564–565.

20. H. Husmann, "Lebensformen und ihr Wandel beim Arbeiter in Hamborn," *Rheinisch- westfälische Zeitschrift für Volkskunde* 4 (1957):145n21.

21. Hans Moser, "Gedanken zur heutigen Volkskunde," *Bayerisches Jahrbuch für Volkskunde* 1954:208–234; see esp. 223. The firm horizon, within which a fashion became valid, general, and binding—i.e., within which it became custom—was of decisive importance here. See p. 54 above.

22. Leopold Schmidt, *Die Volkskunde als Geisteswissenschaft* (Vienna, 1948), 107–108.

23. Leopold Schmidt, "Neuere Passionsspielforschung in Österreich," in *Jahrbuch des österreichischen Volksliedwerkes*, vol. 2 (Vienna, 1953), 114–143; see esp. 143.

24. Adolf Butenandt, "Das Geheimnis des Lebens in neuer Sicht," *Stuttgarter Zeitung*, October 1, 1955.

25. Wilhelm Brepohl, "Das Soziologische in der Volkskunde," *Rheinisches Jahrbuch für Volkskunde* 4 (1953):245–275; see 275; see also Josef Dünninger, "Das 19. Jahrhundert als volkskundliches Problem," *Rheinisches Jahrbuch für Volkskunde* 5 (1954):281–294.

26. Friedrich Meinecke, *Aphorismen und Skizzen zur Geschichte* (Leipzig, 1942), 30.

27. Albert Gutfleisch, "Volkslied in der Jugendbewegung, betrachtet am Zupfgeigenhansl," diss., Frankfurt, 1934, 21.

28. Charlotte Ziegler, "Die literarischen Quellen des Zupfgeigenhansl," diss., Göttingen, 1950, 149.

29. Introduction to the first edition of *Zupfgeigenhansl* (Heidelberg, 1908).

30. Karl Schultze-Jahde, "Dreissigjähriger Krieg und deutsche Dichtung," *Historische Zeitschrift* 143 (1931):257–297; see esp.279.

31. Ibid., 257–297.

32. See Gutfleisch, 16.

33. Alfred Götze, *Das deutsche Volkslied* (Leipzig, 1929), 126.

34. Theobald Kerner, *Das Kernerhaus und seine Gäste*, parts 1 and 2 (Weinsberg, 1913), 122.

35. Karl Pfaff, *Geschichte der Stadt Stuttgart nach archivalischen Urkunden und anderen bewährten Quellen*, vol 2 (Stuttgart, 1846), 174; see also Otto Elben, *Der volkstümliche deutsche Männergesang, seine Geschichte, seine gesellschaftliche und nationale Bedeutung* (Tübingen, 1855), 67, 87–88, 260.

36. Elben, 279; see also 260 and *passim*.

37. Theodor Hornberger, *Der Schäfer. Landes- und volkskundliche Bedeutung eines Berufsstandes in Süddeutschland* (Stuttgart, 1955), 242.

38. *Ludwigsburger Kreiszeitung*, November 30, 1953.

39. Ernst Topitsch, "Zur empirischen Neuorientierung der Kulturwissenschaften,"

Deutsche Universitätszeitung 13 (1958):518–521; esp. 521. It is possible that this complex of problems only attracted attention because of parallel discoveries in the natural sciences, i.e., constituting a sort of Heisenberg effect within the arts.

40. See *Stuttgarter Zeitung,* November 4, 1958.

41. In the opening pages of Vischer's novel *Auch Einer* (Another One), A. E. demands a "Baedecker of Deterrence" when confronted with the sight of the Rigi; he continues: "I would not want to experience the guy in the morning who blows the *Kuhreigen* [cow's tune] at sunrise in his old Swiss costume and then receives his tip in the inn; therefore off, away while it is still night!"

42. See Wein, 199–200.

43. This demand is directed at heritage conservation, where up to now, as far as I know, few attempts at theory have been made, despite much practical work. Important considerations of piety, historical education, and new inspiration of the arts by forms that basically pertain to the past should be supplemented with a refined reception, such as Max Dvořák found in Hellenism: "Old reliefs were installed in state halls and old statues were erected in gardens and in public places, not because of antiquarian considerations, but because of newer, particularly subtle artistic sensations" ("Denkmalkultus und Kunstentwicklung," in *Gesammelte Aufsätze zur Kunstgeschichte* [Munich, 1929], 250–270; see 263).

44. *Der Grosse Brockhaus,* vol. 7 (Wiesbaden, 1955). 25.

45. Theodor Hüpgens, "Grundsätzliches zum Laienspiel," in *Gemeinschaftsbühne und Jugendbewegung,* edited by Wilhelm L. Gerst (Frankfurt, 1924), 125–130; see 128.

46. Arthur Kutscher, *Grundriss der Theaterwissenschaft* (Munich, 1949), 59.

47. See Troeltsch, *Der Historismus und seine Probleme,* 670.

48. Theodor W. Adorno, "Kritik des Musikanten," in *Dissonanzen* (Göttingen, 1956), 62–101; see 68.

49. Leopold Schmidt, "Wurzeln und Wege der dichterischen Gestaltung volkhaften Lebens in Österreich," *Dichtung und Volkstum* 40 (1939):8–31; see 16–17.

50. Richard Weiss, "Alpiner Mensch und alpines Leben in der Krise der Gegenwart," *Die Alpen* 1957:209–229; see 211 and 217.

51. Heinz Maus, "Zur Situation der deutschen Volkskunde," *Die Umschau—Internationale Revue* 1 (Mainz, 1946):349–359; see esp. 358.

52. Leopold Schmidt, *Die Volkskunde als Geisteswissenschaft* (Vienna, 1948), see esp. 19–21.

53. Friedrich Meinecke, "Ernst Troeltsch und das Problem des Relativismus," in *Schaffender Spiegel* (Stuttgart, 1948), 211–228; see 228.

54. Josef Dünninger states in his appreciation of the folkloristic efforts of the Enlightenment, which have often been misunderstood: "Whoever dedicates himself uncritically and indiscriminately to that which is traditional, works without any methodological basis" ("Volkstum und Aufklärung in Franken," *Bayerisches Jahrbuch für Volkskunde* 1957:29–42, see 29).

55. Max Frisch, *Stiller* (Frankfurt, 1954), 325.

56. The concept of "culture lag" or "cultural lag," coined by William F. Ogburn, indicates the "retardation" of cultural adaptation with reference to actual development. See René König, ed., *Soziologie* (Frankfurt: Fischer-Lexikon, 1958), 155 and 235. This catchphrase essentially summarizes what Georg Simmel had in mind when he talked of "the ever widening gulf between the culture of objects and that of men" ("Die Zukunft unserer Kultur," in *Brücke und Tür* [Stuttgart, 1957], 95–97; see also "Vom Wesen unserer Kultur," ibid., 86–94). The objective "culture of objects" includes the highest developments of the arts; the subjective culture always follows it more slowly.

57. Adorno, 67 and 99. In a radio broadcast entitled "Gemeinschaftsbildende Tendenzen der neuen Musik" (Community-building tendencies of the new music), Siegfried Borris defended—against Adorno—the orientation of music toward goals outside the arts and the new impulses this has generated in the works of Hindemith, Fortner, Weill, and Orff.

58. A lecture by Dieter Narr proves that historical observations on the process of the democratization of education can assist in understanding this problem. See "Fragen der Volksbildung in der späteren Aufklärung," *Württembergisches Jahrbuch für Volkskunde* 1959/60:38–67.

59. John A. Waltz, "The Folklore Elements in Hauptmann's 'Die versunkene Glocke,'" *Modern Language Notes* 16 (Baltimore, 1901):89–105 and 130–142; see esp. 100–101.

60. Hans Ulrich Sareyko, "Das Weltbild eines ostpreussischen Volkserzählers," diss., Marburg, 1954, see 24, 29, 37, and 172. See also Mechtilda Brachetti, *Studien zur Lebensform des deutschen Volksmärchens* (Bühl/Baden, 1935), 17–35.

61. Lutz Röhrich, *Märchen und Wirklichkeit* (Wiesbaden, 1956), 146–154.

62. Gyula Ortutay, *Ungarische Volksmärchen* (Berlin, 1957), 85.

63. Richard M. Dorson, "Tales of a Greek-American Family on Tape," *Fabula* 1 (1957):114–143, see 132–133.

64. Friedrich von der Leyen, *Die Welt der Märchen* 1 (Düsseldorf, 1952), 75.

65. See the report "Im Hauptberuf Scheherezade," *Stuttgarter Zeitung,* December 20, 1957.

66. Leopold Schmidt, "Kulturgeschichtliche Gedanken zur Musik im Märchen," *Musikerziehung* 3 (Vienna, 1950):144–148; see also Leopold Schmidt, *Gestaltheiligkeit im bäuerlichen Arbeitsmythos* (Vienna, 1952), 155–156.

67. The phenomenon of requisite freezing is placed here in the context of historicization. However, another process—which we can only allude to in this context—is also essential to the *Märchen*: they not only represent what is older in historical terms but also that which is of mythical origin and archaic; i.e., kingship is not only a historical category. The former shifts in requisites left this mythical essence untouched; however, as the outer reality moves ever farther away from the mythical reality, they threaten to attack the essence—which refers to the "historical" reception of the *Märchen*. These problems are discussed in more detail in Hermann Bausinger, " 'Historisierende' Tendenzen im deutschen Märchen seit der Romantik. Requisitenverschiebung und Requisitenerstarrung," *Wirkendes Wort* 10 (1960):279–286.

68. Special exhibition at the Niedersächsisches Heimatmuseum, Hannover, summer 1954. Julius Schwietering has pointed to the dominance of rococo forms in folk goods; by contrast the historizing empire style was not adopted by the folk culture to the same degree ("Wesen und Aufgaben der deutschen Volkskunde," *Deutsche Vierteljahrsschrift für Literaturwissenschaft und Geistesgeschichte* 5 [1927]:748–765; now in Gerhard Lutz, *Volkskunde* [Berlin, 1957], 143–157; see 154–155).

69. See in this connection the conversation between Albrecht Dürer and Lucas von Leyden in "Sternbald" (*Ludwig Tieck's Schriften,* vol. 16 [Berlin, 1843], 112–113), a conversation on a subject which is more characteristic of the end of the eighteenth century than of the beginning of the sixteenth.

70. Erika Kohler, *Martin Luther und der Festbrauch* (Cologne/Graz, 1959), 95.

71. See Friedrich Sieber, in *Grundriss der Sächsischen Volkskunde* (Leipzig, 1932), 270.

72. Ludwig von Hörmann, *Tiroler Volksleben* (Stuttgart, 1909), 119.

73. Leopold Schmidt, "Formprobleme der deutschen Weihnachtsspiele," in *Die Schaubühne,* vol. 20 (Emsdetten, 1937), 78.

74. Leopold Kretzenbacher, *Lebendiges Volksschauspiel in Steiermark* (Vienna, 1951), 132.

75. Josef Lanz, "Verpflanzung ostdeutscher Volksschauspiele durch Umsiedlung, Flucht und Vertreibung," *Jahrbuch für Volkskunde der Heimatvertriebenen* 3 (Salzburg, 1957):20–55; see 36–40.

76. See Friedrich Heinz Schmidt-Ebhausen, "Zwei ungarndeutsche Weihnachtsspiele in der neuen Heimat," *Zeitschrift für Volkskunde* 50 (1953):271–289; see 276.

77. Adalbert Riedl, "Der Stand der Burgenländischen Volkskunde," in *Burgenländische Beiträge* (Vienna, 1953), 3–14; see 12.

78. Hans Naumann, "Studien über den Bänkelgesang," *Zeitschrift des Vereins für Volkskunde* 30/31 (1921):1–21; see 8–9.

79. See the letter of Hans Lissner of October 1931, in Albert Gutfleisch, "Volkslied in der Jugendbewegung, betrachtet am Zupfgeigenhansl," diss., Frankfurt, 1934, 67.

80. See p. 18 above.

81. A. Birlinger and M. R. Buck, "Sagen, Märchen, Volksaberglauben," in *Volkstümliches aus Schwaben,* vol. 1 (Freiburg i. B., 1861), 283.

82. The dynamic not only inspires people, but also provokes attitudes of stubborn resistance. Moreover, Max Horkheimer has shown how "invariance" is being "somehow sucked up" by the enormous dynamic of our time, but that this also causes stabilization: "Dynamic, the mere change, merges with the eternal sameness" ("Invarianz und Dynamik in der Lehre von der Gesellschaft," *Kölner Zeitschrift für Soziologie* 4 [1951/52]:242–249). In *Das Prinzip Hoffnung* (Frankfurt, 1959), 231, Ernst Bloch criticizes a similar notion in the philosophy of Bergson, who regards "the new simply from the point of view of senselessly changing fashions," and he contrasts this with his "Category Novum."

83. "Der umstrittene Herr Schellenbeck," *Stuttgarter Zeitung,* February 1, 1956.

84. In 1909 Eugen Ritter gave the following advice "to improve the *Fasnacht*": "For once new masks should be made exactly according to the strictly stylized old ones. Furthermore it would be desirable if the '*Narren*' moved about in the streets more than they had in the past and if they stayed as much as possible in the inner city, whose old houses provide a picturesque frame for them" (*Rottweils Fasnacht einst und jetzt* [Rottweil, 1909], 32). In these recommendations the historicizing freezing of forms is as significant as the aesthetic turn given to the *Fasnacht*.

85. See *Schembart* manuscript D 2 in the Germanisches Nationalmuseum in Nuremberg; also the description by Walther Matthey in *95. Jahresbericht des Museums* (Nuremberg, 1950), 49–57.

86. Leopold Schmidt, *Volkskunde als Geisteswissenschaft* (Vienna, 1948), 5–90; see 69–70.

87. Mathilde Hain, *Das Lebensbild eines oberhessischen Trachtendorfes* (Jena, 1936), 21 and 82.

88. Gretel Jekelius, "Deronje," manuscript, Tübingen, 1954, 6 (Folkloristic Investigations of the Ludwig-Uhland-Institut).

89. See Viktor von Geramb, "Zur Doktrin der Volkstracht," *Jahrbuch für historische Volkskunde* 3/4 (Berlin, 1934), 195–220.

90. "Fortschritte in der Kulturarbeit des Heimatbundes," *Schwäbische Zeitung,* September 12, 1958.

91. See the text of the passion play of 1921; also the complete text of the passion play in Waal of 1938.

92. Leopold Kretzenbacher, *Lebendiges Volksschauspiel in Steiermark* (Vienna, 1951), 19.

93. Gregor Römer, "Die Historisierung von Volksbräuchen," diss., Würzburg, 1951; see esp. 36–39, 61–62, 68–86, 101–112.

94. Ibid., 36–39; also W. L. Hertslet, *Der Treppenwitz der Weltgeschichte,* 9th ed. (Berlin, 1918), 213–215.

95. See Albert Fischer, *Villinger Fastnacht von einst und heute* (Villingen, 1922), 42, 50–55.

96. See Eugen Ritter, *Rottweiler Fasnacht einst und jetzt,* 2d ed. (Rottweil, 1935), 31.

97. See *Festschrift zum schwäbisch-alemannischen Narrentreffen am 28./29. Januar 1956* (Riedlingen, 1956), 38.

98. See the review of Rev. Sauter's cultural-historical study *Zur Hexenbulle 1484* (Ulm, 1848), in *Diözesan-Archiv von Schwaben* 2 (Stuttgart, 1885):55–56.

99. See *Festschrift zum schwäbisch-alemannischen Narrentreffen,* 61–62.

100. See Fischer, 38.

101. The late medieval processions and masquerades portray not so much the historical

as the mythical and are more concerned with simply heroic than great historic figures. However, the "presentation" of the historic, as described on pp. 85–86, brings even the historic presentations of our time close to this "mythic" understanding.

102. Adolf Spamer, *Deutsche Fastnachtsbräuche* (Jena, 1936), 10.

103. See Else Gündle, *Brauchtum im alten Gmünd* (Schwäbisch Gmünd, 1953), 15–16.

104. See newspaper announcements in *Stuttgarter Zeitung*, February 7, 1956, February 21, 1956, and July 4, 1956; *Schwäbische Post*, March 11, 1955; and *Frankfurter Allgemeine Zeitung*, July 2, 1958.

105. See newspaper reports in *Schwäbische Zeitung*, June 8, 1956; *Stuttgarter Zeitung*, June 28, 1956, July 17, 1957, July 15, 1957, July 10, 1956, May 22, 1956, and July 9, 1956.

106. See *Stuttgarter Zeitung*, January 7, 1958, and January 11, 1958. Because "contacts" had been established between the *Lützowsche Jäger* and the Federal Armed Forces, this new society received much attention.

107. Fischer, 82.

108. Ibid., 17, 19, 21, 24, 27, 67.

109. *Stuttgarter Zeitung*, January 28, 1957.

110. Dieter Narr, "Volkskundliches zum Brunnenzug und Kuchenfest der Haller Sieder," *Schwäbische Heimat* 7 (1956):131–138; see 132.

111. Ortega y Gasset emphasizes that it is part of "the essence of each custom, including the new, to be old" (*Der Mensch und die Leute* [Stuttgart, 1957], 292). Two different meanings are inherent in the concept "old": our language does not provide for "the opportunity to differentiate a genetic (evolutionary) intrusion of 'older' functions into 'younger' levels from a historical sequence" (W. E. Mühlmann, "Ethnologie und Geschichte," *Studium Generale* 7 (1954):165–177; see 170.

112. Anton M. Keim, "Geschäft schafft Brauchtum—zu den St. Valentinsgrüssen," broadcast, Südwestfunk, February 14, 1959.

113. Friedrich Nietzsche, *Vom Nutzen und Nachteil der Historie für das Leben*. See also Hermann Bausinger, "Volkssage und Geschichte," *Württembergisches Franken* 41 (1957):107–130; esp. 124–128.

4. Social Expansion

1. Friedrich Theodor Vischer, *Ästhetik oder Wissenschaft des Schönen*, vol. 6, 2d ed. (Munich, 1923), 239 (para. 892). Here Vischer mentions the metaphor of the folk as Mother Earth, which has been cited again and again and is regularly attributed to Albrecht Dieterich (see "Über Wesen und Ziele der Volkskunde," *Hessische Blätter Für Volkskunde* 1 [1902]:169–194; now also in Gerhard Lutz, *Volkskunde* [Berlin, 1958], 78–88).

2. See Wilhelm Heinrich Riehl, *Bürgerliche Gesellschaft*, vol. 2 of *Naturgeschichte des Volkes*, 1st ed, (Stuttgart, 1851).

3. Hugo Moser, "Sprachgrenzen und ihre Ursachen," *Zeitschrift für Mundartforschung* 22 (1954):87–111, see 95–96.

4. Otto Elben, *Der volkstümliche deutsche Männergesang, seine Geschichte, seine gesellschaftliche und nationale Bedeutung* (Tübingen, 1855), 273–288.

5. Personal communication from Helmut Dölker, Stuttgart, from Feldstetten/Alb.

6. Rudolf Tartler, "Die soziale Gestalt der heutigen Jugend und das Generationsverhältnis in der Gegenwart," in *Arbeiterjugend gestern und heute*, edited by Helmut Schelsky (Heidelberg, 1955), 263–338, see 292; see also Heinz Kluth, "Arbeiterjugend—Begriff und Wirklichkeit," ibid., 16–174, esp.98.

7. Walther Rathenau, *Die Mechanisierung der Welt* (Schwenningen, 1948), 26.

8. See Willy Hellpach, *Mensch und Volk der Grosstadt* (Stuttgart, 1939), 116–117.

9. *Gedichte*, 2nd ed. Stuttgart and Tübingen, 1839:102.

10. See for example Hermann Gumbel, "Zur deutschen Schwankliteratur im 17. Jahrhundert," *Zeitschrift für deutsche Philologie* 53 (1928):303–346, esp. 322.

11. See the lecture by Dieter Narr, "Fragen der Volksbildung in der späteren Aufklärung," *Württembergisches Jahrbuch für Volkskunde* 1959/60:38–67.

12. See the index volume of Rowohlt's German Encyclopedia, with an introduction by Ernesto Grassi entitled "Die zweite Aufklärung—Enzyklopädie heute" (The Second Enlightenment—Encyclopedia Today), *Rowohlts Deutsche Enzyklopädie* 76/77 (Hamburg, 1958).

13. For parallel observations in the United States, see Merle Curti, *Das amerikanische Geistesleben von den Anfängen bis zur Gegenwart* (Stuttgart, 1947), 796–801.

14. Anton Birlinger, "Sitten und Gebräuche," in *Volksthümliches aus Schwaben,* vol. 2 (Freiburg, 1862), 42–43.

15. See Fritz Fischer, "Restauration in Idee und Wirklichkeit," *Deutsche Universitätszeitung* 14 (1959):78–82; and Wilhelm Heinrich Riehl, *Die bürgerliche Gesellschaft,* 1st ed., 1851. However, Riehl mentions as "forces of mobility" both the fourth estate *and* the bourgeoisie, which he contrasts with the peasantry and the nobility as "forces of stability."

16. Wilhelm Brepohl, *Der Aufbau des Ruhrvolkes im Zuge der Ost-West-Wanderung* (Recklinghausen, 1948); Brepohl, *Industrievolk im Wandel von der agraren zur industriellen Daseinsform, dargestellt am Ruhrgebiet* (Tübingen, 1957).

17. See Johann Mokre, *Grundriss der Arbeiterkunde* (Vienna, 1950), 81.

18. Karl Bednarik, *Der junge Arbeiter von heute—ein neuer Typ* (Stuttgart, 1953), 28.

19. Ibid., 153.

20. Wilhelm Brepohl, "Zur Charakteristik der Industriestädte," in *Biologie der Grossstadt,* edited by B. de Rudder and F. Linke (Dresden and Leipzig, 1940), 31–41; see 39.

21. See Karl Martin Bolte, "Schichtung," in *Soziologie. Fischer–Lexikon* (Frankfurt, 1958), 244–253; also Bolte, *Sozialer Aufstieg und Abstieg* (Stuttgart, 1959); Renate Mayntz, *Soziale Schichtung und sozialer Wandel in einer Industriegemeinde* (Stuttgart, 1958); and Ralf Dahrendorf, *Soziale Klassen und Klassenkonflikt* (Stuttgart, 1957).

22. For example, Carl Jantke describes in detail miners' frequent distrust of the mine inspector, who is generally held responsible for fluctuations in salary, though this does not always hold up to scrutiny. "Bergmann und Zeche. Die sozialen Arbeitsverhältnisse einer Schachtanlage des nördlichen Ruhrgebiets in der Sicht der Bergleute," in *Soziale Forschung und Praxis,* vol. 11 (Tübingen, 1953), 52, 68, 71.

23. In August 1782, in Hohenheim, Count Karl of Württemberg is said to have ridden around the scene of a fire three times and to have subdued the flames with a fire blessing; and even King Wilhelm was said to have proceeded similarly at a fire in September 1861. See Eugen Dolmetsch, *Bilder aus Alt-Stuttgart,* 2d ed., (Stuttgart, 1930), 32–33.

24. Hermann Bausinger, "Strukturen des alltäglichen Erzählens," *Fabula* 1 (1958):239–254; see 242–243.

25. See for example the report "Fein gelungener Dorfabend der Neuravensburger Landjugend," *Schwäbische Zeitung,* May 24, 1956.

26. Wolfgang Hartke, "Die 'Sozialbrache' als Phänomen der geographischen Differenzierung der Landschaft," *Erdkunde* 10 (1956):257–269. Most often, however, we are no longer dealing with *Sozialbrache,* but rather with a *Sozialöde* (social desiccation) or *Sozialwüstung* (social desert).

27. See Gerda Dobbert, "Hainbroch. Eine soziographische Studie über ein deutsches Dorf an der holländischen Grenze," *Kölner Zeitschrift für Soziologie* 2 (1949/50):398–433; see 416–417.

28. See this concept in Peter R. Hofstätter, *Gruppendynamik, Rowohlts Deutsche Enzyklopädie* 38 (Hamburg, 1957), 20.

29. See Johannes Bühler, *Die Kultur des Mittelalters,* 5th ed. (Stuttgart, 1948), 123.

30. Although a distinct self-confidence prevails among certain professions—e.g., truck drivers, coal miners, dock workers,—this can no longer be considered a class consciousness. The cohesion and the self-confidence of such groups merely prove the differentiation, which is very pronounced particularly in the uniform society.

31. See Hans Aurenhammer, "Grossstadtvolkskundliche Untersuchungen an Wiener Wohnungen," *Österreichische Zeitschrift für Volkskunde* 61 (Vienna, 1958):195–204.

32. Johan Huizinga, "Homo Ludens," *Rowohlts Deutsche Enzyklopädie* 21 (Hamburg, 1956), 171; see also 62–67.

33. K. W. Jauss, "Torscha," manuscript, Tübingen, 1952, 31 (Folkloristic Investigations of the Ludwig-Uhland-Institut); and Hannelore Roth, "Veprovac," manuscript, Tübingen, 1952, 5.

34. English as well as Low German and High German origins are posited. (See *Trübners Deutsches Wörterbuch*, vol. 4 [1943], 152–153). Recently Lutz Mackensen has again localized the origin in Munich, where the dialect term *kitschen* means "to scrape together street mud" (*Die deutsche Sprache unserer Zeit* [Heidelberg, 1956], 51).

35. Hermann Broch, "Einige Bemerkungen zum Problem des Kitsches," in *Gesammelte Werke*, vol. 1: *Essays*, edited by Hannah Arendt (Zürich, 1955), 295–309; and Broch, "Das Böse im Wertsystem der Kunst," ibid., 311–350. A comprehensive description of the problem of *Kitsch* should also consider Julius F. Glück, "Die Gelbgüsse des Ali Amonikoyi," *Jahrbuch des Lindenmuseums Stuttgart*, n.s. 1 (Heidelberg, 1951), 27–71. This essay is subtitled "An art-morphological contribution to the problem of *Kitsch* in primitive civilizations"; this unusual broadening of the concept *Kitsch* yields important information on the nature and function of *Kitsch* in higher civilizations. In contrast to Broch, Glück views *Kitsch* merely as an aesthetic, not as a primarily ethical, problem.

36. Friedrich Theodor Vischer, *Ästhetik oder Wissenschaft des Schönen*, vol. 2, 2d ed. (Munich, 1922), 612. The history of sentimentality is one of the more important problems in the intellectual history of the eighteenth and nineteenth centuries and has barely been tackled. More detailed investigations should include the French initiatives (Rousseau's construct of human "naturalness") and the English influences (Sterne's *Sentimental Journey* put the term *sentimental* into circulation), but they should primarily investigate how Schiller's original aesthetic concept of the sentimental was broadened and watered down to become sentimentality. The concept of broken nature is isolated from the merely aesthetic, as is later seen in Kleist's essay on the puppet theatre, but it is simultaneously redirected in a harmonizing manner. Sentimentality cannot endure the tension imposed by consciousness, but feigns a puppetlike security in the situatuion of being broken. A brief attempt to establish a conceptual network on the basis of the oppositon of *naive* and *sentimental* in order to understand folk attitudes appears in Hermann Bausinger, "Beharrung und Einfügung. Zur Typik des Einlebens der Flüchtlinge," *Jahrbuch für Volkskunde der Heimatvertriebenen* 2 (Salzburg, 1956):9–16.

37. See in this connection Josef Dünninger, *Volkswelt und geschichtliche Welt* (Berlin-Essen-Leipzig, 1937), 123.

38. Herbert M. Schönfeld, "Hedwig Courths-Mahler—Ein Erfolgsphänomen," *Schwäbische Zeitung*, February 16, 1957.

39. Richard Egenter, *Kitsch und Christenleben* (Ettal, 1950), see 134 and 167. See also Hermann Bausinger, "Zur Struktur der Reihenromane," *Wirkendes Wort* 6 (1955/56):296–301; and Renate Ludwig, "Für das christliche Haus," *Zeitwende* 1951/2:80–81.

40. See Gerhard Heilfurth, *Das Bergmannslied* (Kassel/Basel, 1954), 184–185, 256, 287–288, 292, and 326; and Hans Commenda, "Der Liederschatz einer Mühlviertler Bauernfamilie," *Jahrbuch des österreichischen Volksliedwerkes* 2 (Vienna, 1953):39–47.

41. See Elben, *Der volkstümliche deutsche Männergesang*, esp. 50–55.

42. See Hermann Schreiber, "Der deutsche Hang zur Schnulze," *Stuttgarter Zeitung*, June 22, 1957. The term *Sentimentalitätsklippe* was coined by Hermann Broch; see his lecture "Einige Bemerkungen zum Problem des Kitsches," in *Gesammelte Werke*, vol. 1, 298.

43. See *Hör zu* 1958/No. 7:2.

44. See Wilhelm Brepohl, *Industrievolk im Wandel von der agraren zur industriellen Daseinsform, dargestellt am Ruhrgebiet* (Tübingen, 1957), 220–221. Brepohl emphasizes that such pictures are "not exclusive to Germany." It would be worthwhile investigating to what extent the "imitation culture" of sentimentality is a common European phenomenon and what differences can be found.

45. It should be mentioned, incidentally, how much the teaching of essay writing—e.g., the often stereotypical insistence on embellishing adjectives—is both predjudiced toward this sentimental style and participates in its development and spread.

46. See Adolf Bach, *Deutsche Mundartforschung*, 2d ed. (Heidelberg, 1950), 289.

47. *Pfullinger Zeitung*, July 12, 1955.

48. See "Almhütten und Rikscha-Kulis sollen nicht mehr für Heidelberg werben," *Stuttgarter Zeitung*, August 30, 1955.

49. Here we are not dealing with the "sour *Kitsch*" discussed in Hans Egon Holthusen, "Über den sauren Kitsch," *Neue Schweizer Rundschau*, n.s. 18 (1950/51):145–151. This "sour *Kitsch*," which, according to Holthusen, denounces the totality of reality as it were with a squint, can be ignored here, as the simple folk has hardly responded to it. Nevertheless certain "hard" types of film, which are spreading in our country, tend toward this kind of sentimentality of the unsentimental.

50. Here the difference in experiencing religious images is helpful, which Rudolf Bultmann expounds (following Fritz Blättner, "Das Griechenbild J. J. Winckelmanns," *Antike und Abendland* I [1944]:121–132): on the one hand the *intentio recta*, which perceives in the image "the godlike portrayed as believed, in the form of an objective" and therefore considers artistic value of no importance; on the other hand the *intentio obliqua*, which pursues the spirit from which the work of art generated, not the graphic meaning (Bultmann, "Das Problem der Hermeneutik," in *Glauben und Verstehen, Gesammelte Aufsätze*, vol. 2 [Tübingen, 1952], 211–235; see 224.

51. Herman Broch, "Das Böse im Wertsystem der Kunst," in *Gesammelte Werke*, vol. 1, 311–350; see 339.

52. Wilfried Wroost, *Deutsche Volkskunst—Mitteilungsblatt der Studien- und Arbeitsgemeinschaft zur Förderung der deutschen Volks- und Laienkunst* 1956/No. 3.

53. It seems an obvious parallel to describe today's high culture as a closed system as well as to point out that it only very rarely turns to folk culture for inspiration. However, for high culture the door to folk culture is neither the only nor the decisive possibility of opening up the system. We can only allude to the difference here; it is best clarified when we attempt to match the above-mentioned request directed at folk culture with an area of high culture. This is impossible, because high culture does not move in such a circle. Broch indicates that the system is nevertheless closed to a large extent.

54. Erwin Ackerknecht, *Der Kitsch als kultureller Übergangswert* (Bremen, 1950).

55. See Hofstätter, *Gruppendynamik*, 10.

56. Johan Huizinga, *Homo ludens*, Rowohlts Deutsche Enzyklopädie 21 (Hamburg, 1956), 127.

57. Ibid., 184.

58. See Johann Künzig, *Die alemannisch-schwäbische Fasnet* (Freiburg, 1950), 64.

59. Anton Dörrer, *Tiroler Fasnacht innerhalb der alpenländischen Winter- und Vorfrühlingsbräuche* (Vienna, 1949), 285.

60. Karl M. Klier, "Das Blochziehen," *Burgenländische Forschungen* 22 (Eisenstadt, 1953):24.

61. See Heinrich Schneegans, *Geschichte der grotesken Satire* (Strassburg, 1894), 59–60.

62. See "Spottmessen," in *Lexikon für Theologie und Kirche*, 2d ed. (1937), vol. 9, sec. 739.

63. Friedrich Ranke, "Zum Formwillen und Lebensgefühl in der deutschen Dichtung des späten Mittelalters," *Deutsche Vierteljahrsschrift für Literaturwissenschaft und Geistesgeschichte* 18 (1940):307–327; see 308.

64. See Leopold Schmidt, "Formprobleme der deutschen Weihnachtsspiele," *Die Schaubühne* 20 (Emsdetten, 1937): 86–90.

65. See, for example, the version of such a duet from Vorarlberg in August Hartmann, *Weihnachtslied und Weihnachtsspiel in Oberbayern* (Munich, 1875), 47; and the spoken intermittent text in the "Scandal Scene in front of the House of the Lover" published by Erk-Böhme in *Deutscher Liederhort*, vol. 2 (Leipzig, 1925), 527–528.

66. Gottfried Henssen, "Wesenszüge der westfälischen Volkserzählung," *Rheinisch-westfälische Zeitschrift für Volkskunde* 5 (1958):75–103.

67. Hermann Römer, *Markgröningen im Rahmen der Landesgeschichte 1550–1750* (Markgröningen, 1930), 85–86.

68. Karl Klunziger, *Geschichte des Zabergäus und des jetzigen Oberamts Brackenheim*, 3 vols. (Stuttgart, 1841), 185–186, after Memminger, *Württembergische Jahrbücher*, 1837.

69. Gerhard Lutz, "Sitte und Infamie. Untersuchungen zur rechtlichen Volkskunde am Phänomen des Verrufs," diss., Würzburg, 1954, 151 and 218–221.

70. In this case the concept is not limited to the tradition, which stems from antiquity, of assigning human roles to animals, such as having the hunter and the game exchange roles. See Ernst Robert Curtius, *Europäische Literatur und Lateinisches Mittelalter*, 2d ed. (Bern, 1954), 104–108.

71. See Hermann Bausinger, "Schwank und Witz," *Studium Generale* 11 (1958):699–710; esp. 706.

72. Jonas Köpf, *Suppinger Liederbuch* (Stuttgart, 1953), 72; for the songs that follow see 46, 8, and 49–50. See also Heilfurth, *Das Bergmannslied*, 115, 292–294, 327, and 483–484.

73. Friedrich Ranke, "Zum Formwillen und Lebensgefühl in der deutschen Dichtung des späten Mittelalters," *Deutsche Vierteljahrsschrift für Literaturwissenschaft und Geistesgeschichte* 18 (1940):307–327. Professor W. Mohr alerted me to this study.

74. See Otto Mahr, *Das Volkslied im bäuerlichen Jahr der Rhön* (Frankfurt, 1939), 127–128.

75. Max Ittenbach, *Mehrgesetzlichkeit. Studien am deutschen Volkslied in Lothringen* (Frankfurt, 1932), 115.

76. Mahr, 78–79, 102, 99, 115.

77. Markus Braun, *Tscherwenka* II, 21 (Folkloristic Investigations of the Ludwig-Uhland-Institut, Tübingen).

78. See Johannes Koepp, "Das Volkslied in der Volksgemeinschaft," in *Die deutsche Volkskunde*, edited by Adolf Spamer (Berlin, 1934), 299–308, esp. 303; and Spamer, "Das Volkslied in der heutigen Grossstadt," in *Bericht über den allgemeinen volkskundlichen Kongress in Jugenheim 1951*, 36–37.

79. *Stuttgarter Nachrichten*, June 3, 1955.

80. See Hans Naumann, "Studien über den Bänkelgesang," *Zeitschrift des Vereins für Volkskunde* 30/31 (Berlin, 1921):1–21; see 1–2.

81. See Mahr, 66.

82. Herbert Schöffler, *Kleine Geographie des deutschen Witzes* (Göttingen, 1955), 70.

83. *Das grosse Roda-Roda-Buch* (Vienna, 1950), 436–437.

84. Georg Simmel, "Die Grossstädte und das Geistsleben," in *Brücke und Tür* (Stuttgart, 1957), 227–242; see 240.

85. Friedrich Nietzsche, *Vom Nutzen und Nachteil der Historie für das Leben.*

86. Friedrich Schlegel, from "Ideen," now published in *Kritische Schriften*, edited by Wolfdietrich Rasch (Munich, 1956), see 93; for the remarks that follow, see "Über die Unverständlichkeit," ibid., 348.

87. Heinz Küpper, *Wörterbuch der deutschen Umgangssprache* (Hamburg, 1955). See esp. the section "Vom Stil der Umgangssprache," 19–28.

88. See Olga Eckardt, "Die Sportsprache von Nürnberg und Fürth," diss., Erlangen, 1937, 29; also the examples on 28.

89. Formerly part of the dialect (see Hermann Fischer, *Schwäbisches Wörterbuch*, vol. 3 [Tübingen, 1911], 176), this form has been ironically adapted in colloquial speech.

90. Translator's note: Derived from the traditional proverbial saying "Das schlägt dem Fass den Boden aus" (lit., This knocks the bottom out of the keg), here changed to a nonsense version.

91. Translator's note: Derived from the saying "Quäle nie ein Tier zum Scherz, denn es hat wie du ein Herz" (lit., Never torment an animal for fun, for it has a heart like you).

92. See Heinrich Schneegans, *Geschichte der grotesken Satire* (Strassburg, 1894), 415.

93. See esp. the fourth act. In this case irony still guards the class boundaries, which are simultaneously educational boundaries, and protects them against renegades.

94. See Eduard Wechssler, *Über den Witz bei Molière* (Heidelberg, 1914), 18.

95. See *Honoré de Balzac in Selbstzeugnissen und Bilddokumenten*, presented by Gaëtan Picon (Hamburg, 1959), 13.

96. Thomas Mann, *Zauberberg*, spec. ed. (Frankfurt: Fischer Verlag, 1954), 709 (chap. vii, para. 9).

97. See Sternberger, Storz, and Süskind, *Aus dem Wörterbuch des Unmenschen* (Hamburg, 1957).

98. See Lutz Mackensen, *Die deutsche Sprache unserer Zeit* (Heidelberg, 1956), 46.

99. See Victor Laverrenz, *Die Denkmäler Berlins und der Volkswitz*, 3d ed., (Berlin, 1896).

100. The same name was given even earlier to the hilly dumping ground of Frankfurt, as Stefan Burger has kindly informed me. According to a comment by H. Dölker, in Swabian skiing circles the ironic use of romance-language names was already common in the 1930s, such as *Piz Mus* for *Musberg*. These ironic denominations of localities also represent important points of orientation and support for the urban spatial awareness (see pp. 35 and 45–46 above). An investigation of the nomenclature of cities should examine to what extent such denominations merely define and differentiate in spatial terms, how far their emotional content specifically carries and determines the *Heimat* awareness of the urban citizen, and how much they fulfil other functions.

101. This process, already recognized by Leibniz, demands, for example, the constant renewal of euphemisms, as each euphemism becomes common over time and thus can no longer be considered a 'euphemizesthai' in the true sense. See Friedrich Kainz, *Einführung in die Sprachpsychologie*. Vienna 1946:32–33.

102. Hans Paul Bahrdt, "Gedanken über einige Formen des gesitteten Betragens," *Deutsche Universitätszeitung* 13 (1958):27–39, see 35–36.

103. Ulrich Engel, "Mundart und Umgangssprache in Württemberg. Beiträge zur Sprachsoziologie der Gegenwart," diss., Tübingen, 1954, 333–341.

104. See, for example, Leopold Schmidt, "Volkskult und Wallfahrtswesen im nördlichen und mittleren Burgenland," in *Burgenländische Beiträge zur Volkskunde* (Vienna, 1953). 45–60, esp. 52; and Hanns Koren, "Die Beziehungen zwischen dem südlichen Burgenland und der Oststeiermark im Spiegel des Wallfahrtswesens," ibid., 61–70, esp. 63.

105. Herlinde Knorr, "Das Volkslied im Leben eines hessischen Dorfes," diss., Marburg, 1945, 73.

106. See Bach, *Deutsche Mundartforschung*, 306.

107. See Klaus Groth, *Über Mundarten und mundartige Dichtung* (Berlin, 1873), 54. How much the size of vocabularies is still underestimated even today is apparent in Arno Schmidt's introductory remarks to his *Gelehrtenrepublik* (Karlsruhe, 1957). Schmidt, who insists on a large vocabulary as well as on numerous new word creations, nevertheless grants his imaginary American author and the German translator a vocabulary of a mere 8,600 words each—and in the case of the translator this number includes 3,000 words of Middle High German!

108. Bach, 272.

109. These dialect recordings were made by Hermann Bausinger and Arno Ruoff for the German Language Archive in Munster. See *Württembergisches Jahrbuch für Volkskunde* 1956:133.

110. See Hugo Moser, "Entwicklungstendenzen des heutigen Deutsch," *Der Deutschunterricht* 2 (1954):87–107.

111. Ernst Jünger, *Der Arbeiter. Herrschaft und Gestalt* (Hamburg, 1932), 203. Even in progress-oriented North America individual voices have considered the "general affluence" endangered by the increasing education of the folk. See Merle Curti, *Das amerikanische Geistesleben* (Stuttgart, 1957), 467.

112. See Narr, "Fragen der Volksbildung in der späteren Aufklärung."

113. Will-Erich Peukert, "Die kleinbürgerliche Welt im Schundroman," *Soziale Welt* 9 (1958):281–288; see 287–288.

114. How decisive the linguistic aspect still is in contemporary England is apparent in an investigation by Alan S. C. Ross, "U and Non-U. An Essay in Sociological Linguistics," in *Noblesse Oblige,* edited by Nancy Mitford (Harmondsworth: Penguin Books, 1959), 7–32. Ross demonstrates that the upper class now can be defined almost solely in linguistic terms.

115. Recently Mario Wandruszka has pointed to "the inevitable advance of the argot" in French society and to the parallel phenomenon of Anglo-Saxon slang. See *Der Geist der französischen Sprache, Rowohlts Deutsche Enzyklopädie* 85 (Hamburg, 1959), 9–10.

116. See for the following section Hugo Moser, "Mundart und Hochsprache im neuzeitlichen Deutsch," *Der Deutschunterricht* 8 (1956, vol. 2):36–61; additional references in Werner Betz, "Neuere Literatur zu Hochsprache, Mundart und Umgangssprache," ibid., 86–92, and Moser, *Mittlere Sprachschichten als Quellen der deutschen Hochsprache* (Nijmegen-Utrecht, 1955).

117. See pp. 90–91 above and the sociological literature cited there.

118. Moser, "Mundart und Hochsprache," 58. See also Werner F. Leopold, "The Decline of German Dialects," *Word* 15 (New York, 1959):130–153, esp. 133–134.

119. Hans Lipp, "Sprache, Mundart und Jargon," *Blätter für deutsche Philosophie* 9 (1935/36):338–400; see 400.

120. See, for example, Olga Eckardt, *Die Sportsprache von Nürnberg und Fürth,* 27–28. It lists many different phrases for a badly shot ball: it starves, it dies, it needs food stamps, it comes in instalments, it stutters, etc.

121. Anton Pfalz, "Formwucher," in *Festschrift Max H. Jellinek zum 29. Mai 1928 dargebracht* (Vienna and Leipzig, 1928), 97–104. See also Hildegard Himmelreich, "Volkskundliche Beobachtungen an der Umgangssprache in Gelsenkirchen," diss., Münster 1939, 166–168.

122. See Adam Wrede, *Neuer Kölnischer Sprachschatz,* vol. 1 (Cologne, 1956), 4; and as a supplement Heinrich Lützeler, *Philosophie des Kölner Humors,* 10th ed. (Honnef: Rheinbücher N.F.V., 1955), 37.

123. Vischer, *Ästhetik oder Wissenschaft des Schönen,* vol. 6. See p. 88 above. Interestingly, the word "mass" here does not yet have a negative connotation.

124. In another context Vischer took up the same problem: In the diary entries from Palermo his A. E. differentiates between pure religion and, as Lessing has said, its "supports," or, as Vischer says, its "image world," its "pigment." He recognizes that a large part of the folk has "outgrown the image world" but has now reached pure religion: "The old reverence is gone, but they cannot find a reason for a new one." Even though it is highly questionable whether education can ever realize "pure religion," these reflections are again concerned with those "who exist in the indeterminate middle"—it is the Pygmalion problem transferred from language to religion.

5. Relics—and What Can Become of Them

1. Translator's note: At this point Bausinger refers the reader to the earlier discussion of fundamental concepts in *Volkskunde.*

2. Translator's note: Heine coined the word *sich-herauflassen* from the common term *sich herablassen,* "to lower oneself."

3. Translator's note: Mark Twain, "The Jodel in the Native Wilds," in *A Tramp Abroad,* edited by Charles Neider (New York, 1977), 188.

Index

HERMANN BAUSINGER, Professor of Ethnology and Folklore at the University of Tübingen, has been the Director of the Department of Empirical Culture Science at the Ludwig-Uhland-Institut. He has written several books and published more than one hundred articles on folklore, socio-linguistics, cultural history, and popular culture.

ELKE DETTMER, a native of Germany and a folklore scholar, has published a study of blue jeans in the folklore series of the Tübingen Vereinigung für Volkskunde.